43.50

P9-CTO-919

Seine Fishing

Bottom fishing with rope warps
and wing trawls

SEINE FISHING

Bottom fishing with rope warps and wing trawls

incorporating *The Seine Net –*
its origin, evolution and use

David B Thomson

 Fishing News Books Ltd
Farnham · Surrey · England

British Library Cataloguing in Publication Data
Thomson, David B.

Seine fishing. – Rev. ed.
1. Seining
I. Title   II. Seine net
639′.22   SH344.6.S4
ISBN 0 85238 113 1

Published by
Fishing News Books Ltd
1 Long Garden Walk
Farnham, Surrey, England

The Seine Net first printed in Great Britain by The Whitefriars Press Ltd
Seine Fishing set by Inforum, Portsmouth in 11/12pt Plantin
Printed in Great Britain by Page Bros (Norwich) Ltd.

To my father, Skipper Jimmy Thomson,
and to Seine Net Fishermen Everywhere

All author's royalties from the sale of this book
will be donated directly to the Royal National
Mission to Deep Sea Fishermen

Contents

Illustrations
and tables

Preface to the revised edition

Thirteen years have passed since the original edition of The Seine Net was published. What changes have come about in that period! And who could have foreseen them all? Some of them we were aware of and some took us by surprise. The hydraulic revolution was just beginning in 1968 as vessels began to be fitted with power blocks and hydraulic winches. But what a quantum leap occurred in vessel size, power and sophistication. And how much greater was the rise in vessel costs as inflation eroded the value of money. Fish prices also shot up, though in less proportion. The most expensive seine net boats were costing £70,000 in 1968. Ten years later, they were costing over £750,000. In 1968, many people believed that seine net fishing had 'peaked' and would soon decline in importance. But it prospered as never before. When the deep-sea crisis hit the trawling firms, pushing them out of their traditional distant waters back on to grounds nearer home, they found that they could not compete with the smaller more versatile seine netters. When the big trawling companies then started to build more compact and economical vessels for near-water fishing, they turned by and large from otter trawling to seine netting and pair trawling.

For the writer, the past decade brought about a change in his view of the subject. In 1968, he felt he could still write as an 'insider' with personal knowledge of the industry. But that was thirteen years ago and in the interim he has been involved in various parts of the world with almost every other type of fishing and fish farming. So he now feels he has much less personal affinity with the fishery, yet if so, perhaps he can write of it more objectively and with less personal bias.

Thinking back over a quarter century to the time when he first sailed as an apprentice-cum-galley-boy on a seine netter, when his wage was £3 per week plus 10 shillings per £100 grossed, the writer can recall how the crew could get a good wage if the boat grossed a mere £240. Who would have thought that within a generation some seine net boats would gross over £24,000 for a week's work. He remembers hauling coil after coil of rope from the winch, and helping the crew pull the nets in by hand every single drag, despite wind, tide and motion. He often wondered whether the job could be done by machine, but certainly never envisaged the remarkable degree of automation that was to be achieved. Ropes were shot, and fish gutted on the open deck in all weathers until very recently. Now, on the best modern vessels, most of the work can be carried out in the relative comfort of a shelter deck. But those vessels are fishing further afield and working in weather that would have been too much for the boats of the early 1950s.

What a contrast is seen between these large modern seiners and their predecessors. The 70ft (21.3m) 152hp seiner made its appearance shortly after the Second World War, and for over fifteen years it was considered to be the last word in vessel technology for seine netting. Some even thought such craft were too big for the job. Yet larger and more powerful craft were introduced in the early 1960s, and by the 1970s, seiners of 80ft, 85ft, and even 90ft in length (24.8, 25.9 and 27.4m) were in operation. Some were built of steel and had engines of over 500 or 600hp, plus a multitude of sophisticated acoustic, radio and electronic aids to navigation and fish detection. And these large vessels were remarkably successful, many of them out-fishing much bigger deep-sea trawlers. What would Jens Vaever or John Campbell have thought of it all!

Of course there were still plenty of small boats around and many of them continuing to fish well. But they were much beamier, fuller craft, than the former fifty-footers (15.2m). They had more than twice the power of their predecessors, plus most of the electronic aids used by the bigger vessels. The catching power of seine netters had increased so that annual landings by Scottish seiners rose from 60,000 tons to over 100,000 tons in the period 1954 to 1976. Landings by bottom trawlers actually declined during the last ten years.

Despite the remarkable progress, for seine net fishermen, life is far from easy today. The sea is as dangerous and as cruel as ever. Fish are more scarce than at any time in the past, and international pressure has brought about a grim situation on the North Sea grounds. Fishing rights have been bartered away by politicians, catch quotas have been enforced and the prospect of even stricter controls and more severe competition looms now on the horizon.

But we cannot stay the relentless tide of events and must face each new situation as it comes. The questions of fishery management and international control are beyond the scope of this little book.

In submitting this updated account of seine netting, the writer would like to pay two brief tributes. The first is to the former generation of seine net fishermen who have passed on and who now sleep in deep waters or in churchyards hard by the sea. What an intrepid group they were. For integrity, perseverance, character, and spirit, we will surely not see their like again. They served their day well and left their mark on fishing history. May we always honour their memory.

And now a new generation has taken their place, a generation no less intrepid and no less blessed with the pioneering spirit. Wherever they fish, from the Viking Bank to the Butt of Lewis, and from the Fladen Ground to Dubh Artach light, the writer wishes them God speed, safe and successful voyages, and continued prosperity in the years to come.

David B Thomson
Manila, Philippines

Preface to the first edition

One cannot but wonder at the way commercial fishing has progressed in the past fifty years. From a supposedly primitive (but in reality, highly skilled) art, it has become a science—a science that demands and utilizes the best and most advanced equipment and materials that man can produce. It has also come from the realms of obscurity to where it can be studied and documented in detail.

The documenting of fishing gear and methods is extremely important in these days of expanding techology. In the past a fisherman gathered his vast store of information from years of hard experience, by keen observation, and by word of mouth, the accounts of others and the tales and folklore handed down for generations. Today, the pressure of time and competitive industry demand a far greater and much faster dissemination of information.

Progress has been made in this direction, but it is still insufficient. Of all the sections of the fishing industry, the fish-catching side has been most poorly documented. There are a number of reasons for this; the inaccessibility of facts, the natural reticence of some fishermen to share knowledge and so on, but these facts alone do not excuse the ignorance of commercial techniques that exist.

There is a strong trend towards specialization in today's fisheries. Two types of fishing gear account for roughly two-thirds of the entire world catch. These two are the otter trawl and the purse seine. Interest in fishing gear tends to concentrate on these two methods and this is quite proper. But as a result, lesser known methods tend to be ignored.

'New' concepts in fish catching, such as air bubble curtains, electric shock, fish pumps and fish farming, are receiving publicity far in excess of their relative importance. With the exception of fish farming in fresh water and shellfish harvesting, which has been carried on for many years, their present contribution to the industry is relatively negligible.

The seine net has been in use now for over one hundred years. It is presently being used in more than ten countries with well-developed fisheries, and by many thousands of vessels. It is estimated that the gear catches annually nearly one million tons of fish, practically all of which goes for human consumption.

The seine net has also bred its own type of fishermen. Since its operation requires skills like those needed in the finer points of both trawling and seining, a seine net skipper must be expert in locating fish, in pin-pointing fishing grounds, in the accurate rigging of gear, and in the cunning arts of the operation of the net itself. It is a reliable gauge of the skills required in a seine net skipper that any who have taken up a different method of fishing have done exceptionally well at it.

This gear has probably reached its peak of use in Europe and possibly Japan, but it is only beginning to reveal its effectiveness in Canada, the United States and the temperate countries of the southern hemisphere.

There is a human side to the story of the seine net fisheries. It is responsible for the welfare of countless numbers of families whose livelihood depends on the success of the gear, and it is the most real and most meaningful part of any fishery. It can be touched upon only briefly in the following pages, but it should be borne in mind nevertheless, and, for those who have only slight acquaintance with fishermen, it will explain why that breed of men is so singularly independent, cautious, and sometimes resistant to change. Their knowledge and skill has been acquired in the hard school of experience and from the success of their endeavours they obtain the wherewithal to provide for their people. Some fisheries have been beset with problems caused by fluctuating conditions in nature or in the markets ashore, but in the main the seine net fisheries have been fairly stable and have provided a steady year-round income for the fishermen engaged in them.

Here, then, is an account of the history and development of this gear. The work is by no means complete but it is as comprehensive and as detailed as time and means available have permitted. I present it in the hope that it will be of interest and help to any who would like to know more of the seine net, its origin, evolution and use.

David B Thomson
University of Rhode Island, USA
December, 1968

Acknowledgements

Sincere thanks are extended to the many friends and acquaintances who provided data for both the original edition of 'The Seine Net' and this revised work. The writer is indebted to them all and also to the numerous fishermen and fisheries technicians who have readily shared their knowledge with him over the years. Often a chance word or comment in a passing conversation was as helpful or as illuminating as a formal letter.

Many who assisted unselfishly are no longer with us. The generation of fishermen who developed seine netting between the two world wars and who helped rebuild the fleet in the immediate post-war period has largely disappeared. Some of these pioneers are still around however and they are a wonderful source of much fascinating information.

Special mention has to be made of individuals who have responded tirelessly to requests for help. D M Baikie, the writer's uncle is again the source of the majority of the photographs used. Leslie Innes of Fraserburgh provided valuable data on fishing gear, from his vast store of knowledge on the subject. The writer's uncles and cousins in the industry gave much helpful advice. Willie Campbell and Gordon Eddie gladly permitted use of their WFA interview. Jimmy Allan of the Lossie Hydraulic Company responded freely with technical information as did D F Sutherland the winch manufacturer and most of the boat builders in the country. Willie Stewart of Lossiemouth provided valuable data in his FAO report on Danish Seining in Korea. The staff of Fishing News and Fishing News Books were a constant source of excellent material and advice. The fisheries statistics staff of the Department of Agriculture and Fisheries for Scotland regularly contributed data. From Japan most generous assistance was provided by Dr Y Iitaka and Dr M Nomura.

David B Thomson

1 History and development

The nineteenth century witnessed the start of the major methods of fish catching used in the world today. Previously, long-lines and drift nets were the chief means of fish capture. Beam trawls, beach seines and trap nets had also been used for centuries, but to a lesser extent. The first recorded use of the purse seine as we know it today, was in the United States in 1826. It is believed that the otter trawl was first used in England or Ireland around 1860 to 1870.

Between those two dates, in 1848, the seine net, or rather its method of use, was invented. It originated in Denmark, the southermost of the Scandinavian countries, and was first used to catch flatfish (plaice) in shallow water. The principle of the operation of the seine net was that of using ropes to catch fish, the ropes acting both to keep the net open, and to herd the fish towards it.

Because of its origin in Denmark, the gear was later to be termed 'the Danish seine'.

We do not know for certain who was the first to use an otter trawl net, or who first used a purse seine, but we do know from reliable sources the identity of the originator of the Danish seine—Jens Laursen Vaever, a fisherman of Limfjord, Denmark (*Fig 1*).

Jens Vaever was born in Kralbjerg, Skive, on 6th November 1822. His father, Laurs Clausen was a peasant-farmer and fisherman.

As a young man, Jens helped his father on the small farm which he eventually took over. He often worked as a cattle drover, walking south with herds to the market in Holstein. But it was the fishing that interested him, and not the farm, and he often spent time thinking of ways to improve his father's gear and methods.

There were two kinds of nets used by the fishermen of Skive at this time. They were called the nedet and the kratvoddet, both of which were used to catch plaice in Salling Sound. The kratvoddet was a large type of beach seine which was set out from the shore by means of a row-boat (*Fig 2*).

1

Young Jens Vaever wondered how a similar net could be used in the deep water of the sound where huge quantities of plaice were congregated.

The story goes that he was on his way to get medicine for a neighbour when an idea occurred to him. He thought that it might be possible to make a small net the same shape as the kratvoddet and set and haul it from a boat anchored in the sound.

In Skive, Jens bought the necessary hemp which his aunt spun into yarn for him. An old fisherman who knew something about making gear, helped to construct the net.

Apparently, like many other innovators, Jens did not receive much encouragement. Most people thought he was a bit off his head in trying to catch plaice with such a small net. But Jens minded his own business and let the rest of them talk.

In mid-December 1848, the net was ready, and Jens and a friend tried it for the first time. Unfortunately, the anchor they used for the main vessel was not up to the job and, instead of the net coming to the boat, the boat came to the net and they caught only 15 plaice.

There was great merriment on the beach when Jens Vaever came ashore with his new invention. As he explained it later himself, he 'walked around as the town fool that day'.

But the following month, January 1849, he borrowed a larger anchor, and then things went better.

With his borrowed anchor on the boat, Jens rowed out to sea followed by condescending smiles from the men on the beach who were happy if they caught 40 or 50 plaice in a day's work. When Jens rowed ashore that evening with 2,640 plaice, there was no more laughter. The next day he caught nearly 4,000 plaice and the men rushed to order the same kind of nets (*Fig 3*).

In two days, Jens earned enough money for his wedding and in February he was married to Anna Marie Nielsdatter (Niels-daughter).

Jens Vaever was very short of stature. It was partly because of this that he was on hand to use the seine in 1848 as he had been rejected by the army that year. However, he was accepted into the army shortly after, despite his height, and fought in the latter half of the three-years war.

He was fond of reading his Bible and would always take some fish from his catch to the local minister, saying that they who receive the Word should support those who minister the Word.

Fig 2 The kratvoddet or beach seine which was used before the seine net. (*W. Thomson*)

Jens Vaever lived to a good old age and was honoured by his countrymen in many ways. He was given a Danish fisheries medal and a money prize in 1896 and was also made a 'Danzkburger', and an honorary member of the Danish Fishermen's Association.

3

Fig 3 How the seine net was first used in Salling Sound, Denmark. (*W Thomson*)

He lived to see the use of his invention spread to the sea fisheries off the coast of Denmark and even further abroad. On 31st January 1914 he died in Skive, in the same house in which he was born.

The Danes named the gear 'snurrevod', 'vod' meaning 'net', and 'snurre' from the vibration of the ropes which formed such an important part of the gear.

From Limfjord the use of the snurrevod spread to other areas in Denmark. One of the first seaports to adopt the gear was Frederikshavn where fishermen began to use seine nets around 1880. The vessels used at this time were sailing cutters of 40 to 60 tons in size. These vessels were fitted with live fish-wells where the catch was kept. These fish-wells, common to many line fishing vessels in the North Sea, worked surprisingly well by today's standards. The method adopted for setting out the net from the fishing vessel is shown in *Fig 4*. An early type of seine net is shown in *Fig 5*.

Around 1885, some Danish fishermen were using otter boards on their seine nets. The reason for this is not clear. It may have been simply experimental or it may have been to help keep the net open longer. The only times that otter boards were used on seine nets later was when they were being used to catch prawns (Norway lobster) on soft bottom.

4

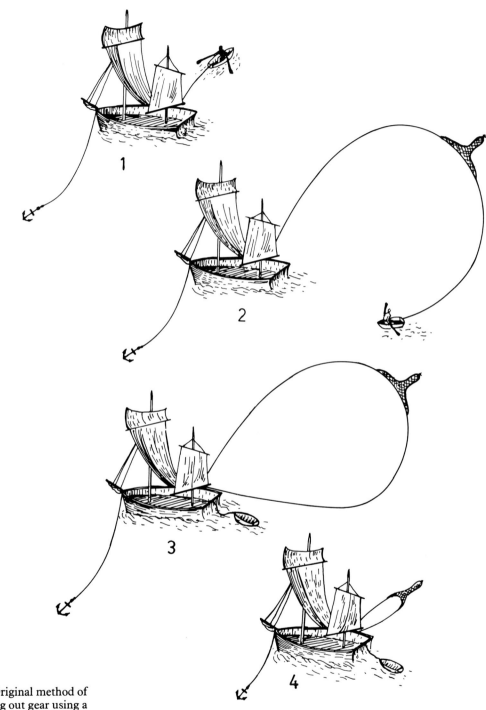

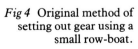

Fig 4 Original method of
setting out gear using a
small row-boat.

5

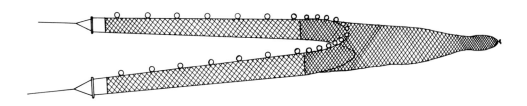

Fig 5 Early seine net.

The seine net ropes were hauled in by hand on these early sailing cutters. A primitive type of winch was used, run from a 'pumping'-type hand-operated capstan. As can be appreciated, the lack of power was a severe limitation on the length of warp which could be set.

Around the turn of the century, steam engines were first installed in seine net vessels, to drive winches. Although the power available was not very great, it was sufficient to haul in the gear, and also to pull up the sails. This was a big step forward as it meant that the gear could be operated with a smaller crew, and that longer warps could be set, paving the way for fishing in deeper offshore water.

These steam engines were first used at Frederikshavn and Greenshavn, and their use later spread to the west coast. The seine net had been used most extensively on the east coast at first, and the fishermen on the west coast adopted it somewhat later.

Perhaps it was a good thing for Denmark's fisheries that their country did not have an abundance of coal, and the use of steam engines soon declined. While the steam winches were an improvement, they were never really satisfactory and once diesel engines were installed in vessels, they began to decline in use. There were no attempts to power seine net boats by steam and this was just as well considering the size of these vessels.

Motor engines were installed in fishing boats in Denmark from 1903 onwards. The first engines were semi-diesel types and had no propeller clutch. Clutches were installed in the larger cutters in Greenshavn around 1906 to 1908.

With the mechanization of the vessels, it became possible to dispense with the row-boat for setting the gear, since it could be done by the main vessel. The vessels were now large enough and powerful enough to fish many miles away from home, and the North Sea grounds, rich in plaice and ideal for seining, beckoned them on.

A glimpse of the type of fishing vessels used and of the fishermen who manned them about the turn of the century is given in *Figs* 6 and 7—that of the marketing scene at Esbjerg is particularly impressive.

Fig 6 Early Danish sailing vessel *Grønne Erno* E 117, used in seine net fishing 1909. *(Esbjerg Fisheries)*

Fig 7 Fishermen landing their catch, Esbjerg, 1892. *(Esbjerg Fisheries)*

Post-war plenty Fishing activity in the North Sea had been reduced to a minimum during the war, and the stocks of fish, unchecked by man, multiplied rapidly. By 1918, the North Sea fishing grounds were teeming with fish. The great abundance of plaice made the efficiency of the Danish seine appear all the more remarkable. The small seine net boats were able to load up with enormous catches in a relatively short time.

In 1914, at the start of the First World War, Danish seiners began to fish on the Dogger Bank, and by 1918, at the close of the war, they first landed fish in English ports.

What these vessels achieved on the Dogger Bank grounds is really amazing (*Fig 8*). Denmark's share of the Dogger Bank catch grew from nothing in 1913 to 9% in 1924, and 75% by 1938.

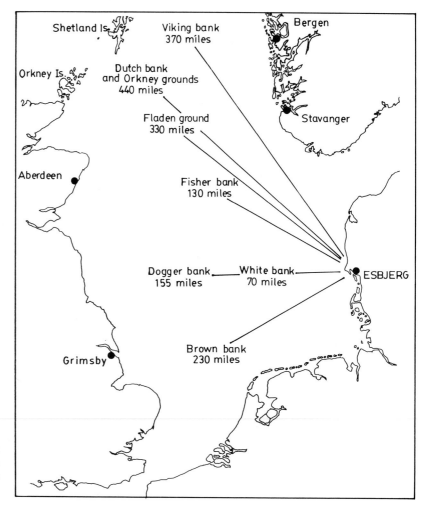

Fig 8 Distances of the port of Esbjerg from the main fishing grounds of the North Sea.

8

Working alongside steam trawlers sometimes twice their size, these small wooden, diesel-powered vessels caught more fish than their big neighbours, and caught them with a much smaller expense in crew, gear, fuel and stores.

The Danish seiners began to use ice around 1920. They started to gut and clean all fish and pack them in ice, therefore making it possible for them to stay at sea for trips of two to three weeks' duration.

The tremendous expansion of Denmark's seine net fishery in the North Sea, brought about the development of a major fishing port on its west coast. The port, the largest in Denmark today, and one of the major ports of the world, is Esbjerg, located on the southern part of Denmark's west coast.

Though Esbjerg's fishery is more diversified today, it is a port that was built up almost wholly around the seine net.

The seine net first came to Esbjerg in 1886, the same year that saw the establishment of the first harbour there.

Some decked vessels had previously been brought to Esbjerg from Norway. The small fleet soon grew with additional Danish cutters, and a few vessels bought from England. By 1899 Esbjerg had its first power-driven vessel.

The following year saw the start of fisheries control in the port. Denmark's fish inspection system is very strict and, consequently, the high quality of Danish fish is widely recognized. It is interesting to note, however, that the fishermen did not take too kindly to the inspection to begin with, and when the first control officer arrived at the port in 1900, they duly dumped him in the harbour!

The last two years of the First World War saw great haddock fishing for Esbjerg's fleet. The expansion of the fishery to more distant grounds further helped the growth of the port, and by 1922 an auction-sales system had been introduced in the fish market. A large auction hall was in use by 1924.

Following World War II, during which fishing activities were curtailed, the seine net continued to be the chief means of capture for Esbjerg's fish. However, by 1952 otter trawls were being used successfully, especially to catch large quantities of small herring and haddock for reduction to fish meal.

The trawl fishery continued to grow and by 1964 the number of trawls being used at the port had exceeded the number of seine nets. Today the bulk of all the 'industrial' fish in Denmark is landed at the port of Esbjerg, but the port still obtains much of its revenue from fish for human consumption.

Today, Esbjerg is a model port—one of the most modern and best equipped in the world (*Fig 9*). It has an extremely well laid out two-basin harbour, and a large fish market and auction hall.

Esbjerg also has several shipyards, machine works, net makers

9

Fig 9 The modern port of Esbjerg, Denmark. (*Esbjerg Fisheries*)

and marine service firms. There are many fish processing establishments and cold stores, and a number of industrial plants producing fish meal and oil.

In many ways, trends in the fishery from Esbjerg, are typical of Denmark's fishery as a whole. The seine net is still being used to a great extent, but industrial fishing has increased enormously. This may account for the slight decline in the number of seine nets.

It is estimated that there were around 800 Danish seiners in 1966 and these landed 31,500 tons of fish, worth about 86 million kroner.

The profitable grounds of the Dogger Bank from which so much wealth has been and is drawn, are shown in *Fig 10*.

Englishmen took note English fishermen were the first in Britain to observe the seine net at close quarters. They witnessed its effectiveness on the Dogger Bank and were able to have a close look at the vessels and their gear when they first landed fish in an English port in 1918.

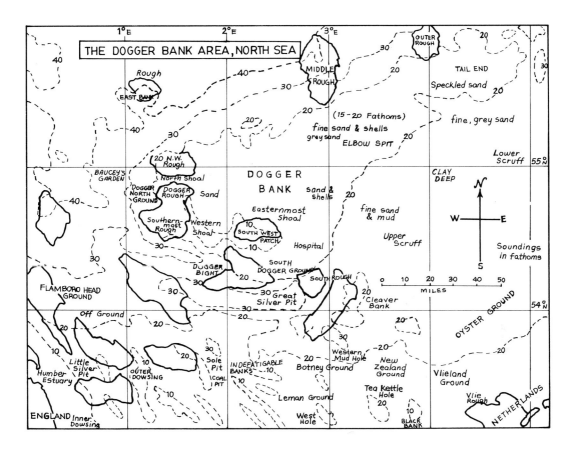

The map labels include:

THE DOGGER BANK AREA, NORTH SEA

1°E 2°E 3°E

40

Rough 40 30 OUTER ROUGH 20 30

EAST BANK MIDDLE ROUGH 20 TAIL END Speckled sand 20

20 (15-20 Fathoms) fine, grey sand

20 fine sand & shells grey sand ELBOW SPIT 20 Lower Scruff 55°N

20 N.W. Rough BAUCEY'S GARDEN North Shoal DOGGER BANK sand & shells 20 CLAY DEEP

DOGGER NORTH GROUND DOGGER ROUGH Sand fine sand & mud N

40 Southernmost Rough Western Shoal Eastermost Shoal 10 SOUTH WEST PATCH 10 Upper Scruff W E

30 Hospital S Soundings in fathoms

DOGGER BIGHT 30 20 SOUTH DOGGER GROUND SOUTH ROUGH 20

FLAMBORO HEAD GROUND 30 30 Great Silver Pit 20 Cleaver Bank 0 10 20 30 40 50 MILES 54°N

Off Ground 20 20 30 30 20 30 20 OYSTER GROUND 20

10 Little Silver Pit 10 20 30 Sole Pit INDEFATIGABLE BANKS 10 Western Mud Hole 20 New Zealand Ground Vlieland Ground

Humber Estuary OUTER DOWSING COAL PIT 10 Botney Ground Tea Kettle Hole 20 Vlie Rough NETHERLANDS

ENGLAND Inner Dowsing 10 Leman Ground West Hole BLACK BANK 10

Fig 10 The Dogger Bank area, North Sea, showing the fishermen's map for locating special grounds.

Most of the fishermen had served with the Royal Navy during the war, and after being discharged, they returned to their home ports to refit their trawlers and drifters which had been used for minesweeping and patrol work. The North Sea grounds were rich with fish following the fallow time they had experienced during the war years, but the smaller Danish seiners were able to take advantage of the prolific fishing more effectively.

Often these little motor boats arrived in Grimsby from the Dogger Bank so heavily laden with fish that they had very little freeboard remaining. The sight of such remarkable catches provoked considerable interest in the new method and many Grimsby fishermen bought sets of gear to use on their steam trawlers.

English steam-powered vessels continued to use the seine net until the outbreak of the Second World War. A detailed description of the gear and the equipment they used is given in an old catalogue of the Great Grimsby Coal Salt and Tanning Company. Winches and coilers were not much different from those used today, and the anchor mooring was almost identical to that used by Danish vessels.

11

Danish seining in English has been associated largely with one port—Grimsby. Danish vessels have now been landing fish in this port for more than fifty years. Many Danish fishermen settled in Grimsby and quite a number of the companies operating there have connections in Denmark.

Other ports in England to acquire Danish seiners were Fleetwood, Whitehaven, North Shields, Whitby and Hull. The Hull fleet was the largest in Britain next to that of Grimsby. Seining activity continued at most of these ports for over thirty years. By 1970 there were seiner fleets at only Hull and Grimsby and by 1979 only Grimsby had any 'anchor-draggers'—the term used to describe Danish seiners.

Some English fishermen were later to go seine netting Scottish style known as 'fly-dragging'. At North Shields on the Tyne, a modern fleet of 'fly-dragging' seiners was built up over the years after the war, due chiefly to the influence of visiting fleets of Scottish seiners.

Grimsby anchor seiners numbered over a hundred by the 1960s. They sailed on trips of up to 20 days, icing down their catch in bulk or in shelves in a similar way to the side trawlers. With a crew of only four men they could land from 100 to 400 kits (6 to 25 tons) from a single trip. These catches were worth from £1,000 to £3,000 each in the 1960s and from £5,000 to £15,000 by 1980.

In the late 1970s the little Grimsby seiners were to become of great importance to Grimsby. When the deep sea trawler fleet was diminished in size after the extension of the fishery limits around Iceland, Norway, Faroe and Greenland, there was a consequent slump in landings which threatened the whole fish industry in Grimsby. Then the port came to rely chiefly on fish landings by the little anchor-draggers and other small craft like pair trawlers, line boats and gill netters.

Fish landings by seine net boats in England rose to over 30,000 tons annually after the war.

The fly-dragging vessels in North Shields worked much shorter trips, usually from two to five days. Their catches were in the region of 2 to 20 tons, worth from £1,500 to £15,000 by 1980.

Used in Scotland Until World War I, the fishing industry in Scotland was chiefly concentrated on herring. In 1913 Scottish drifters landed well over 200,000 tons of herring and this total has not been surpassed since. The herring fishery was dependent on overseas markets and each year vast quantities of the fish were sent to Europe and Russia. The war resulted in the loss of most of these overseas markets and the export of Scottish herring was drastically curtailed.

On resuming this fishery in 1919, the drifter fishermen were faced with poor prices at which it was almost impossible to maintain an economic operation. Many men who owned their vessels and houses lost all in attempting to pursue the fishery. There was no lack of herring and catches were good, but there was very little demand for the fish.

As a result of the deflated market for herring, many fishermen turned their attention to the demersal or 'white' fish which could fetch better prices. Unfortunately, most of these men operated from small ports and harbours which were not equipped to cope with large scale trawler operations. Long-lining was an alternative method, but it involved laborious work both ashore and at sea, and the 'liners' could not compete with the larger trawlers. Many herring fishermen left the sea to seek work ashore because of the hardships they endured at this time.

This was the situation that confronted the Scottish herring fishermen when they sailed south to share in the herring fishery at East Anglia after the end of the war. They were bound for the ports of Yarmouth and Lowestoft, but stopped in at Grimsby for gear and stores; it was there that they first obtained a close look at Danish seiners and their gear.

Strange to say, an English vessel, the *Brash*, was the first to operate the Danish seine in Scottish waters. It used the gear in the Moray Firth in the winter of 1919–20. Though the local fishermen were curious to know what the *Brash* was doing, they apparently did not have much opportunity to find out at that time.

Six of the drifters from Scotland obtained sets of seine net gear in Grimsby in 1920, after their skippers had observed the effectiveness of the Danish method. Most of the gear was purchased from the Great Grimsby Coal Salt and Tanning Company which also supplied converted steam winches for the operation. Winches were also made available by Chapman Engineers and coilers were imported from Mollerups, Esbjerg, Denmark.

Suitably equipped for the operation, the drifters made their way back to the Moray Firth where they started to work for haddock, cod, plaice and lemon sole. Most of these boats belonged to the port of Buckie, but soon many other ports in the Moray Firth were to adopt the gear. One of the ports that was soon to lead the way in seine netting was Lossiemouth, from where the gear was first used in 1921.

Some older fishermen had predicted that seine nets could not be operated in the Moray Firth due to the rugged nature of many parts of the sea bed. However they were soon to be proved wrong. In 1921, 760 tons of fish were caught in the seine net. In 1922 the total was 2,500 tons, and by 1924 it had risen to 4,360 tons.

By 1922 it was well apparent that Germany, Poland, Russia and the Baltic States which had previously imported large quantities of cured herring from Scotland, were no longer able to do so, lacking finance. Many of these countries were beginning to exploit their own herring fisheries instead. The Scottish markets dwindled in consequence and sometimes hundreds of tons of herring had to be dumped back into the sea. Many fishermen left home and emigrated to Canada, Australia or the United States.

The more successful herring fishermen continued to pursue the fishery despite the limited home market for their catch but many of them changed over to seine netting. The seine net was adopted as a part-time gear at first—a method to be used in the off-season—but some vessels began to use it all the year round and ceased to use drift nets altogether.

The gear was operated from the steam drifters in the traditional method of anchor-dragging which the Danes had perfected. The winches and coilers were situated in a fore-and-aft position on the deck.

Some vessels used their steam capstans instead, and coiled their ropes by hand. This was a laborious process and the use of the capstan was soon discarded in favour of a proper winch and coiler.

Fly-dragging The Scots soon developed their own method of seining called 'fly-dragging', which does not involve the use of an anchor. It is not clear how fly-dragging was first evolved but it is believed that to begin with, the use of the anchor was discarded to help escape the strong arm of the law! Most of the vessels worked fairly close to the shore and sometimes within the prohibited limit of three miles. When the fishery cruiser appeared, the boats did not have sufficient time to haul up the gear and the anchor before it came alongside. By eliminating the use of the anchor it was possible to make a more speedy departure from prohibited waters when necessary!

It became apparent that by fly-dragging, *ie* by towing and heaving at the same time, it was possible to catch more round fish (haddock, whiting, cod) than by anchor-dragging. It was also an easier method to use in grounds where there was a limited amount of clean or smooth bottom and allowed the vessels to shift their grounds more quickly. The Scottish seine net boats all gradually changed over to fly-dragging though it was awkward to work on the vessels with fore-and-aft fitted winches. Many steam drifters towed the gear stern first as their skippers felt that they could not go ahead slow enough. This, obviously, was an awkward and unsatisfactory arrangement, but nevertheless it achieved results.

Fly-dragging demanded faster hauling speeds on the winch, in ratio to engine speed and the single-speed Grimsby steam winches were inadequate in this respect. Some fishermen replaced them with stronger closed-in Elliott and Garrood type winches. In 1925 a Lossiemouth engineer, James Main, made a two-speed winch out of an old Grimsby steam winch. The conversion was designed and

14

instigated by Joseph (Doff) Thomson and fitted on the motor boat *Challenger*, a wooden vessel, 50ft × 13.5ft × 5ft, (15 × 4 × 1.5m) powered by a 36hp Gardner FNM paraffin engine. The two-gear winch worked successfully and many other steam winches were similarly converted as the demand for gear models increased.

In 1920 the fishing fleet in Scotland was composed of 4,658 sailing vessels, 854 steam drifters and liners, 354 steam trawlers and 1,947 motorized vessels. These motorized vessels were powered by petrol-paraffin or semi-diesel engines and were used for long-lining and herring fishing. Many of them were converted to work seine net gear.

Two traditional types of vessels were prominent in Scotland at the time of the early use of the seine net. These were the zulu and the fifie (see *Figs 11* and *12* and also *Figs 13* and *14*).

The fifie, an earlier model than the zulu, was double-ended with a vertical stem and a very slightly raked stern. The first zulu was built in Lossiemouth in 1879. It had a similar stem to the fifie, but carried a rake of 45° on the stern. This modification was borrowed from the older scaffie vessels which were built on lines resembling the Viking ships.

Steam drifters were excellent craft for the job for which they were originally designed but they were rather heavy and cumbersome for the requirements of the seine net operation. During the 1920s and 1930s the price of coal rose and made the drifters increasingly uneconomical to operate. They also required a large crew and this added to the expense of their operation.

Once the use of the seine net was established in Scotland, it became evident that vessels would have to be specially designed and built for the job. The first of these vessels was the *Marigold* which

Fig 11 Scottish zulu under full sail.

15

Fig 12 Zulu and fifie.
Left to right: *Margaret Ann*
BF 336, and
Felicity BF 538.

was built for John Campbell of Lossiemouth in 1927 (*Fig 15*). His action was to be as significant to Scotland's fishery as the building of the first steam drifter a quarter of a century earlier.

The *Marigold* was built of wood, of fifie lines, by Wm. Wood & Sons, Lossiemouth. She was 50ft (15.2m) overall, with 16ft (4.9m) of beam, and was powered by a three-cylinder 36hp 3T4 Gardner semi-diesel engine. The accommodation was forward and the engine-room aft. The vessel carried only one mast and the winch, built by the Macduff Engineering Co, was situated in front of the wheelhouse. It was driven by a chain from the main engine. This gave no flexibility and had to be modified later.

The *Marigold*, with a crew of four men and a boy, soon proved to be very suitable for the job of seine netting. Its advantage over the larger drifters was evident, and with a 36hp engine, it was far more economical.

The introduction of the seine net to Scotland's sea fishery was a providential stroke for the industry. Had Scots fishermen not adopted the seine net when they did the result may have been the eventual disappearance of many of the smaller ports. Instead, the inshore fishery received a new lease of life and these ports began to flourish again.

Before World War II, approximately three-quarters of the Scottish seine net catch came from the Moray Firth. Although seine net fisheries were established in most other areas of Scotland, the Moray Firth continued to be the chief centre of seine netting after the end of the war.

Shortly after the seine net had been introduced in the Moray

16

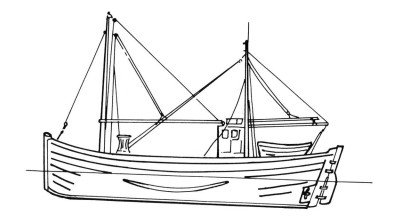

Fig 13 Motorized fifie.

Fig 14 Scottish zulu.

17

Fig 15 MV *Marigold*, the
first vessel built exclusively
for seine net fishing in
Scotland—John Campbell
was skipper-owner.

Firth it was tried out on the east coast, and also in the Firth of
Clyde.

The chief centre of seine net activity on the east coat was at
Arbroath although many vessels landed at the trawling port of
Aberdeen. By 1925 there were 32 boats in Arbroath using seine
nets. They worked the seine net for six months each year and
long-lines for the remaining six months. Long-lining activity in
Arbroath did not cease until 1966. The early seine netters in
Arbroath were small vessels with no winches, and all the pulling
had to be done by hand.

The evolution of Scottish seining is indicated by *Figs 16* and *17*.
The first shows the motor vessel *Prestige* with seine net gear aboard
in Lossiemouth Harbour in 1923, and the second shows the motor
vessel *Olive Leaf*, built in 1934 and the prototype of the modern
large seine net vessel.

Farther south, the ports of Anstruther, St. Monance, Port Seton
and Eyemouth, did not pay much attention to seining until after the
Second World War.

In the Firth of Clyde, seine nets were worked by fishermen from
Ayr, Campbeltown, and Tarbert though development was slow
until the war years.

Fishermen from the Moray Firth helped to develop many of the
ports on the west coast, notably from 1947 onwards. Some fishing
had been carried on from Oban, before and during the war, and this

Fig 16 MV *Prestige* INS 159, with seine net gear in Lossiemouth harbour.

Fig 17 Seine net boat *Olive Leaf* INS 96. This vessel, launched in 1934, was 60ft by 17ft (18·3 by 5·2m) and powered by a 72hp Gardner J type engine. She was a prototype of the modern large seine net vessel.

effort was increased considerably. Farther north, Moray Firth fishermen established bases at Lochinver and Loch Clash and landings at these places increased greatly during the 1950s.

In the Shetland Isles, there had been little activity with the seine net until after the war, but it increased rapidly then, and catches rose accordingly.

The post war years showed a marked increase in the amount of fish caught by Scottish seine net vessels. In 1939 they had taken only 11,000 tons. By 1945 this was more than doubled to 25,000 tons, and in 1947 a new high of 50,000 tons was reached. This greatly increased catch was made up chiefly of haddock, whiting and cod. The relative quantity of flatfish caught diminished from

19

over 25% just before the war, to just over 8% in the early 1950s, while their relative value decreased from over 50% to less than 20%.

The Scottish seine net catch continued an over-all increase in the 1960s, and in 1964 it reached over 100,000 tons. This was increased to over 130,000 tons in 1965.

The 1964 catch made the seine net the chief means of capture of demersal fish for the whole of Scotland. In 1938 the seine net catch comprised only 10.4% of the total demersal catch in Scotland, while the catch by otter trawls made up 75.7% of the total. In 1964 the percentage caught by the seine net was 47.9% and that of the otter trawl was 46.3%. The leading place of the seine net was further established in 1965 when its catch constituted 54.2% of the total, and the percentage of trawl-caught fish decreased to 41.1%. During the period 1960 to 1965 when the seine net overtook the otter trawl in catch, Scotland's total demersal landings increased from 168,000 tons to 258,000 tons.

The value of the seine net catch also increased over that of the otter trawl in Scotland. In 1965 it amounted to £7,150,000, over £400,000 more than the trawl catch. The following year the seine catch realized over £500,000 more than the trawl catch.

The result was that Scotland became the leader in seine net fishing in Europe and indeed in the world, with the exception of Japan whose seine net fishery does not seem to have been copied in any other country. Scotland has made the seine net its own in such a way that when the fly-dragging method is referred to, the gear is called 'the Scottish seine net'.

The statistics of Scottish landings of seine net catches are impressive. In 1938 they totalled 13,000 tons worth £347,827. Increased post war activity lifted the catch by 1958 to 95,450 tons and the value rose to £5,457,325. But expansion did not cease. It continued and by 1966 the catch was 120,448 tons while the value was returned at £7,775,531. By 1971 it had reached a peak volume of 120,621 tons worth over £10,000,000. Thereafter, due to overfishing and quota restrictions, the catch fluctuated between 80,000 and 120,000 tons, but its annual value rose to nearly £40,000,000.

Some pioneers of seine net fishing in Scotland

John Leask was probably the greatest of all the seine net fishermen that Scotland produced. He was a giant, both in stature and character; and his seamanship and fishing prowess are still talked about in fishing circles.

Born in Burra Isle, Shetland in 1903, John began life as a line fisherman along with his brother William and progressed to being skipper of his first seiner the *Budding Rose*, a 40 to 45ft (12.2 to 13.9m) vessel. He later engaged in drift netting for herring as skipper of the *Thistle*, and during the war he was awarded the BEM for running vital supplies to the Royal Air Force in a force 10 gale. As drift netting began to phase out in the early fifties John bought the 50ft (15.2m) vessel *Prossom* from Buckie and renamed the boat *Wave Sheaf*. In this boat he concentrated on seine netting only, and worked a system of fishing all week and running to Aberdeen on Friday evening, to land on Monday morning.

In the late fifties the whole family left Shetland, and moved to Aberdeen and John had the 48ft (14.6m) seine netter *Fear Not*, built in Richard Irvins in 1958. Although much older than most of his rivals he blazed a trail with spectacular trips from the Shetland and Fair Isle grounds. One of these was a two-day catch of 24 tons of large haddock, which at that time was outstanding.

A deeply religious man, with strong Christian convictions, John Leask was highly respected. In all his years at sea, it was his proud boast that he never needed to fish on a Sunday and it was a poor fisherman who wouldn't make a trip from Monday to Friday. He died in late 1978, and the fishing community felt his loss greatly.

Among pioneers of seining from Banffshire ports, who had copied the method from their close neighbours in Lossiemouth, were the Farquahars of the MV *Corinth* and James Bruce of the *Celerity*. Both these vessels worked amongst very stony ground, fly-dragging with six or seven coils of rope and catching mostly codling and haddock.

After the 1939–45 War, and with the introduction of the Grant and Loan Scheme for fishermen, many new 65ft (19.8m) wooden seiners were built and fished very successfully by a new breed of men, who were willing to go out and about and exploit new grounds. One of these was Alec Reid of Port Gordon who found rich fishing grounds at the Butt of Lewis and ran a constant stream of large trips of prime fish in his 60ft (18.3m) vessel *R.P.W.*, built by Jones Shipyard in Buckie and powered by a 152hp Gardner diesel. Others who participated in this movement were Alec Phimister of the *Capella*; Joe Humphrey of the *Briar*, Jim Bruce of the *Diligent*, and Joe Mowat of the *Prolific*. These four skippers once sailed to the Norwegian Coast, in 1948, and found a rich fishing bank twelve miles from Alesund. They returned to Buckie filled to the hatches with extra large haddock and cod, and with boxes and hold lockers absolutely filled. From the Norwegian coast the Buckie fishermen focused their attention to the rich North Sea grounds and became very adept at seine netting on the Ling Bank, Bressay Shoal and similar areas.

With the untimely deaths of Jim Bruce and Joe Mowat other younger skippers came to the fore among whom was George Murray of the the *Opportune*. George is probably the best known of Buckie seine net skippers, and throughout the past two decades, has kept up a really consistent record of good fishing. He has an immense knowledge both of the inshore and far distant grounds, and he might be found at the Bellans, six miles from Buckie and shooting five coils of rope or, on the next trip, on the Outer Shoals, 280 miles from Peterhead, and using both short and long fleets of rope as fishing dictates.

Ireland

It was a Danish fisherman who first used a seine net in Ireland. He came to Arklow around 1922 and started to use it on the anchor-dragging principle, but with limited success owing to the strong tides. He moved farther north to Skerries or Balbriggan where he had more success.

Apparently this stimulated local interest in the gear. A Balbriggan fisherman shot a seine net in Dundrum Bay and caught so much fish that he could not get the net up. Eventually, after a tremendous struggle he managed to take 80 boxes of plaice out of it!

One of the men who was led to adopt the seine net from this incident was the grandfather of Victor Chambers of Annalong. The Chambers family used the gear from small boats, anchor-fishing, until the early 1930s.

Around 1933, these fishermen came into contact with Scottish fly-dragging seiners, and were quick to see the advantages of their more versatile gear. Chief among the Scottish skippers they learned from was Willie Thomson, then in command of the *Olive Leaf*.

Fly-dragging was introduced to Ireland's west coast in 1936. Until this time a few small boats had been anchor seining near the beaches but there was not any great effort in this direction.

In the year in question, a Scot, James McLeod, had arrived in Donegal, and was fishing with a local man Francie McCallig, in a little half-decked boat. They were using lobster pots and lines but had little success. A number of small trawlers from County Kerry, 36ft (11m) long with 28 to 36hp Bolinder and Scania engines, were doing better.

In answer to some advertisements in *Fishing News* and partly at the instigation of Francie McCallig, James McLeod wrote off for details of some 40ft (12.2m) Scottish seine net vessels. A trip to Scotland followed, and in November of that year, the fishing vessel *Martha Helen* was purchased and taken back to Donegal.

Though greatly assisted by his crew's knowledge of the local grounds, James MacLeod's efforts were not initially a great success. This was due to their lack of knowledge of the technical aspects of the gear in particular. The first real break came in October 1937 when large quantities of haddock and whiting showed up at Point Head, Donegal Bay.

For about five weeks the *Martha Helen* had hauls of up to 15 boxes per tow, and 60 to 75 boxes per day. The local Sea Fisheries Association agent to whom the fish were being landed was asked by

22

Dublin where he was getting the 'rest' of his fish as they knew of only one boat that was landing to him!

Following this success, other local fishermen followed suit and obtained vessels to use the same gear. Tommy Swan bought two 44hp boats, the *Jeanette* of Ayr, and the *Pursuit* of St. Monance. The *Mary Buchan* was built at Meevagh for Francie McCallig and a Scottish zulu, the *Mulroy Bay* was fitted with a 44hp K2 Kelvin engine, and taken over by Martin Moore and his brothers. They had previously been fishing in the Kerry trawlers.

The *Martha Helen* continued to fish until 1947, although her skipper spent the war years in the Merchant Navy. She was wrecked on Islay in 1947, in a 65mph gale of wind, when *en route* to Scotland for an overhaul, but her skipper, James McLeod, and his crew all got ashore safely.

In 1949, a fleet of vessels, under the command of the family of Thomson brothers of Lossiemouth, began to fish around Ireland, landing their catches to H J Nolan & Co Ltd, Dublin.

Two of the vessels, the *Kincora* and *Casamara* were built in Ireland by John Tyrrell & Sons, Arklow, and the other two, the *Moravia* and *Kittiwake*, were Scottish built.

The influence of these Scottish fishermen added to the impetus that the seine net was already experiencing in Ireland, and the fleets of seine netters continued to grow. The main ports that vessels were working from were Skerries, Howth, Dunmore East, Helvick, Berehaven, Galway and Killybegs. Vessels also operated from a large number of smaller ports.

One factor that hampered fishing in Ireland, was that the only fish market of note was located in Dublin. Most of the fish had to be hauled overland to the market, which was often glutted, especially with large quantities of whitings.

From 1960 onwards, Ireland's fishery became increasingly dependent on herring rather than white fish. The huge stock of whiting in the Irish Sea was drastically reduced following the increased pressure by fleets of trawlers chiefly from France. Many Irish boats began trawling for prawns for much of the year and tried herring trawling in the winter. Today a handful of Irish boats still practise seining, particularly in the North West. But many of the prominent skippers in Ireland today commenced their careers on seine net vessels over 25 years ago.

Scandinavia

From Denmark the use of the seine net spread to the other Scandinavian countries of Norway and Sweden, and to Iceland. These countries adopted the gear to a limited extent only and continued to use the long-lines, gill nets and trawls in addition to the snurrevod.

Sweden

Seine net fishing was first introduced in Sweden in the year 1868 by

23

Olof Larsson of Öckero, and some months later August Andreasson from the neighbouring village of Hono became a pioneer in this field. In the first few years all the seine netting was done in the Kattegat and Skagerrak but with the success in fishing and the enlargement of the fleet, skippers began to venture further afield. In 1913 Emil Eriksson of Hono sailed to Hirtshals in Denmark and began exploratory fishing in the North Sea. By the year 1919 seine net fishing had reached such proportion that over 1,968 tons (2 million kg) of prime fish were landed in a twelve-month period. 689 tons (0·7 million kg) of this total was made up of large haddock and the remainder of plaice and lemon soles.

As the North Sea venture progressed, two Swedish vessels sailed into Grimsby in 1921 with huge catches of plaice taken on the Dogger Bank. These vessels were the *Carnegie* and *Ymer* from Gothenburg. Later in that year Gustav Claesson of Hono went seine netting as far south as the English Channel and even called into Yarmouth on his way north to land the catch in Grimsby. At this time Johan Abrahamsson and his brothers August and Albert placed an order for a 50ft (15.2m) seine netter to fish the Dogger Bank, and land regularly at Grimsby. They named the vessel *Zita*; and at that time she was the pride of the fleet; with mizzen and foresail, two-cylinder diesel, mechanical winch and coiler, log line, and anchor arrangement for riding out North Sea storms. *Zita* is still going strong as a trawler and has even been re-engined with a 320hp Mercedes diesel.

By 1935 over 1,000 Swedish fishermen were using the seine net, in 200 vessels, and at the same time there were 900 seine netters in the North Sea, from Skagen, Hirtshals, Esbjerg, Thyboron in Denmark, and also from Hull, Grimsby and Aberdeen. With the advent of the wing trawl in 1956 to 57, the fall of seine netting was as sudden as its rise, and in 1970 only 15 vessels were using this method in Sweden. By the end of that decade, only two vessels fished the North Sea, the *Kennedy* and *Crosby*.

Swedish fishermen worked the North Sea during the war years and several landed regularly in Buckie. The *Hispano*, *Ragnhild*, *Linnea* were amongst these, and the quality of their fish was outstanding. Such was the care of the catch that even after being iced for several days the fish appeared to be line-caught.

Norway   Seine net fishing was taken up by Norwegian fishermen following Denmark and Sweden and gradually spread along the entire Norwegian coast from the Skagerrak to the Arctic circle. At one time around 500 vessels used the seine net for all or part of the year. Those using the gear part-time also worked with long-lines, hand lines, gill nets or trawls.

The Norwegians developed their own method of seining which

24

was similar to both anchor-dragging and fly-dragging. They use no anchor but neither do they tow the gear. Instead, the vessel maintains its position by balancing the propeller thrust against the pull of the warps. Power blocks, hydraulic winches and rope reels were introduced in late 1960s and early 1970s.

Norway's fishing industry has been predominantly a herring purse seine fishery for many years. But like many other countries which went in for industrial fishing, they over-invested in large purse seiners and fish meal factories. The stocks were overfished and many fishermen and fishing companies suffered economically when fishing had to be curtailed.

A study by the Trondheim Fisheries Institute in 1979 revealed that small inshore fishing boats like seine netters, long-liners and gill netters produced up to four times as much fish per ton of fuel consumed as the large offshore trawlers. Owing to the better economic performance of such vessels and the remarkable success of Scottish seiners on grounds bordering on Norway, from 1965 there were several attempts by Government and industry to encourage more investment in seine netting.

Iceland The situation in Iceland is similar to that in Norway, as the vessels using seine nets there also use gill nets or long-lines at other times in the year. The gear is used for only part of the year because of the legislation governing Iceland's fisheries.

When the fishing limits of Iceland were increased to 12 miles, the Government prohibited the use of otter trawls within that area. This law applied to Icelandic as well as foreign vessels. The use of the seine net was also prohibited except in certain regions during a season from 15th June to 31st October. The chief area of its use is off the southwest coast, but it is also allowed in Eyjafjordur and Skjalfandi (north and northeast of Iceland). Some fishing also takes place along the northern part of the west coast.

Cod, haddock and plaice are the main species caught by seine nets in Iceland.

The catch in 1965 totalled 21,121 tonnes, having risen to that figure from 15,878 tonnes in the preceding year. Since 1965 the increased use of the seine net has been notable as mechanical aids, mentioned later, came into use.

Many of the Icelandic vessels use a trawl or purse seine winch when seine netting. Wire warps are used instead of ropes and they are simply wound on to the winch drum, thus avoiding the necessity of a rope coiler, and the labour involved in its use.

USSR Seine nets were used in the Soviet Union in some inshore fisheries of the Baltic, the Barents Sea, the Black Sea and the Pacific Ocean, and also in some inland lakes. The gear was probably modelled on the Danish snurrevods, but this is not certain. Apparently it was used on the shores of the Baltic in the early stages of development. At one time it was claimed that fishermen in Ostashevo used the gear before the Danes did, and that the term 'Danish' seine was unjustified!

The nets are called 'mutniks' and 'snurrevaads' in Russian books. Those used in the Sea of Azov were designated dredges and those in the Baltic were termed bag nets. They were used by the smaller fishery combines and co-operatives in the Soviet Union, and not by the fleets of middle- and distant-water trawlers whose finances were more centrally controlled. Operating on a co-operative basis the small fishery combines may use only one or two well-equipped vessels, and have the other basically-equipped boats work under the direction of the searcher or commodore vessels.

Haddock and plaice were taken in the Barents and Baltic Seas while gobies figure prominently in the Azov and Black Sea catches. Flounder and pollack were caught in the Pacific. Some Japanese influence was evident in the Russian use of warps of large and varying thickness. Originally the warps were made of tarred hemp cable.

Australia As early as 1923, attempts were made to operate the seine net in Australian waters. These first attempts were not really successful, difficulty being experienced in handling the gear owing to the depths of water and the tide encountered.

The method first used was anchor-dragging. It was used intermittently until 1931 when it was discarded in favour of fly-dragging which was initially successful.

Most of the seine net vessels in Australia operate on the southeast coast, chiefly from the State of Victoria. They work with very small crews, often only two men, and use some techniques they have developed on their own. They shoot their gear always to port, and tow always with the current. Their vessels are fitted with a deckhouse forward and thus have a clear working space aft. Apart from this, their gear differs little from that of most Scottish seine netters.

A fisheries economist and marketing expert Mr. John L. Dibbs, who began his career as a seine net fisherman in Australia in the early days, described the development of the fishery there thus:

'The use of Danish seine gear in Australian waters dates back to the late 1930s, introduced in New South Wales by fishermen of Italian origin working from Sydney Harbour and a south-coast fishing port of Ulladulla, some 150 miles south of Sydney.

'Steam trawlers had been introduced by a state enterprise in 1924, but this venture was unsuccessful and the company was sold

26

to private interests and was finally closed down in the mid-fifties. The fleet was reduced as vessels became old and repair bills mounted. Although marketing catches contributed to this failure, the nature of the narrow continental shelf extending from 20 to a maximum of 60 miles, with a patchy bottom of rock, sand, gravel and mud, limited the areas of operations for the larger otter trawlers. The Danish seiners on the other hand were able to work in small areas of clear bottom. The largest trawl grounds were located off the small south coast town of Eden on Twofold Bay, close to the Victorian state border. Here the clear grounds extended to a width of approximately 60 miles and extended southward towards Bass Strait.

'Catches in the pre-war years were good and a sizeable fleet was developing mainly in the 50ft to 70ft (15.2 to 31.3m) class.

'The war in the Pacific virtually stopped all coastal fishing, as small vessels were impounded for fear of invasion, and the new Danish seine vessels were taken into service in the island campaign to the north of Australia, where the 'small ships' and their crews performed magnificently in supplying the hard pressed land troops fighting in the coastal tropical jungles.

'There were many casualties amongst the small ships but those surviving were either returned to their original owners or were auctioned off to eager fishermen at the end of hostilities.

'A new generation of fishermen entered the industry immediately after the war. Many of these were ex-servicemen who had received some suitable training during their war service. Danish seining, as the first almost fully mechanized fishing method for medium sized vessels, attracted the new fishermen. Within three to four years the fleet grew to over 300 vessels working from Newcastle, 100 miles north of Sydney, to Eden, 500 miles south on the state border, and to Lakes Entrance in Victoria.

'Danish seiners ranged in size from 45ft (13.9m) with a two man crew to 80ft (24.4m) with crews of up to six men. Although vessels were licensed, there were no qualifications required for skippers, mechanics or fishermen. Engines were mainly in the 80 to 180hp range. Most vessels were double-enders suitable for crossing river bars where surf is encountered, although a number stuck to the more conventional tuck or square stern. Practically all vessels had the wheelhouse forward with galley and accommodation, engine room midships; with ice fish hold aft. The combined winch and coilers were placed over the engine room with belt or chain drive from the main engine. Some of the larger vessels had sunken wells for ropes, but most stowed the coils along both sides of the afterdeck.

'In the immediate post war years $3\frac{1}{2}$in (89mm) manila ropes were used exclusively but as prices rose a change was made to hard laid sisal ropes. Nets were made with hard laid cotton seine twine with wings and bunt of minimum mesh 3$\frac{1}{8}$in (79mm) by government regulation. Nets were the conventional design from Europe.

'A government regulation forbade Danish seining within the 3 mile territorial limit. Average depths fished were 30 to 40 fathoms (55 to 73m) extending to 60 fathoms (110m) on the far south coast.

'The peak years for the Danish seine fishery were between 1946 and 1953. At that stage catch per unit effort was showing a marked decline, indicating overfishing on the limited grounds. As a management measure mesh sizes were increased to 3$\frac{1}{2}$in (89mm), but the economics of the fishery, the discovery of ocean spawning grounds and the introduction of pole and line fishing for southern bluefin tuna, led to conversion of many of the Danish seine vessels to other fishing methods.

'Marketing statistics over the last ten years indicate that the Danish seine fishery has stabilized with very minor fluctuations in total landings. The main trawled species are flathead (sand and tiger), redfish, morwong and john dory, which comprise well over half the fresh table fish sold through the Sydney Fish Market each month. This indicates that Danish seining is a small but viable method of fishing for the coastal waters of southeastern Australia.'

New Zealand   The seine net was also introduced to New Zealand where a small fleet continues to operate from the southern part of Auckland. In both Australia and New Zealand the gear is used in a rather elementary fashion. Net designs, techniques and machinery are more akin to that used in the Scottish fishery thirty years ago, in the immediate post-war era.

New Zealand is one of the few countries in the world with relatively untapped fishery resources on its doorstep. The extensive demersal stocks could be harvested in abundance using either seine nets or bottom trawls. But the chief constraints to the development of the fishery is the limited local market, the distance from overseas markets, and the tarriffs or regulations governing entry to those markets.

Canada   It is only in comparatively recent times that the seine net has been used in Canada's maritime region. A fisherman in Nova Scotia is reported to have used it in 1951. By 1953 several vessels were working the gear in Newfoundland, Nova Scotia and New Brunswick waters. The Fisheries Research Board of Canada carried out a programme of exploratory Danish seining in Newfoundland and Cape Breton in 1953 to 1954.

These early attempts in Canada were with anchor-dragging and they achieved only limited success. The catches consisted mostly of flounder, witch or grey sole. It was not until fly-dragging was

28

introduced at the instigation of the Federal Government that the gear came into prominence.

The Canadians continued to develop their seine net fishery through the 1970s. Developments in Scotland were watched with such great interest that when Scottish fishermen visited the fisheries exhibition in Nova Scotia in 1977, they were surprised to find themselves treated with respect and admiration.

A Scottish seiner was chartered in 1978 to conduct exploratory fishing operations in the vicinity of the Grand Banks of Newfoundland. The vessel from Peterhead, was the 86ft (26.2m) steel boat *Juneve IV* skippered by W Strachan. Large areas of the famous Grand Banks are now quite barren, and the cod fishery is under strict control. Despite the scarcity of fish, the *Juneve* obtained some record catches of sole and round fish, outfishing trawlers twice her size on the same grounds. The demonstrations proved that seine net gear could be used effectively in a number of offshore areas. After the success of the *Juneve*, the Canadian Government chartered two more seiners from Scotland in 1979, namely the *Lothian Rose* and the *Lothian Rose II*.

USA Seine net gear has been tried out from time to time in the United States in places as far apart as Maine and California. In 1967 the Bureau of Commerical Fisheries funded a project supervised by Skipper R Barry Fisher, then operating out of New Bedford, Massachusetts. Some years later Barry Fisher organised seine net demonstrations in Oregon with the co-operation of two Scottish skippers. Another Scottish fisherman was recruited to operate a small seiner equipped and chartered under a project managed by Robert Taber of the URI Marine Advisory Service in Rhode Island.

The first successful commercial use of the seine net in America was by Phil Rhule an enterprising fisherman who had worked at different times for shrimp, swordfish, lobsters and hake, in waters off Massachusetts in the north and Florida in the south. On his converted Gulf of Mexico type wooden shrimp trawler skipper Rhule persevered with the seine net until he had mastered its skills the hard way, by which time he was bringing in catches of prime fish, well in excess of those of other local trawlers.

As labour costs results in very small crews and 60%:40% crew: boat shareouts in America, the seine net was not a really attractive proposition to US fishermen until rope reels and power blocks made seining with small crews a viable proposition. A 39 ft (11.9m) long-liner/inshore trawler, the *Destiny*, of Chatham, Rhode Island was successfully equipped with reels for an experimental project in 1977. But the project staff later concluded that the boat was too small and that a vessel of at least 45ft (13.9m) in length was needed for successful seine netting in that area.

29

The future What of the future of seine net fishing? In view of the serious problems now threatening the fishery industries of industrialised and developing countries alike, can we foresee a useful role for bottom seining as a method of harvesting fish?

It is evident now in Europe and Scandinavia that there are two distinct types of seine net operations evolving. One is dependent on the use of powerful and sophisticated vessels with all possible aids to mechanization and vessel safety. Such craft can fish the open waters of the North Sea throughout the year. The other depends on the use of smaller, more economical craft working within a few hours steaming distance of the market.

As the cost of fossil fuels rises, the larger vessels may have to undergo considerable changes to make their power units less energy expensive. During the 1980s, fuel costs will be likely to increase astronomically. By the 1990s, the fishing industry may have to use substantial amounts of substitute fuels. Unlike the otter trawler, its chief competitor, the small Scottish or Danish seiner, has very low power requirements. It will, therefore, be a more attractive proposition than high fuel consumption fishing vessels.

The serious situation regarding fish stocks in the north Atlantic has been brought about largely by the almost uncontrolled use of purse seines and industrial trawls to catch fish for reduction to meal or silage. In very few cases where fish have been caught solely for human consumption have fish stocks been diminished to such low levels. The seine net is used only to obtain fish for human consumption. It is therefore a method of fishing which should be retained while industrial fishing ought to be stopped or, at least, very strictly controlled.

Not only does the seine net produce fish exclusively for human consumption, but it produces high quality fish which is ideal for the fresh fish trade. Despite the increase in supplies of frozen fish for restaurants and supermarkets, the housewife still prefers fresh fish. Appearance and quality are essential for the fresh fish trade, and these the seine net can provide. The introduction of insulated and chilled fish rooms, and comfortable fish working decks will help seine net fishermen maintain their reputation as the main suppliers of quality fish for the retail trade.

The automation of the seining operation with hydraulic rope reels and power blocks has at last made the method attractive to American and Canadian fishermen who are so conscious of labour costs. Once these advances are also introduced to Australia and New Zealand, there may be renewed interest in the gear there. So it is possible that its use will continue to spread in suitable fisheries in the temperate zones.

30

The seine net has come a long long way since its inventor rowed out into Salling Sound over 130 years ago, with his simple little seine made of hemp on the stern of the vessel. A fitting tribute to Jens Vaever is inscribed on the bust erected in his memory at the port of Esbjerg (*Fig 1*). It reads:

Fra Limfjordsstrande
Til
Havdybs Vande
Hans Vod
Gilk Sin Sejrsgang

'From the Limfjord beaches to the deep seas of the ocean his snurrevod blazed its trail of victory'

2 Anchor-dragging: the Danish method

The anchor-dragging method of seining is particularly suited to the capture of flatfish and is still used extensively by the Danes for plaice and cod in the North Sea. It requires considerable stretches of smooth, sandy bottom with an absence of snags or fasteners, and the gear must always be set so that it is hauled in against the tide. It is carried on mostly in daylight hours and in shallow water.

While these may be regarded as limiting factors, anchor-dragging has advantages of its own. It can be carried out by a smaller crew than can fly-dragging. Most Danish seiners carry a crew of three or four men compared with a crew of five or six on a Scottish seiner. The winch only is used to haul in the gear and as a result, less power is required than when the gear is towed and hauled in at the same time.

Traditional Danish seining vessels are very full, stoutly-built vessels with engine room aft and accommodation forward. The wheelhouse is situated aft, and the winch and the coiler lie forward of it, in a line with and over the keel (*Fig 18*).

The anchor winch is usually driven off the main seine net winch and is situated in front of it, but with its drum facing foward to take the anchor line which will be led from a roller near the stem. Previously, smaller seiners hauled the anchor up by hand, or with the aid of a capstan.

Larger Danish seiners may have their accommodation aft as in Scottish vessels, with direct access to the wheelhouse.

Inshore Danish seiners are mostly about 15 to 25 gross tons in size, though some may run as small as five tons. The distant-water or North Sea seiners lie mostly in the 40 to 50 ton range.

Danish seiners carry a foresail and mizzen. While these are used for added propulsion, their main purpose is to stabilize the vessels while lying to an anchor.

The engines used are slow running diesels of about 100 to 200bhp. The Scandinavian-produced engines are generally slower running than those produced in Britain.

Fig 18 Layout of typical Danish seiner of the 1950s and 1960s.

Fig 19 Anchor buoys and warps as used by a Danish seiner.

The winch used has to operate at slightly faster speeds than those on fly-dragging seiners. Speeds when closing the gear are from 100 to 200ft (30 to 60m) per min, and 350ft (106m) per min when heaving up. Most anchor-dragging seiner winches have three gears.

The ropes are usually coiled all on one side, usually the port side, and the net is laid on a platform aft.

Danish seiners may set from 10 to 18 coils per side, *ie* 1,200 to

33

2,160 fathoms (2200 to 4000m) per side. The warp used is mainly manila seine net rope of 2¼in to 2³/₈in (57 to 60mm) circumference (*Fig 19*).

Operation   Upon reaching the fishing grounds, the anchor is dropped in a likely place. The anchor weighs about 180lbs (82kg) and has large flukes to give it extra holding power. Next to the anchor is attached a length of chain and a long 'spring', now usually of synthetic rope, 6 to 9in (152 to 228mm) in circumference. A length of ½in (13mm) diameter wire may separate the chain and the spring and the mooring gear is attached to a wire at the other end of the spring.

The mooring buoys and marker dhan are set out as shown in the diagrams (*Fig 20* and *21*), and the end of the first warp is made fast to them. The vessel then steams away from the buoys in the direction of the set, laying out the first warp. The warp is prevented from 'travelling' aft on the vessel's rail by a vertical roller, the 'shooting bolt'.

The gear is always laid out with the tide. That is, so that the tide flows directly into the net. Therefore, if the vessel is setting the gear to starboard, the first part of the warp will be laid with the tide on the vessel's port quarter. If shooting ten coils, the first turn will be made when eight coils have been set.

Fig 20 Layout of mooring gear for anchor seining.

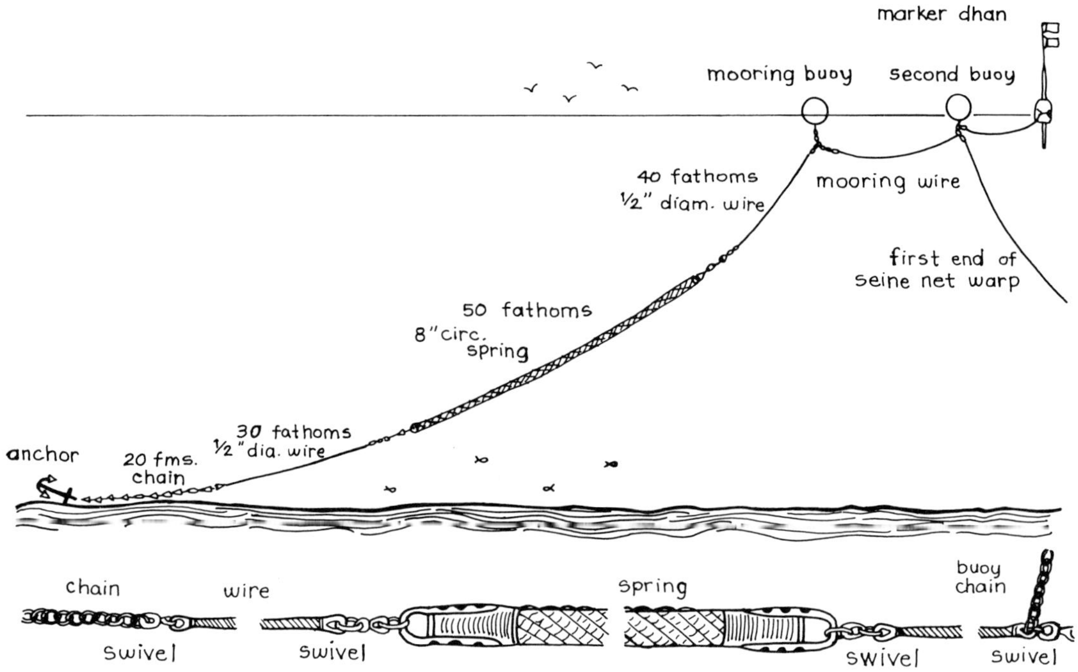

34

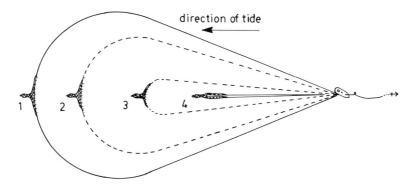

direction of tide

Fig 21 Anchor-dragging operation, showing various stages: 1 Hauling commences. 2 Net advancing. 3 Gear closing. 4 Gear closed.

The last end of the first warp, and the first end of the second warp are brought aft and shackled to the respective net bridles. The net will be laid on the platform aft with its bag on the port side since the vessel is turning to starboard.

As the last half coil of the first warp runs out, the bight of the warp from the net will be put over the shooting bolt and the skipper will slow the vessel down for the net to be set.

By this time the vessel will be at right angles to the mooring buoys. The net will run over the side so that its mouth faces directly into the tide.

As the shoulders and mouth of the net run out, the bag is thrown clear of the headline and the footrope. The second wing followed by the sweeps, if any, and the bridle runs out, and the vessel is put full ahead once more, for setting the second warp. (The parts of a seine net are illustrated in *Fig 52*, p 88.)

The second warp is set in a similar manner to the first. While it is running out, the far end, or winch end, is laid on to the winch barrel and into the coiler. The last few fathoms of warp should run out as the dhan and buoys are approached, and the vessel will be slowed down once more.

The mooring gear is usually made fast on the opposite side to that on which the gear will be towed. The end of the first warp is disconnected from the buoy and made fast to the winch on the appropriate side. When the gear is all properly fast and the warps are lying clear, hauling may commence (*Figs 22, 23* and *24*).

The vessel is now lying stationary to the anchor and the propeller will not be used again until the drag is over.

The warps are led to the winch from two separate rollers in the rail amidships. A crew member will feel the tension on each warp from time to time in case they may be snagging on the sea bed. The warps will also be kept level in the water to prevent one end of the net from coming in ahead of the other.

35

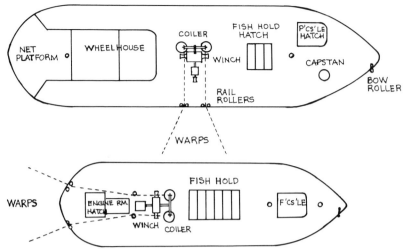

Fig 22 Deck layout of an anchor-dragging seiner and (bottom) of a small inshore vessel towing over the stern.

In first gear, the ropes will be drawn in at a speed of 130 to 160ft (40 to 50m) per min. As the warps are coiled up, they are drawn away in bundles and stacked by the crew in preparation for the next haul. As in Scottish seining, one side of ropes must be inverted in preparation for setting the first warp on the next drag.

After about two coils of rope are in, and the warps are beginning to close together, the winch will be put into second gear. This will draw the rope in at 160 to 200ft (50 to 60m) per min. This closing stage is critical and care must be taken to keep the warps level as the bulk of the fish will now begin to enter the net.

Once the net is closed, the winch is put into third or top gear. This will increase the hauling speed to around 300ft (90m) per min or faster. Once the last coil splice has come in, a watch will be kept for the 'marks' which will be situated at about 20 fathoms from the net. As soon as these appear, the winch is slowed down, and then stopped when the bridles are up to the rollers.

The net is unshackled from the warps, taken aft, and hauled on to the platform in preparation for the next set. Two crew members haul one wing on to the platform, and two, the other wing on the side deck. If there are three of a crew, one man will haul the wing on the deck side himself.

If, as is likely, the bulk of the catch is plaice or flounder, the bag will not float to the surface, but will hang down from the net. The crew haul it up to the surface, shaking down any stray fish in the process. The codend is brought forward to the fish tackle, a becket is put around it, and it is then lifted on board, and the codend knot released. The fish fall into the pounds which lie on either side of the hold hatch.

36

Fig 23 Danish seiner
hauling in the warp.
(*Esbjerg Fisheries*)

Fig 24 Taking the codend
on board. (*Esbjerg Fisheries*)

Should the catch be too much to take on board in one lift, the bag may be 'split'. If necessary, the propeller is put astern, and its wash will help the crew to pull up the lower end of the codend, so it may be split evenly. The 'lazy decky' or splitting line is pulled up and the fish are taken on board in two separate lifts. Once the catch is all aboard, the work of sorting, gutting and washing the fish commences.

Anchor-dragging seiners do not usually box their fish, instead they are iced and shelved, or packed in bulk, in the hold. Since a Danish seiner's trip may last as long as a side-trawler's, a large quantity of ice is needed. A single vessel may land as much as 400 kits (25 tons) of fish from a two-week trip. This is quite an achievement for a small vessel with only three or four of a crew.

Anchor-dragging seiners work only in the daylight hours. In the summertime, this means that they may have seven or eight hauls in a single day. Each haul is made with the gear lying out from the anchor in the direction of the tide. As the tide shifts round, this will enable them to cover all the ground around the anchor in four or five hauls.

Star-Ringing A method of covering even more bottom in a single drag or series of drags is known as 'star-ringing'. The first warp and the net are set out as usual, but the second warp is set in a straight line from, and in line with, the wing of the net. After all of the second warp is set out in this way, the end is made fast in the winch, and the vessel 'tows' the warp back to the dhan (*Fig 25*).

This warp will scare more fish in towards the centre of the ring as it is towed back over the sea bed. When hauling this warp back to the dhan, the vessel will be kept heading somewhat to the outside of the flag.

By making similar sets around the anchor, a vessel can cover an immense area of the sea bed in a matter of hours. Needless to say, the grounds where this method is used must be smooth and free from snags of any kind. Individual skippers will have their own preferences as to how and when to use the star-ringing technique, but some ways of setting out the gear are illustrated in the diagrams (*Figs 26* and *27*).

It sometimes happens that a Danish seiner has what is termed a 'fly-drag' in order to determine whether there are any fish in the area.

On arriving at a likely spot, the first warp is set out attached to a free-floating marker buoy. The rest of the gear is set out in the conventional pear-shape, and the vessel arrives back at the marker dhan. The dhan and buoys are taken on board and the first warp is made fast to the winch. Then, and only then, the anchor is dropped, and hauling commences.

38

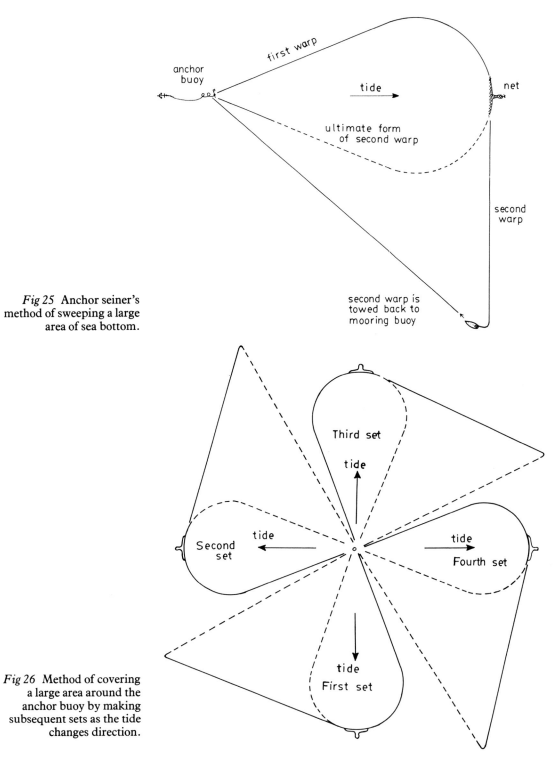

first warp

anchor
buoy

tide

net

ultimate form
of second warp

second
warp

Fig 25 Anchor seiner's
method of sweeping a large
area of sea bottom.

second warp is
towed back to
mooring buoy

Third set

tide

Second
set

tide

tide

Fourth set

tide

First set

Fig 26 Method of covering
a large area around the
anchor buoy by making
subsequent sets as the tide
changes direction.

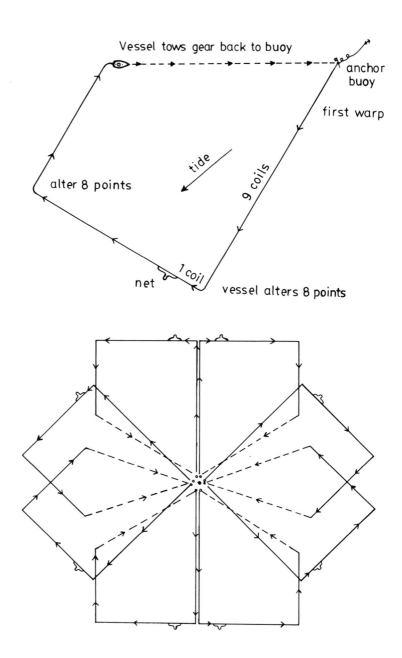

Vessel tows gear back to buoy

anchor
buoy

first warp

tide

9 coils

alter 8 points

1 coil

net

vessel alters 8 points

Fig 27 Top: Method of 'star ringing' as outlined in Glanville's (FAO) work on Danish seining. *Bottom:* Setting around the anchor buoy as the tide changes direction.

This method is useful when a quick drag is desired to find out whether there are any fish in the area. If the drag is successful, the moorings are properly secured and the normal procedure commences. If the drag produces very few fish then the anchor is lifted, and the vessel moves elsewhere in search of fish.

To clear a snag When a snag is encountered at the commencement of a drag, the following procedure is carried out. At the first indication that the warp is snagged the winch is stopped. The skipper may try to free it by heaving very slowly, but with great care lest the rope be broken. If this does not clear the snag, then the free or un-snagged warp, is taken out of the winch and made fast to the mooring buoy. The mooring gear is released, and the vessel heads back over the path of the snagged warp, hauling on the winch at the same time. Hauling is done at high speed, in this case, as fast as 500ft (150m) per min.

Once the vessel is directly over the snag, the winch is slowed down, and the rope pulled in cautiously until it is cleared from the snag. The 'bar'-like tension on the warp will suddenly give way and the warp will become very slack, then assume normal tension. The rope is then taken out of the winch and re-set, this time on the 'inside' of the snag or fastener.

On arriving back at the anchor buoy, the free warp is taken on board again, and hauling resumes.

If the gear is snagged near the close of a drag, it will be necessary to let go from the anchor moorings, and go back to both warps. This is because the net could be seriously damaged if it was drawn over the fastener. In this case the drag will be spoiled and no fish will be caught.

Anchor-dragging is usually carried on in shallow waters, that is, up to about 50 fathoms (90m), though it is possible to fish in up to 100 fathoms of water. However, at that depth it becomes difficult to drop and hold an anchor. The strain on the winch is also much greater in deeper water.

Norwegian techniques Norwegian fishermen have used Danish seines since the turn of the century but not to any great extent.

The advent of a complete Decca Navigator chain on the Norwegian coast has also given impetus to the use of the seine net.

Since most of the Norwegian grounds lie in deeper water, the fishermen have discarded the use of an anchor. Instead, they have developed a method which is somewhere between anchor-dragging and fly-dragging.

The gear is set out much in the same way as by a fly-dragging seiner, with a free-floating buoy. After picking up the buoy, the vessel does not tow the gear. Instead, the engine is put in ahead at a speed which will just prevent the vessel from being drawn astern by the warps. With the propeller keeping the vessel in approximately the same position, the winch is put into gear and the warps are hauled in at about the same speed as on an anchor-dragger.

This method of seining has accounted for large quantities of cod off the Norwegian coast, especially around the Lofoten Islands in the spring of the year.

Highly profitable   Anchor-dragging is the method used today by the seine net fleets of Denmark, England and Iceland. It is also used to a limited extent in Norway and some other European countries.

The smaller anchor-dragging vessels operate on a day to day basis close to their home ports, but most of the larger anchor-dragging vessels remain at sea for periods of up to 21 days. In this respect their operation is not unlike that of deep-sea and middle-distance, 'wet fish' trawlers.

The crew gut, wash and pack the fish in ice, the usual measure being one basket of ice for each basket of fish. The bulk of the catch usually consists of plaice which will fetch about twice as high a price as cod. In 1966, the average price paid for plaice in English markets was just short of £1 per stone. By 1979 it was £2.50 per stone or 40p per kilo. The better the condition the fish are in when they reach the market, the higher will be the price paid at the auction sales, therefore careful icing and storage are essential.

For a vessel with a crew of only three or four men, an anchor-dragger can earn a remarkable amount of money. The top seine net boats at Grimsby have an average grossing from £5,000 to £15,000 per trip.

Gear   The gear used by anchor-dragging seiners is very similar to that used by fly-draggers. The ropes are made of manila or synthetic fibre and are $2\frac{1}{4}$in to $2\frac{1}{2}$in (57mm to 64mm) in circumferences.

Icelandic techniques   Most Icelandic seine net vessels operate in a similar way to Danish anchor dragging vessels. One point of interest is that many of these boats use wire warps instead of manila ropes. The wire is wound on a trawl or purse seine winch drum and in this way there is no need for a coiler which would be awkward to operate with wire warps. The warps are run off the winch drum directly when shooting the gear and they appear to wear extremely well although one warp is turned 'end to end' each time the gear is used. Most seine net fishermen would tend to think that wire warps would dig too deeply into the sea bed, but this does not seem to be the case where they are used in Iceland. Comparative trials however, have shown that wire seining is much less efficient than rope seining. *Fig 28* illustrates some seine nets.

There was little basic change in the design of Danish seine net boats from 1930 to 1970 although considerable advances were made with electronic equipment and synthetic wing trawls (*Fig 29*). The boats remained the small economic units they had been since their inception in the 1920s. Many seine skippers began to diversify their operations around 1970, switching over to pair trawling or wreck gill netting. Those who continued to seine full time replaced their mechanical winches and coilers with hydraulic winches and rope

42

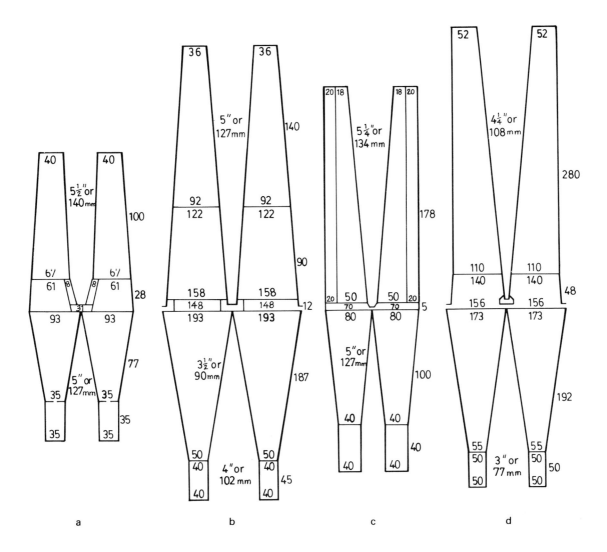

Fig 28a Plan of plaice seine net used in Denmark. Material, nylon; headline, 105ft (32m); footrope, 110ft (33·5m); twine size 210/60; floats, 20 × 5in (127mm) plastic; leads, 120 ×4oz (113g).

Fig 28b Plan of a seine net used for catching haddock, *R Larsen*, FAO No 202. Material, cotton; headline, 162ft (49·4m); footrope, 162ft (49·4m); floats, 20 × 5½in (191mm) glass; leads 220 × 2½oz (71g); twine size (tex) 700.

Fig 28c Plaice seine net used in Iceland. *Harry Franklin, Grimsby*. Materials, lower wings, shoulder and upper bag, cotton; headline, 140ft (42·7m); footrope, 142ft (43·3m); floats 20 × 5in (127mm); weights 120 × 4oz (113g), lead or equivalent. Twine size, cotton, Nos. 18, 21, 33, 43; manila, Nos. 112½ and 180.

Fig 28d Another Franklin net used for seining in Iceland. Material, cotton; twine sizes 15, 18, 21, 36; headline, 168ft (51·2m); footrope, 172ft (52·4m); floats 22 × 5in (127mm); leads, 130 × 4oz (113g).

43

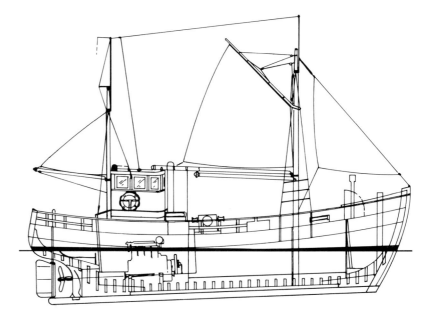

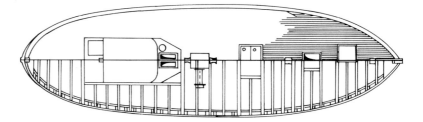

Fig 29 Layout of a Danish
seiner designed by J Miller
& Sons Ltd, Scotland 1960
(50ft × 15ft ×7·25ft)
(15·2m × 4·6m × 2·2m).

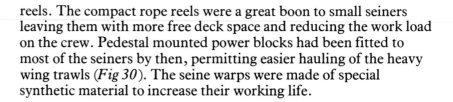

reels. The compact rope reels were a great boon to small seiners
leaving them with more free deck space and reducing the work load
on the crew. Pedestal mounted power blocks had been fitted to
most of the seiners by then, permitting easier hauling of the heavy
wing trawls (*Fig 30*). The seine warps were made of special
synthetic material to increase their working life.

Fig 30 Net hauling with a power block.

3 Tow-dragging: the Japanese method

The fishing industry of Japan is undoubtedly one of the greatest in the world. Japanese vessels engage in a global search for fish which takes them many thousands of miles from home. Their annual catch of around 10 million tons of fish is equalled only by that of the Soviet Union.

Japan's fisheries are extremely diversified and many specialized techniques are used to take the great variety of fish species caught. The bulk of the fish catch is taken by dragnets, purse seines, lift nets, pole and line gear and long-lines. The type of dragnets used are pair trawls, otter trawls, beam trawls, midwater trawls and Danish seines. These Danish seines are the chief means of capture used for bottom species.

The Japanese developed a method of Danish seining of their own without any apparent influence from Europe. They have developed this method so well in the past that today Japan probably catches more fish by seine netting than the rest of the world put together. Seine nets are used in almost all the coastal and off-shore fishing grounds around Japan. They are used in depths up to 500 fathoms (900m) and take a variety of fish species including cod, herring, sea-bream, sharks, squid, crab, lobster, shrimp, and eels. The main species caught are pollack and flounder.

Before 1900, Japan's fishery was largely un-mechanized. Many different types of nets were used to catch fish in the shallow coastal waters and amongst these were numerous beach-landing and boat-landing seines. From these seines the fishermen developed a small drag net, which they used with long ropes for warps. The gear was towed by small vessels and hauled on board by hand. It was from this type of net that the Japanese seine net was developed. 'Danish' seine nets are known as 'issobiki kisen soko-biki ami' in Japan.

Mechanization of fishing vessels began in 1909 but did not really catch on until 1913. From then on, engines were installed in an increasing number of fishing craft, and in 1917 motorized winches and capstans began to replace man-powered haulers. It was around

46

this time that otter trawls were being introduced from Britain and cotton webbing was gaining widespread use in trawl nets. Pair trawling was first started around 1920 in Kyushu, the southern part of Japan. The vessels used at this time were of about 10 tons in size and their fishing trips lasted for only one or two days. They rarely fished more than 10 miles off shore and their catches were made up mostly of sea-bream and flatfish. The number of boats using seine nets increased and the government saw fit to prohibit the use of them in certain inshore waters. The fishing limit varied in different localities from three to ten miles.

Pair trawling or 'bull trawling' as it is called in Japan, was being developed at the same time. The seine net boats used nets which were very similar to the bull trawls. The pair trawls were very efficient but they were used mainly in shallower waters of up to 50 or 60 fathoms (90 or 110m). The seine net vessels operated in the deeper waters often over 100 fathoms (183m). In 1924, latitude 130°E was set up as a boundary for administrative control of the fishery. The waters west of this line were opened for pair trawling and those east of the line for seine netting.

By 1935 the number of seine net vessels had risen to 1,432 and their average gross tonnage was 21·7. Apparently the large number of boats engaged in this method of fishing caused the government some concern and in 1937 a strict control of the number was enforced. In 1943 there was a limit of 1,345 vessels. These vessels caught about 18,000 tons of fish annually, the catch per unit effort being about 15 tons. The main species caught were oil shark, atka mackerel, sea bream and flatfish.

During the Second World War, the number of seine net vessels declined and in 1945 there were only 849. Two years after the end of the war this number had risen to 2,630. The average tonnage of these boats was low, less than 15 tons, but their annual catch amounted to 150,000 tons. The vessels operating from Hokkaido caught mostly cod, pollack and rockfish. Those operating in the south-west areas of the Japan Sea caught flatfish, shark, cod, pollack and sea bass. For deck arrangements see *Fig 31*.

Fig 31 Deck arrangement on Japanese seiner of the 1950s and 1960s.

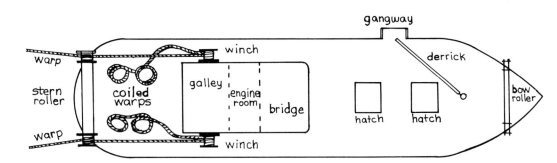

The size of the vessels in the seine net fleet increased steadily and by 1951 it came to 28·8 gross tons, average. The gear was worked in deeper waters, the general range of fishing being from 50 to 250 fathoms (90 to 450m).

The size of the seine net fleet grew steadily and the extent of their operations increased. Vessels began to operate from motherships based in waters thousands of miles from their home ports in Japan. The use of the seine net spread to the north Pacific and into the Bering Sea. By 1964 there were over 1,100 seine net vessels in the size range of 15 to 100 gross tons and on average, 50 new steel vessels of over 50 tons were being built annually. Their annual catch rose to 655,000 tons—approximately 10 per cent of the total catch of Japan. By contrast, the catch of otter trawlers was only 14,000 tons in 1963.

Japanese mothership operations started in 1940 but were interrupted during the war. Today motherships operate as far north as the Bering Sea from Cape Olyutorsk, north of the Kamchatka peninsula in the USSR, to Unimak Island, near Bristol Bay in Alaska. They fish mainly for flatfish, pollack, sablefish, rockfish, shrimp and halibut. A mothership with reduction facilities may use a fleet of 25 seine netters as catcher vessels. The seine netters would be vessels of about 60 to 70 gross tons with about 250 to 270hp and a crew of around 18 persons. In some cases the fleets of catcher vessels are made up of both pair trawlers and seine netters.

Large new stern-dragging vessels have been developed to work seine net gear and they have been fitted with the latest electronic and hydraulic equipment. Stronger, long-lasting warps have been made out of compound synthetic and wire ropes, and nets have been made of advanced design. Seine netting has been found to be a practical operation in much greater depths than was previously thought possible, and it has been proved to have certain real advantages over other methods (*Fig 32*).

Vessels Japanese seine net vessels are mostly built of wood though some larger vessels are now being made of steel. In many ways they resemble typical Japanese pair trawlers and otter trawlers, having their engine rooms aft and their wheelhouses and superstructure located above the engine room. In size they range from 15 to 100 tons and there are obviously considerable variations in design. They are commonly known as 'one boat medium trawlers' (without otter boards).

The two winch drums protrude on either side of the wheelhouse. Each drum carries a smaller whipping drum and the whole winch is run off the engine by means of a chain drive. Hydraulic winch drives allow for a more flexible operation. When the winch and propeller are both run directly off the main engine it is difficult to

48

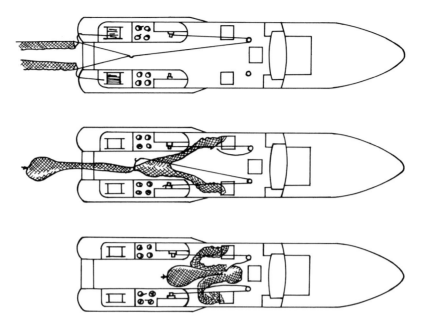

Fig 32 Hauling procedure on a large stern-dragging Japanese seine netter.

control their relative speeds which can be critical at the closing stage of the seining operation. A roller is often fitted across the stern to make it easier to haul the net aboard.

Rope coilers have not been used much on Japanese seiners. Instead, the warps are wound on to large reels as they come from the winch. On the smaller and older vessels, the warps were coiled by hand. The use of compound ropes makes this laborious process nigh impossible and rope reels are used by practically all of the newer vessels. A modern stern-trawling type of seiner may use a hydraulic winch with 'V-wheel' shaped barrels. These have a pull of $2\frac{1}{2}$ tons at a speed of 295ft (90m) per min or $1\frac{1}{4}$ tons at 394ft (120m) per min.

On conventional Japanese seine netters, the warps are coiled aft, or on either side of the wheelhouse casing, and the fish are taken aboard on the fore side of the bridge. When the wings of the net are taken up aft, the bag and codend are pulled alongside and a tackle from the derrick on the foremast is used to lift the bag on board. The fish are emptied into pounds on the deck, from where they are gutted, washed and lowered into the hold to be packed in ice.

In 1964, a revolutionary type of vessel, the *Sankichi Maru No. 51*, was built to operate the seine net from the stern in a manner similar to the operation of modern stern trawlers. The *Sankichi Maru* was 122ft (37m) long, 300 gross tons and was designed for fishing in the Barents Sea. She was of diesel electric propulsion and

49

her port and starboard winch barrels could be controlled independently from the bridge. She was also fitted with a variable pitch propeller.

The *Sankichi Maru* proved to be a great improvement over vessels with traditional hauling systems, and a number of similar vessels have been built. The latest vessels are built with a stern ramp and can take catches as high as 15 tons on board in a single haul. Once on board the fish are released into the factory deck amidships. The ropes and winches are located on the higher side decks on either side of the trawl deck and ramp. The deck layout and hauling operation on one of these vessels is shown in *Fig 32* on p 49. The specifications of the vessel shown are:

Main engine, 510hp	Crew, 15
Max. speed, 11·5 knots	LOA, 100ft (30·5m)
(21·28km per hr)	LBP, 85ft (25·9m)
Gross tons, 96	Breadth, 20ft (6·1m)
Fish hold, 3,450ft³ (97·7m³)	Depth (i), 8·2ft (2·5m)
Fuel oil, 6,160 gals	Depth (ii), 7·3ft (2·2m)
(28,000 litres)	Completed, Sept. 1965.

Electronic equipment carried by the Japanese seine net vessels includes radio telephone and telegraph, echo sounders, fish finders and DF. Extra power is supplied by an auxiliary engine generator. The more modern types also carry radar, loran, gyro-compass, and other navigational aids.

A fishing trip normally lasts from three to ten days but as the size and range of the vessels has increased, so has the length of the trips. This has made some form of freezing or refrigeration necessary as fish will keep for only a limited period on crushed ice. A few boats use refrigerators but a more satisfactory method has been found to be brine cooling. By pre-cooling the fish with a brine of about 28°F temperature, it has been found that they will keep much better in a refrigerated hold.

Vessels using this equipment stay at sea for two weeks or more. To speed up discharging on freezer vessels, a belt conveyor system is used when landing the catch.

Since a number of vessels operate from motherships, their fishing trips and mode of fish handling differ accordingly. The catch is stowed in the fish hold until the time comes for trans-shipment. The catcher boat then approaches to within 40 yards (37m) of the mothership. The fish are packed in baskets and suspended over the side in loads of about 10 tons. Wire ropes are payed out from the mothership and connected to strops on the load which has been made ready. The fish are then pulled on board the mothership. The catcher vessels obtain their stores from a ferry boat that plies between them and the mothership. They do not normally moor up alongside the main vessel unless for refuelling purposes.

Mothership-based seine net operations in the Bering Sea are carried on from April to September. Some vessels continue to operate beyond this period when the weather is suitable but normally the winter conditions are too difficult for the small catcher vessels.

Operation The Japanese method of seine netting can best be described as 'tow-dragging'. The gear is set from a free floating buoy and then towed forwards in a way similar to fly-dragging except that the winch is not used until the two warps have come together and the net is closed. The warps are then hauled in and the net is brought up. The other main differences lie in the gear itself. The nets are mostly box-type and are more complicated in design than European seines. The warps are much thicker and usually vary in thickness from the net to the vessel, the thicker parts being next to the net, or at the bight of the warp. The warps also carry weights at the bight to increase friction and keep the gear open for a longer period (*Fig 33*).

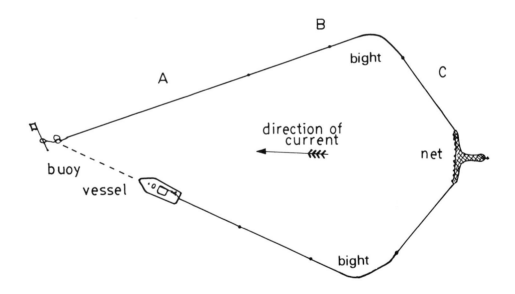

Fig 33 Typical set of a Japanese seine net (*Japan Fisheries Agency 1965*). Warps A: 1,000 fathoms (1,828·8m) length, 3½in (89mm) circ; material, manila. Warps B: 330 fathoms (603·5m) length. 3¾in (95mm) circ; material manila. Warps C: 330 fathoms (603·5m) length, 3½in (89mm) circ; material manila. (Note: weights are often inserted between the three lengths of warp).

51

A single vessel may set around ten 109 fathom (200m) coils on each side of the net. If working in depths of over 200 or 300 fathoms, fifteen coils per side may be used. The length of warp varies at a ratio of from 8 to 15 times the depth of the water. The gear is set out roughly in the shape of an isosceles triangle, the exact shape depending upon the preferences of the fishing skipper. From the marker buoy, the gear is set into the tide or current so that the tow may be made with the tide.

The marker buoy may be the keg or barrel type, with a flag pole supported by a few glass floats, or more sophisticated plastic buoys may be used. The end of the warp is attached to the buoy which is thrown overboard at the required spot. The vessel then heads up-tide with the current two points on either bow, depending on whether the set is to port or to starboard. If setting ten coils per side, an eight-point turn is made when about seven coils have run out. The remaining three coils are run out and the vessel slows down for the net which runs out over the stern, wing for wing, and the bag is thrown clear of the headline. If necessary, the vessel turns two or four points gradually as the net and bridles run out. The second warp is set out in a similar form to the first and the vessel returns to the marker buoy which is taken on board. When both warps are made fast on their respective winch barrels, towing commences (*Fig 34*).

Fig 34 Set of a Japanese type seine with synthetic rope warps (*Toyama Fishing Net Co 1967*). Warps A: 250 fathoms (457·2m) 3in (76mm) circ. Kuralon. Warps B: 50 fathoms (91·4m) 6in (152mm) circ. compound. Warps C: 110 fathoms (201·2m) 3in (76mm) circ. compound. Warps D: 15 fathoms (27·4m) 6in (152mm) circ. compound. Warps E: 110 fathoms (201·2m) 3in (76mm) circ. Kuralon.

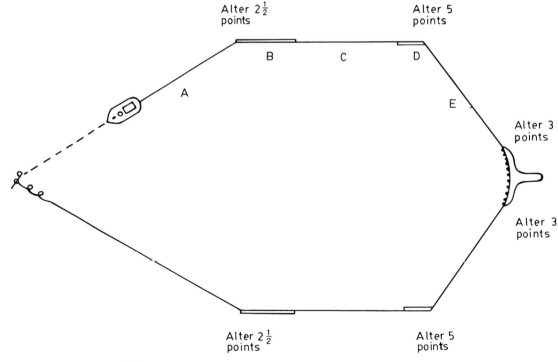

Towing speed is slow—between one and two knots plus the effect of the tide or current. Normally a vessel will tow about one gear length (1 mile to 1½ mile or 1.6 to 2.4km) in a drag of around one hour's duration, including the time taken to heave up the warps. Since the winch is not in motion during the towing period, the operation is much less critical than anchor-dragging or fly-dragging. Studies by Japanese scientists indicate that the fish enter the net during the 'closing' stage of the operation. The net may begin to close about 10 minutes after towing commences, and should be fully closed 15 to 20 minutes later, just shortly after hauling has commenced.

The engine is slowed down or stopped and the winch drive engaged before the ropes have come completely together. The angle between the warps, when hauling commences, is about 10°.

Once the warps are hauled in, the net is pulled on board by hand and the codend lifted up by means of a derrick. Since most of the vessels resemble side trawlers in layout, the codend is taken on board on the fore side of the bridge, but some of the modern stern-trawling seine netters pull their codends up a ramp in the stern.

Net performance Observations under water indicate that the warps are hard on the bottom for most of their length. As the gear is towed forwards, the ropes disturb the bottom and kick up 'clouds' of mud about 1½ to 2½ft high. This appears to have the effect of herding fish in towards the net. The weights at the bight of the warps help to keep the gear open and make it assume a shape more diamond-like than pear-shaped. *Fig 35* shows the movement of warps as towing proceeds.

When towing starts, the wing ends of a 250ft (76m) headline net would be around 150ft (45m) apart. As the gear is drawn forward, this distance decreases to 100ft (30m)and then more gradually to about 30ft (9m) when hauling begins. Ten minutes after hauling has started, the wings should be together. The wings of the net are nearly vertical during the operation and the headline rises gradually from a height of about 3ft (1m) at the dan leno to around 8ft (2.5m) at the square. It takes about thirty minutes to reel in the warps, and a further ten minutes to haul the net. The total operation of setting and hauling takes about one and a half to two hours to complete.

The advantages of Japanese seine net fishing over pair trawling and otter trawling are said to be three-fold. The gear can be used successfully in deep water, 150 to 300 fathoms (274 to 548m), where pair trawl and otter trawl operation is difficult. It can also be used on sloping or inclined areas of the sea bed, apparently with equal success. A third advantage is that the fish caught in the seine net are not crushed as much as they would be in an otter trawl and

53

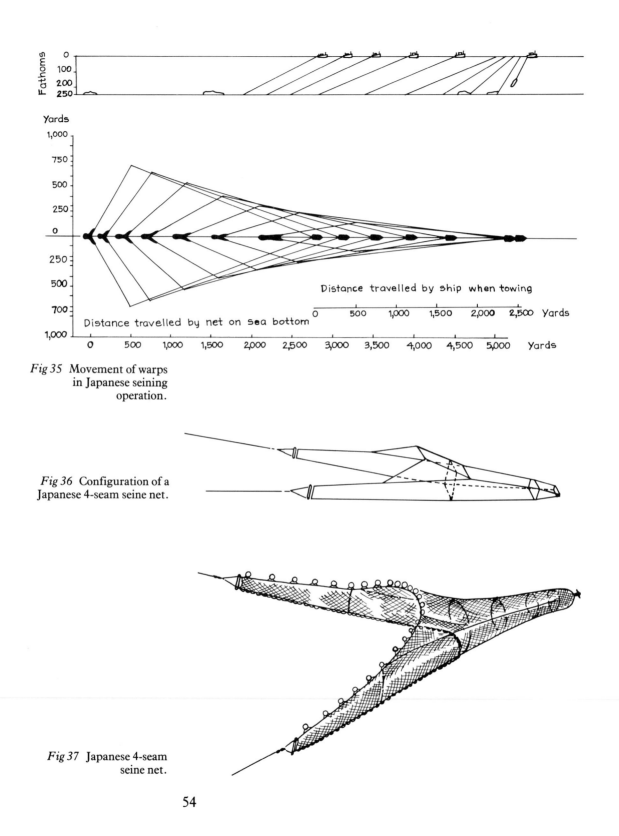

Fig 35 Movement of warps
in Japanese seining
operation.

Fig 36 Configuration of a
Japanese 4-seam seine net.

Fig 37 Japanese 4-seam
seine net.

54

the light gear does not damage the fishing grounds.

Measurements made by fishery scientists in Japan indicated that in a single drag, when the towing period lasted for 32 minutes, the seine net gear covered an area of 667,646yd² (558,400m²). In the same time, two pair trawlers covered an area of 569,082yd² (475,776m²).

Figs 36 and *37* show the outline achieved by typical Japanese 4-seam seine nets.

Gear   The warps used by Japanese seine net boats come in various thicknesses and are usually supplied in coils of 200 metres length. A single vessel may use from 8 to 15 coils per side. The thicker warps are used next to the net, or at the 'bight' of the set where the vessel makes a six- or eight-point turn when laying the gear. In general these warps vary from 3in (76mm) to 4½in (114mm) in circumference though smaller or larger vessels may use lighter or heavier ropes according to individual preferences and requirements.

Practically all seine net warps were made of manila until the late 1950s. Under normal conditions, a 'fleet' of manila rope will last approximately four months. If a vessel is using 10 coils of rope on each side, it would have to purchase 60 coils a year. Synthetic rope was introduced in the hope that its better wearing characteristics would offset its greater cost. It was found to last for about one year, thus wearing three times longer than conventional manila rope.

Unfortunately, most of the synthetic ropes preferred for this purpose have a specific gravity of less than 1·0 and are buoyant in water. Some heavier material must be added to ensure that the rope sinks properly. A good example of a combined synthetic fibre rope designed for this is the Tetoron (Polyester)—Kuralon (Polyvinyl Alcohol) combination. In this case the tetoron fibre contributes both weight and strength to the finished rope. Combination wire and synthetic rope has been produced and is becoming popular. This rope carries a lead core in each of the three strands to weigh it down. Ordinary combination (wire and manila or wire and hemp) rope has been tried but it is difficult to handle and cannot be used without large warp reels.

Most of the larger seine net boats now use some kind of synthetic or combination rope for warps but the smaller vessels continue to use manila rope since it involves less initial expenditure. It has been estimated that about 15% of the inshore fleet of seine net vessels use synthetic ropes for warp.

Weights of chain or similar material are attached to the warp in various places. In general two weights are inserted in each side of ropes. One is dropped on the net side of the bight, and the other between the bight and the vessel. These lengths of chain may weigh from 50 to 100lbs (22 to 45kg) each. They are inserted to keep the warp on the bottom, and to help the gear to stay open for a longer period.

Nets The Japanese seine nets are large, 200ft (60m) headlines being quite common, and are remarkable for their complicated box-type design. A single net may be constructed of as many as 30 different net panels. They were previously made of cotton but synthetic twines are now being used.

The parts of a typical Japanese seine net are the extension wing, wing, square, batings, belly, side panel, upper triangle piece, lower triangle piece, flapper, extension piece and codend. The codend often carries an extra flap to give it a box-shaped end. A fairly small mesh size is used, except in the wing extension or outer wing which may carry a mesh of from 4 to 6in (100 to 150mm) stretched length. The mesh in the bag and codend may be anything from ¾in to 3in (19 to 76mm) size, depending on the type of fish sought.

The wings of the net are hung quite tight, the amount of slack allowed being as low as 15% of the stretched length of the webbing. This is slightly slacker than the hanging ratio used in wing trawls in Europe.

The headline is usually made of 2in (50mm) circumference manila rope and the footrope may be somewhat thicker. About 2½ft (·76m) of extra slack is allowed in the footrope along the wings. An additional manila rope, of the same size as the headline, but of opposite twist, is used to carry the floats which are threaded on to it. This rope is lashed securely along the length of the headline.

Glass floats, 5in (127mm) diameter are mostly used but synthetic types are also available. The number of floats carried, may be as high as 200. Torpedo-shaped porcelain weights of from 4 to 8ozs (113 to 226g) in size are fitted to the groundrope. There may be as

Fig 38 Wing end details of a Japanese seine net.

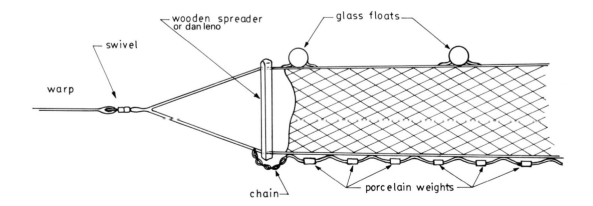

many as 400 of these. The groundrope may be a plain manila line, but occasionally a large grass or straw rope may be used. Lead weights may be substituted for porcelain, and short lengths of chain may also be used. Some weight is also added to the codend and the codend rope is fitted on the end meshes or on a separate opening on top and slightly forward of the bottom of the codend.

The dan leno or spreader pole is made of wood and is $2\frac{1}{2}$ or 3ft ($\cdot$76 or $\cdot$91m) long. It has a 6ft (1$\cdot$8m) bridle made of rope which is attached to the warp with a shackle and swivel connection.

Fig 38 shows the wing end detail of a Japanese seine net and *Figs 39a, b* and *c* give the layout and measurements of typical Japanese nets.

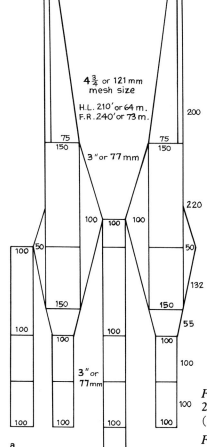

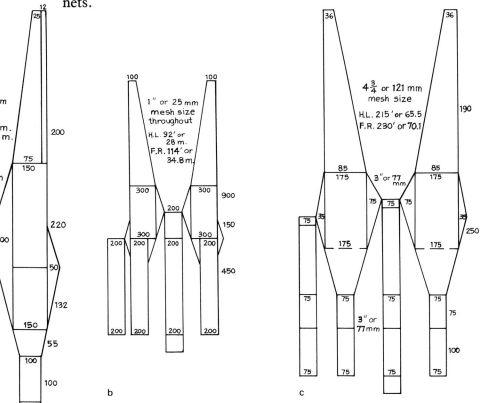

Fig 39a Cotton seine net, Japan (*Japan Fisheries Assn*). Material, cotton; headline, 210ft (64m); footrope, 240ft (73m); bag length, 90ft (27$\cdot$4m); floats, 122 × 4$\frac{3}{4}$in (121mm) glass; weights 184 × 4oz (113g), 30 × 13oz (369g) porcelain.

Fig 39b Polyethylene seine net, Japan (*Toyama Fishing Net Co*). Material, polyethylene; headline, 92ft (28m); footrope, 114ft (34$\cdot$7m); mesh size 1in (25$\cdot$4mm) throughout; floats, 50 × 5ins (127mm) glass; weights 100 × 4oz (113g) porcelain.

Fig 39c Kuralon seine net, Japan. Material, Kuralon; headrope, 215ft (65$\cdot$5m); footrope, 230ft (70$\cdot$1m); bagropes, 110ft (35$\cdot$5m); floats 50 × 6in (152mm) glass, 40 × 4$\frac{3}{4}$in (121mm) glass; weights 180 × 4oz (113g), 112 × 7oz (198g).

57

4 Fly-dragging: the Scottish method

Fly-dragging has been proved to be the most versatile method of seining. It enables the gear to be worked more independently of the tide and in areas where there may be patches of hard bottom. The length of warp used can also be varied considerably as the conditions require.

This method of seining is ideal for use in the mosaic of rough and smooth grounds found around Scotland. It has also proved to be highly effective in catching the faster and higher–swimming cod, haddock, and whiting, in addition to the slower flatfish.

A number of other countries have adopted the Scottish fly-dragging technique after finding it to be particularly suited to their fisheries. Amongst these are Ireland, Australia, New Zealand, Canada, and more recently, the USA.

Operation In the fly-dragging operation (*Fig 40* shows progress of operation) the winch and the propeller are used simultaneously to pull and close the gear. It is a delicate operation requiring the correct ratio of speeds between the propeller and winch if they are driven off the same main engine.

The vessel must tow through the water at about a half to two knots (0·9 to 3·6km per hr) when with the tide or in little or no tide. If towing into the tide, the vessel's speed should be increased to about one and a half to three knots (1·3 to 5·6km per hr), depending on the tide's strength. The majority of seine netters tow at about three-quarters of their engine's maximum speed. In most cases this will be at about 750rpm.

The winch must be able to draw the warps in at speeds varying from 50ft to 100ft (15 to 30m) per min while towing is in progress. When the gear is closed, the pulling speed must be increased to between 200 and 300ft (60 and 90m) per min.

Before setting the gear, the skipper will take note of the direction of the tide and the lie of the grounds. He may set his gear to tow with the tide, into the tide, or slightly across the tide, but he will

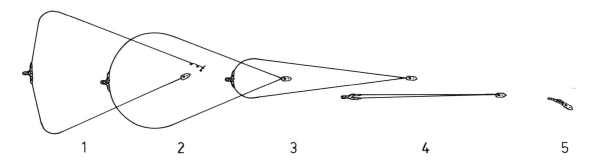

Fig 40 Fly-dragging operation: 1 Gear set out; 2 Towing commences; 3 Gear closing; 4 Gear closed; 5 Net up.

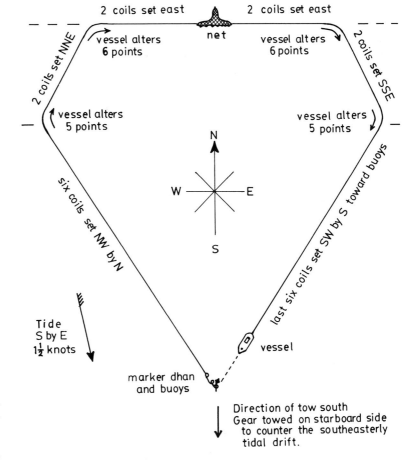

2 coils set east   net   2 coils set east

2 coils set NNE

vessel alters
6 points

vessel alters
6 points

2 coils set SSE

vessel alters
5 points

vessel alters
5 points

N

W —— E

S

six coils set NW by N

last six coils set SW by S toward buoys

Tide
S by E
1½ knots

marker dhan
and buoys

vessel

Direction of tow south
Gear towed on starboard side
  to counter the southeasterly
  tidal drift.

Fig 41 Typical set of a
Scottish seine net with
vessel setting 10 coils a side
on clean bottom and the tide
setting 1½ knots (2·78km
per hr) S by E.

59

never shoot his gear directly across the tide unless it is very weak. *Fig 41* outlines a typical procedure in relation to the compass and tide.

In particular he must not set it with the first warp across and towards the tide. Otherwise it will be swept into the ring and, by the time the second warp has been set, the ring will be almost closed and the drag will be spoiled.

The gear is towed on the weather side of the vessel in order to offset the leeway. This will be determined by the wind, tide or swell, or by a combination of these factors.

Scottish seiners have their warps stowed on either side of the deck, forward of amidships. The net is laid on a platform aft as on the Danish seiners, but the winch lies athwartships on the foredeck.

Fly-dragging vessels can set either to port or to starboard. A set to port is called a port shot, and a set to starboard is known as a starboard shot. The direction of the tide, and the proximity of hard bottom may determine to which side the gear must be set.

The first warp may be set from either side. There is not a general rule for this, and the side used as the dhan side will depend on what is the handiest for the crew.

The shape in which the gear is set will depend on the skipper's preference, the nature of the sea bottom, the strength of the tide, and the number of coils to be set. Generally it will take the form of a rough triangular or pear shape as shown in the diagrams.

The end of the first warp is made fast to the marker dhan and buoys. Usually one dhan and two buoys are used. There are two ways of doing this: the end of the warp may be simply connected to a link on the dhan, or a bundle of about 12 fathoms (22m) of the warp is lashed to the first buoy. This length of rope is sufficient to be passed around the fairleads and on to the winch when it is taken on board. When it is not made ready in this way, a separate length of warp is made fast to the winch while the ropes are being set, and when brought on board, the first end is simply shackled into this.

The dhan and buoys being ready, the other end, or net end, of the warp is brought aft and shackled to the bridle of the net.

When the skipper gives the word, the dhan and buoys are thrown overboard, and the warp snakes out after them. The gear is shot at full speed unless the weather is bad, and the rope man must pay careful attention to the coils as they run rapidly over the side.

A vertical roller, or shooting bolt, prevents the rope from 'travelling' aft on the rail. Otherwise it could come foul with the net or roller aft, or worse still, could knock a crew member over the side.

The danger involved in shooting the ropes cannot be over-emphasized. Many men have lost their lives through being dragged overboard when trapped in a bight of rope.

60

The rope man will stand on the fore side of the warps, and he will have a sharp knife at hand in case of any emergencies. When, as often happens, part of a coil is fouled by the outgoing rope, he will throw the tangled bights overboard, and then take the strain on the warp until the foul part is cleared.

When all but half a coil of the first warp has run out, the rope man will warn the crew aft, and then take the rope running to the net and pass the bight of it over the shooting bolt.

At this point the skipper will slow the vessel down for the net to be set. The last of the rope will run out and the men at the net will hold on to the dan leno until the warp is taut. Then the dan leno will be pulled out followed by the sweeps and the wing of the net.

Setting the net The net is laid on the platform in such a way that it can be set end for end. The headline will be on one side, and the footrope on the other. The bag is pulled out as far as it will come, and is laid on the side rail so that it can be thrown out behind the net. If the vessel is shooting to port the bag will be on the starboard side, and vice versa. Should the net be laid on for a port shot and the skipper decides to set to starboard, the crew will have to turn the net so it can be set to face in the appropriate direction.

As the shoulder of the net runs out, one or two crew members will throw the bag and codend as far as possible so it lies well clear of the headline in the water.

The second wing of the net and then the sweeps and dan leno will run out followed by the first end of the second warp which the rope man will have passed over the shooting bolt on its side.

The second side of warps is paid out in much the same way as the first. While he is watching them the rope man will make the tail end fast in the winch. Before doing this he will check with the skipper to see which side they are to tow on. The skipper will be watching the set of the dhan and buoys to indicate the direction of the tide or leeway. After the end is in the winch, the bight is brought aft and placed in the towing roller.

The towing roller is placed in one of at least three holes or sockets made in the side rail for this purpose. If the weather is fine, the roller is placed in the aftermost hole. If, however, there will be considerable leeway caused by tide or wind, the vessel will tow the gear from the second or third roller position.

When the last of the ropes is running out, the bight from the roller is passed over the shooting bolt and over the heads of the crew, should they be gutting on the side deck.

If all the ropes have not run out by the time the dhan is reached, the rope man will throw the remaining bundles over the side.

It may be noted here that there is no danger of the ropes fouling the propeller as long as the vessel is moving fast through the water.

61

As soon as the boat slows down or stops, however, the rope must be held up aft to make sure it is clear of the screw.

Picking up the dhan

As the vessel approaches the dhan, the crew stand by to pull it on board. The rope man will use a light grapnel on a heaving line, or else a long boathook to get a hold of the dhan and buoys. It is important they they be caught at the first approach as the strain on the second warp, which will be taut by now, will make it difficult for the vessel to manoeuvre.

The dhan and buoys are pulled on board, and the end of the warp is laid on to the winch. About five or six turns of the rope are laid around the winch barrel, and then the tail is passed into the V-wheel and spout of the coiler. A coiler gate at the 'neck' of the spout is opened to allow this. The crewman aft shouts when the warps are clear and the skipper puts the vessel ahead once more.

Drawing in the warps

The skipper will tow ahead until the strain comes on both the warps, and then he will slow the engine and signal for the winch to be put in first gear. The engine speed is increased to about three-quarters of the maximum rpm. This will allow the vessel to tow ahead at about a half to two knots (0·9 to 3·6km per hr) while the warps are drawn in at about 50ft (15m) per min.

At this stage in the operation, the crew may go below for a meal or a cup of tea. One or two men will watch things on the deck and if the boat needs to be steered, the cook will relieve the skipper in the wheelhouse.

For the first coil or so, the second warp will be higher than the first, but then they will become even. Thereafter any rise in one of the warps will mean it must be slacked back a fathom or so to make it even with the other. This is accomplished by pulling on the tension wheel in the coiler.

In addition to watching the level of the warps, the skipper or the mate will feel the tension on them from time to time, especially if there are any snags or obstacles in the vicinity.

If there is any swell or motion, it is most important that the towing roller be lashed securely in position and the gate on the roller be tightly closed. A serious accident could result if either the warp, or the roller, broke loose.

After about one coil, the winch is put into second gear. This will bring the ropes in at a speed of between 60 and 80ft (18 and 24m) per min.

The men on watch at the winch will shake the coils of rope down under the coiler, and pull them away in bundles of about 30 to 60 fathoms (55 to 110m). These bundles are stacked tidily in preparation for the next set. The ropes on the 'dhan' side must be turned upside down so they can be paid out from the first end. The

62

ropes on the other side are not turned since they are set from the net end first.

When about two coils of rope have come in, the winch will be put into third gear which will increase the pulling speed to between 80 and 100ft (24 and 30m) per min.

The first few coils will be connected by links and the man at the winch must be careful to pull these down through the coiler to prevent them from jamming. The same is true of splices in the warp, but usually it is sufficient to help them down between the V-wheel and the tension wheel.

Closing stage
After three or four coils are in, the gear will be closed. The closing stage is the most critical one since it is the stage at which the fish enter the net. Any snag or hold-up at this point could result in the loss of the catch. The skipper will therefore watch for any slight unevenness in the warps as they come together.

Once the gear is closed, the winch is put into fourth or top gear (sixth gear in a six-speed winch). The pulling speed will now be increased to between 200 and 300ft (60 and 90m) per min. At this speed it requires two crewmen to tend the winch and pack the ropes.

At the fast speed also, the crew men must be careful to avoid the danger of having their oilskins caught in the winch. They must not lean over the winch or stand too close to it, especially in bad weather.

When only half a coil remains to come in, the crewman on the control side of the winch will stand by to stop it. The winch is stopped simply by pulling up the jockey pulley handle which acts as a clutch and allows the winch to be put out of gear. The crewmen must not try to engage or disengage the winch without using the jockey pulley handle.

The warp is marked at about 16 or 20 fathoms (29 or 37m) from the net end. When this mark comes up, the crewman standing-by aft will signal or shout to the man at the winch. The skipper will slow down the engine and if the propeller clutch has been disengaged during the 'heaving up' period, it will be put in ahead once more.

The winch is stopped when the bridles come up to the roller, and the crew stand by to haul the net.

Hauling in the catch
Once the net has been towed up to the surface, the skipper will give the boat a 'kick' astern, and hauling commences. If there is any quantity of fish in the net, the codend will float to the surface. If the catch is large, the bag 'bursts' to the surface and the sight is greeted by cheers from the crew.

Hauling is always done on the weather side of the vessel, at the

63

stern. Two crew members will haul one wing directly on to the net platform, and the other wing will be hauled on the side deck. If there are four men hauling the net, two will take a headline each, and the other two will take a footrope each.

A wing trawl is somewhat heavier to haul than a seine net and if one is being used, it may have a 'lazy-line' from the bosom to the wing end. This line will be disconnected from the wing end and pulled in by the winch to draw up the heavy groundrope in a manner similar to the quarter ropes on a deep sea trawl.

Once the wings and bosom are on board, the crew pull in the bag of the net. If any fish are in the upper part of the bag, they are shaken down towards the codend.

The codend is pulled alongside and the fish tackle is made ready to lift it on board. If the bag contains too much fish for one lift, it is 'split' by means of the 'lazy-decky', a light rope passed around the meshes in the middle of the codend. The bottom of the codend is pulled up with a boat hook to spill some of the fish back into the main part of the bag. The lazy line is then pulled up and a becket passed around the codend. About half a ton or 1,000lbs (454kg) of fish are taken aboard in one lift.

As the codend comes up, a line is passed around it to prevent it from swinging outwards with the motion of the boat. As it swings in over the side-deck, the winch man drops the bag slightly to help keep it inside the rail. A crew member tugs on the codend rope and the fish are released to fall into the pounds. *Fig 42* shows a sequence of hauling splitting and lifting a bag of cod.

Once all the fish are on board, the net is hauled back on to the platform, the codend is retied and the gear made ready for the next set.

The crew scoop the fish into boxes and start to gut, select and wash them before icing and packing them in boxes in the fish hold.

Fig 42 (a,b,c,d) Hauling, lifting and splitting a bag of cod. (*See also following pages.*)

(*a*) A bag of cod has surfaced. While the crewmen haul in the net, a deckhand stands by with a boathook.

(b) The boathook has snagged the line at the codend and the crewman is pulling it alongside. In rough weather the crew would winch the bag forward and alongside, using a lazy-line attached to the splitting strap.

(c) The bag of fish is now alongside. A crewman will pull up the circular splitting strap (barely visible behind the boathook). A strong becket or lifting strap will be bent around the bag and the first lift will be hoisted on board.

(d) The fish are brought on board in 'lifts' of up to half a ton. This picture shows the last of several lifts coming aboard. The tackle used is wire, nylon or other synthetic with a 3-fall purchase from the top of the derrick. The weather is fine, otherwise the crew would use a bag rope to prevent the codend from swinging overboard again.

Resetting the gear   While the ropes were being drawn away from the winch, the crew men on duty will have kept a watch for any parts that are frayed or broken. Should any parts require splicing these will be pulled out for the attention of the rope man. Quite often, splices need to be re-done as they may jam in the coiler if they are too soft.

Should a whole coil be badly worn, it may be cut out completely, and a new coil spliced in. New coils are usually joined in the fleet at or near the dhan end, but it is important to keep a good coil just next to the net.

Under normal conditions, a coil of seine net rope will last for several months, but sometimes ropes are 'scored' or stranded on rocks or wrecks and whole coils or more may be lost on a snag or fastener.

If there was any damage to the net during the haul, this will be attended to by the crewman or men responsible. The lacing may be broken in several places or a number of ground-rope ossels may be missing. Often, the nylon float lashings may be frayed or partly broken. These are minor matters and require little time to put right.

Unless the grounds have been excessively rough, the net itself will not be damaged. The nylon, polyethylene or polypropylene twine does not tear easily, but it may happen that there is an extensive tear in the wing or shoulder of the net. If there is time before the next set, and if there is not too much fish to attend to, it will be repaired there and then. However, time is usually limited and the tear may be simply laced or 'scunned' together for the next few sets, and repaired properly later on.

Should the net be damaged beyond the point of immediate repair, it will be taken off and another put on in its place. A vessel may carry two, or even three, spare nets at one time.

The nets are overhauled properly at the end of each week. This work is usually done ashore on a Saturday morning.

Procedure when 'fast' Since the gear is often set very close to rocks or wrecks, it sometimes happens that one of the warps becomes fast or snagged on the sea bed. This can be noticed by a great increase of tension in one of the warps, or by the fact that the vessel will cease to make headway through the water.

Immediately this happens, the winch must be stopped. If not, the warps will be broken. Once the winch is stopped, the skipper may try to tow the gear clear of the obstacle. The propeller speed will be increased to help this, but care must be taken to avoid breaking any of the ropes. Towing the gear forward will raise the angle of the warps and make it easier for them to come over any obstacles.

If the rope 'jumps' and then assumes normal tension, it will have cleared the snag and the drag may be resumed. The winch will be started again and the warps evened-up in the water.

There are two ways of clearing a fastener if it cannot be towed free. One is to put the safe warp on to a floating buoy, and go back to the snag with the snagged warp, heaving it in in the process.

67

Once directly above the snag, the rope can be freed, and then the warp is reset well clear of the obstacle. The dhan and the free warp are picked up and then the drag recommences. This method is used only when the snag occurs at the commencement of the drag, and when there are at least eight coils of rope set out per side.

When a snag occurs in the later stages of a drag, or when there are only six coils, or less, of rope per side, it is wiser to go back with both warps. This is because the net may be damaged badly if it is drawn over the snag.

When going back over the snag with the gear, the ropes are hauled in at great speed, about 500ft (150m) per min, until the snag is reached. The winch is put into low gear and the vessel stopped when directly above the fastener. Once the rope is clear, the high speed of hauling back may continue.

Should a warp be broken in the course of a drag, the whole gear must be hauled back on a single rope.

It sometimes happens that both ropes are broken, usually when the net itself is suddenly snagged. The procedure then is to drop a 'creeper' and tow it slowly over the spot where the net was lost. If successful, the creeper will hook on to part of the net which then can be drawn up to the surface. This procedure is greatly simplified with the use of the Decca navigator.

The creeper mentioned here is a bar of steel about four or five feet (1·2 or 1·5m) long. Several sharp prongs protrude from the stock in the direction in which it will be towed. A length of chain is usually attached to the fore end of the creeper to make sure it lies right on the bottom.

When the vessel is fast 'up and down' to its net and cannot clear it, the help of a second vessel is required to free the gear. The second vessel simply sets two coils of rope, with a weight between them, around the gear, and tows it off in the opposite direction to that in which it was snagged. This method usually works remarkably well. It is rather seldom that seiners have to resort to this, but when necessary, it is a very helpful technique.

Fish handling   A great variety of fish is taken by fly-dragging. The main species caught in Scotland are haddock, whiting, cod, plaice, dogfish, skate, lemon sole, and hake. In an average drag, a vessel will get a preponderance of one species, say, haddock and a sprinkling of a few other kinds of fish.

Once the fish are in the pounds and the empty codend is pulled out of the way, the crew starts to fill the fish into boxes for gutting. The boxing is done with scoops which do not damage the fish in any way.

If there is a large percentage of trash fish (fish of no marketable value), these will be dumped over the side. The number of species

68

in this category decreases every year as more and more of them find some marketable outlet.

Skate, dogfish, angler fish, and other ammonia-secreting species are thrown into a pound by themselves to prevent them from damaging or contaminating the 'clean' fish. Cod are also thrown into a pound by themselves, but this is simply because they are too large to box before gutting.

When gutting commences, a number of boxes or baskets are placed in order to receive the various selections of fish. The fish are selected for size and species. There may be as many as four selections of haddock, 'jumbo' (extra large), large, medium, and small.

The crew sit on the rail while gutting, with their heads inclined into the wind to shield them from any spray. The gutting knives are short, wooden handled, pocket knives, known by such trade names as 'Nest', 'Cock', 'Venture', *etc*.

The gut is removed with remarkable speed. At the same time the crew take care to avoid piercing the flesh of the fish. The whole gut must be removed, especially the liver which decays quickly.

The gutted fish is thrown into the box or basket containing its particular selection. As these baskets fill up they are taken to the tub or pound where the fish are washed. The fish are poured out into the water under a running hose. Large fish are washed directly by the hose. After being shaken around in the water, the fish are poured into a fresh basket, and lowered down into the hold.

In the hold, the fish are packed in boxes, each holding about 7 stones (98lbs or 44·5kgs). A shovelful or two of ice covers the bottom of the box, and fish are packed on top of this until the box is three-quarters full. Another layer of ice is placed over this and a further layer of fish completes the packing of the box. A greaseproof paper covers the top layer of fish to shield it from water dripping from other boxes in the hold.

Fly-dragging seiners in Scotland land all their fish to a fresh fish market. There are over twenty such markets around the coast of Scotland. These fresh fish markets demand a prime quality product, and the auctioning system often results in considerable fluctuation of price due to the landed condition of the fish.

Vessels working for small haddock, or whiting cannot take the same meticulous care with their catch as those fishing for large haddock, cod, or plaice. This is due to the fact that they must catch and handle much larger quantities to achieve a similar return.

Usually around the spring of each year, the boats are laid up for two to three weeks for an overhaul. The vessel is scrubbed and painted, and the engine and equipment serviced. Worn parts are replaced, and the nets are overhauled. A number of skippers have their boats' hulls painted again in the late autumn.

69

Fly-dragging seiners catch a much larger amount of fish than do anchor-dragging vessels. This makes it necessary for them to carry a larger crew. The average Scottish seiner carries a crew of six though some vessels carry as few as four, and some, as many as eight.

The variety of fish caught by fly-draggers is also much greater. While they work for haddock, whiting or cod most of the time, in certain places and at certain times, they may work specially for other single species such as plaice or sole, skate, dogfish, herring, sprat, or Norway lobster.

Operating conditions

Fly draggers operate all the year round in Scotland. In summertime they work almost non-stop with very little sleep for the crews, but in the winter their hours are much shorter. They work in winds up to force 7 (28–33mph), in strength, and in tides of up to three and a half knots. They rarely fish in waters deeper than 120 fathoms (220m).

Unlike anchor-dragging, which is carried on mainly in the day-time, fly-dragging can be equally successful at night. Scottish seiners fish a lot at night, particularly in the summertime. Fishing at night is usually carried on in the shallower water, up to 60 fathoms (110m). Canadian fly-draggers also work extensively at night.

When fishing at night, a small dhan light or 'winkie' is used to help guide the vessel back to the marker and buoys. This light may be a simple torch-type affair operated on flashlight cells, or it may be a more elaborate flashing type buoy light.

Large modern seiners in the 78 to 86ft (23 to 26m) class which may have engines of 500 to 800hp operate all year round in the North Sea, over 200 miles from their home port. This is a treacherous exposed part of the ocean where the relatively shallow water and strong winds combine to produce extremely bad sea conditions, particularly in the winter time. When gale force or storm force winds prevent fishing, the large seiners 'dodge' with their boat's head to the wind until the gale is past and the sea subsides enough to enable them to fish. To protect the crewmen on deck the boats are fitted with whalebacks and gutting shelters or even full-length deck shelters.

The bigger seiners work slightly longer trips of from four to eight days duration. They land larger catches of from 200 to 400 boxes (9 to 18 tons). Some remarkable catches of over 600 to 1,000 boxes (27–45 tons) have been landed by these vessels.

Some typical Scottish seining vessels are shown in *Fig 43*.

70

Fig 43 Typical Scottish
seiners.

Argonaut

Arnhem

Excelsior

71

Atlantis

Leander

Swiftsure

72

5 Techniques used in fly-dragging

Mr W Dickson, a well-known Scottish gear technologist, has aptly said that compared with trawling on a heavy ship, seining is the rapier to the sledgehammer—not necessarily more effective in all circumstances, but requiring a difference of outlook and technique. The late Ronnie Balls, MBE, described fly-dragging as 'the nearest thing to the dustpan and brush in fishing' and called the seine net's capacity for catching fish as 'cunning outmatching force'.

Almost all who have written about the gear have stressed that its successful operation requires skill, experience and considerable knowledge of local tides and the nature of the sea bed. These factors must be borne in mind when considering the more advanced techniques used by seine netters.

Setting close to hard bottom

Being such a light gear, a seine net can suffer extensive damage if it is pulled over rough grounds. Some grounds which are used regularly by otter trawlers, are inaccessible to seine netters. To offset this disadvantage, seine net skippers have developed their own techniques of setting their gear on smooth bottom close by dangerous rocks and snags.

Patches of clean bottom close to hard ground are known as 'rooms'. These rooms may be surrounded by rough ground on three sides. Obviously the gear must be set with extreme precision in order to avoid snags or damage to the net. The setting of the gear is further complicated by the action of the tide which may carry the warp or the net over the snags before they sink to the bottom.

Fish will often gather around a wreck or peak on the sea bed and seine net fishermen often drop their nets close to these to take advantage of this.

A typical example of a 'room' used by seine net vessels was the 'double corner' in the Moray Firth. This particular ground is situated on the southeast side of Smith's Bank in a stretch of rocky bottom known as the 'reef'. It extends for one and a half miles (2·4km), is about quarter (0·4km) mile broad, and is composed

73

mainly of sand and shingle, hemmed in on three sides by rocky ground.

Before the advent of the Decca Navigator, there were two landmarks used when shooting into this room. The first was the 'Main Tap' or peak of Morven in the saddle of the Braemores, and the second was the Braes of Helmsdale. By keeping these hills in their respective positions a seine netter could set its gear within the narrow confines of the room. Since the angle between the two landmarks was rather small (45°–50°), one had to be extremely precise when shooting gear. A slight error on either side could result in considerable damage to the net. As a result, only the more daring fishermen made a practice of working this particular ground.

In times of poor visibility the room was left well alone. Sometimes a whole week would go by before the land became clear enough to allow a vessel to shoot its gear there. Immediately the land was clear, boats would head for the area, and a marker dhan would be dropped in place in case the landmarks were obscured again during the day's fishing.

There are a multitude of 'rooms' like this, used by Scottish seine net fishermen. Each has its own particular difficulties and rewards. Fish are not always present in these rooms but may be relied on to appear at certain times or seasons, or following a ground swell or gale of wind from a certain direction. Inshore fishermen like to give names to their favourite rooms or fishing grounds. The names may be taken from a nearby wreck, rock or landmark, or from the boat or fisherman who was first to fish there.

Today almost all small narrow fishing rooms can be worked by any skipper, young or old, in any kind of visibility, with far more precision than was possible with the landmarks. The instrument that makes it possible is the Decca Navigator which gives a near 90° cross-bearing fix on almost every position within the Decca range.

Where the Decca plotter is also used, the fisherman may mark the snags or the bounds of the rooms on the recording paper. This gives the skipper a visual impression of the closeness of his gear to the rocky bottom.

Each particular room poses its own problems and the gear must be set with due regard to the dangers prevalent. The warps may be laid in almost any shape along the edge of the hard bottom. Obviously a drag under these circumstances will not be ideal, but the presence of larger quantities of fish near the hard ground will compensate for the difference in the lay-out of the gear from the ideal form.

When hard bottom is encountered unexpectedly while shooting the warps the vessel will slow down and the rope man will take a few turns of the bight of the warp around the stringer. The skipper will then tow the warp away from the hard ground. Once the rope is clear and the echo sounder registers clean bottom, the bight of the rope is released and the rest of the warp is set in the usual manner.

It sometimes happens that heavy shoals of fish are located in a ground where there is room for only one vessel's gear at a time. If the fishing has been plentiful there for some time, or if there are many boats in the vicinity, there may be as many as six or seven vessels waiting to shoot into the one room.

The boats form an orderly 'queue' by agreement of the skippers who will keep in contact by radio-telephone. The skipper next in line will wait until the first skipper has started towing his gear, and has taken in about half a coil of warp. Then he will drop his dhan and start shooting his gear. By the time he has set his gear and started towing, the first vessel will have begun to heave up. In this way, several vessels may make sets in the same room in a relatively short period of time.

To see this in progress, one might be surprised that there could be any fish left after the first few hauls, but on occasions, a small patch of ground may yield good catches of fish continuously for a whole day or more.

Sometimes a room will yield good catches at only certain times of the day, usually around dawn or dusk. When this is the case, only one vessel may profit from it at a time, and there may be a rush by several boats to obtain the 'darkening' or 'daylight' drags as they are called. Then it is a matter of 'first come—first served', though the fishermen must be careful not to set too soon or too late.

Where there is an argument between two vessels as to which one set his gear first, the one which first dropped its dhan into the water is usually recognized as the first to start shooting. Should one vessel's gear be set on top of another's, the other's drag will be spoiled and its headline stripped of floats.

Setting in areas of strong tide

Under normal conditions, fly-dragging vessels can work their gear in tides of up to three knots (5·5km per hr) strength. In currents beyond this strength it becomes increasingly difficult to operate.

The most common spoiling effect of the tide is a 'fouled bag'. This occurs when the codend is swept over or under the net while the gear is sinking to the bottom. To help prevent this, one or two floats may be attached to the codend. These may be tied directly on or inside the codend, or be attached to it at the end of a nylon line of about three or four fathoms (5·5 or 7·5m) length. Sometimes a piece of chain or a few lead weights will prevent the codend from being swept about by the currents. Once towing commences the net will take the strain as it is drawn through the water and the bag will not be fouled. The period when the net is sinking to the bottom is the critical time for fouling to occur.

75

Another effect of the tide is to sweep the warps in towards the centre of the ring and thus spoil the shape of the set. If this occurs, the gear will not 'open' when the vessel commences to tow, and no fish will be caught. To avoid this, the first warp must never be set with the tide across it and towards the centre of the ring. If the lie of the grounds makes it necessary to set the gear across the tide, the first warp must be laid so that the tide will sweep it out from, and not towards the centre of the ring. That is, with a starboard shot the tide would be on the starboard side when setting the first warp, and on the port side when setting the first warp with a port shot.

Where one has a choice of direction to tow and the tide is strong, the gear will be towed either into, or with, the tide. Towing with the tide will allow the gear to cover a large area of the sea bed before it is closed. This is the practice where there is plenty of clean bottom. Towing into the tide will greatly lessen the distance the gear will travel, but it may be expedient to do this if there are snags or hard bottom ahead.

It is common practice to work with shorter warps in areas of strong tide. Also seine net fishermen are usually careful to obtain a good set at the period when the tide is turning. The 'slack tide' drag as it is called, often yields the best results in a day's fishing.

Ringing dense shoals and fishing on hard bottom Practically every seine net skipper has had the experience of gazing enviously at a dense shoal of fish on the echo sounder display, and feeling rather galled because it is lying on an inaccessible part of the sea bed, beyond the reach of a seine net.

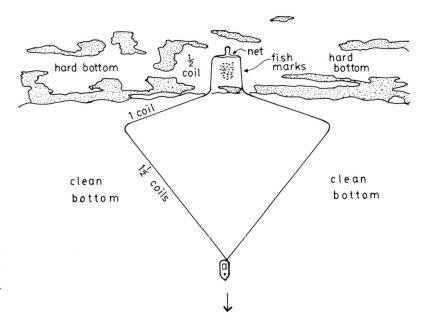

Fig 44 Method of setting around a shoal of fish lying on hard ground close to clean bottom. Length of warp three coils per side.

76

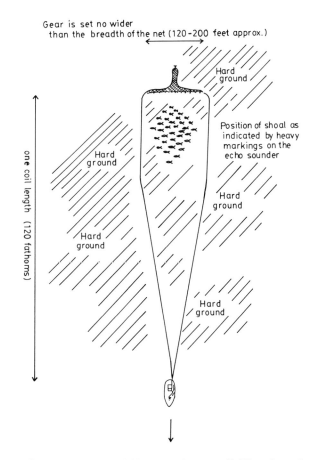

Gear is set no wider
than the breadth of the net (120-200 feet approx.)

Hard
ground

Position of shoal as
indicated by heavy
markings on the
echo sounder

Hard
ground

Hard
ground

one coil length (120 fathoms)

Hard
ground

Hard
ground

Hard
ground

Fig 45 Method of ringing a shoal of fish located on hard bottom. The normal allowance in this case is one coil of rope per side for every 10 fathoms (18·3m). (Gear will close in less than five minutes during which time the net will have travelled approximately one gear length. Once inside the bag, the fish will tend to buoy the net up off the sea bed.)

Many a fisherman, gambling on the possibility that the net might 'come home', has set his gear around such a shoal on extremely rough grounds—with disastrous results! However, most seine net skippers appear to be gamblers by nature and through perseverance, various techniques have been developed whereby the gear can be used on such dangerous grounds.

The first step is to reduce the length of warp to be set to the absolute minimum (*Figs 44* and *45*). For a normal drag, a seine netter will rarely set less than five coils a side, but for rough bottom, three, two or even just one coil per side, is used. This, of course, is only when surrounding dense shoals of fish as the net will stay open for only a few minutes. This technique was used with remarkable success to capture large quantities of herring in Ireland. Seine net vessels there encountered dense shoals of herring near Dunmore East in 1954. The herring were lying in 10 to 15 fathoms (18 to 27m) of water on hard bottom. By setting their nets on top of these shoals, and using only one coil of rope per side, these vessels were able to catch as much as 100 crans (20 tons) of herring in a

77

single haul lasting only ten minutes. The nets used were conventional haddock nets fitted with small mesh herring brailers or bags (*Figs 46a, b, c and d*).

Fig 46(a, b, c, d) Catch of herrings using seine net with small meshed brailer. Net was set around school using only one coil of warp on each side. (*See also following pages.*)

(*a*) The net surfaces ten minutes after shooting with 20 tons of herring inside.

(*b*) The crew haul in the net, shaking the herring down and concentrating the catch in the last half of the bag.

(*c*) While the crew pin the front part of the bag around a cleat aft, the engine is given a kick astern and the brailer full of fish is drawn alongside.

(d) The bag is 'split' repeatedly and over 40 lifts taken on board till the last half ton of herring is hoisted inboard. Note the pounds brim-full of fish, as are both side decks and the fish lockers in the aft end of the hold.

This remarkable herring fishery lasted from December to February each year. Seine net vessels prosecuted it in 1955, 1956, and 1957, but their numbers decreased gradually as more vessels converted to ring-netting or vinge trawling. However, it proved that the seine net could be used to catch pelagic species under certain conditions and the same technique was used later to catch sprat in the Moray Firth and other areas of Scotland.

Each winter in the Moray Firth, cod congregate in large quantities for spawning. The cod fishery is an exciting one since the fish are so 'spotty'. They are either caught in quantity or not at all and this results in a 'hit or miss' type of fishing.

In the early 1950s, seine net fishermen began to set their gear around shoals of cod, even if they were located on rough bottom. About two or three coils of rope were used per side. It was found that if the net caught the fish it became buoyed up by the quantity of the catch and consequently suffered no damage from the sea bed. If, however, the net missed the fish, then it remained on the bottom and as a result was often torn to shreds.

79

Fishermen experimented with different types of groundrope rigs in an attempt to minimize the damage suffered on rough bottom. In 1964, a seine net skipper suggested that ordinary car tyres cut in half across their diameter could be arranged on a groundrope to support the seine net on the rocky bottom and allow it to pass over obstacles without suffering any damage. The White Fish Authority agreed to assist experiments with the proposed gear, and supplied divers to study the effect of the tyres under water.

As a result of the divers' observations, the gear was modified slightly and then used on grounds where conventional nets would have been severely damaged. The tyre-mounted net came over the bottom without suffering any damage whatsoever (*Figs 47* and *48*).

Fig 47 'Bouncer' type rough bottom groundrope gear showing the metal dan leno encased in a car tyre.

Fig 48 Net laid out for inspection.

Several good hauls were obtained with the tyre-mounted gear which was named the 'bouncer' because of its action in coming over rough bottom. Catches as high as 100 boxes were taken in a single haul on grounds normally inaccessible to seine net vessels.

The success of the bouncer net led others to devise different types of rough bottom groundrope gear for seine nets. Boris Net Company, Fleetwood, produced special bobbins made of lightweight metal or plastic, for use on rough bottom. These bobbins are fitted between spacers made of rubber hose and rubber discs.

Setting on hard bottom When setting around a shoal of fish lying on hard bottom close to clean grounds, it is possible to set longer warps without further endangering the net. However there would be little advantage in setting more than five coils a side in this case. The warps are set out in the normal shape except that the last coil or half coil next to the net is set on the hard bottom and at right angles to the net. The width between the warps at this point is equal to the length of the net from wing-tip to wing-tip. This leaves very little room for error if the shoal is to be surrounded accurately.

If the shoal is located on rough grounds with no smooth bottom in the vicinity, then it is wise to use very short warps of about one coil per side. In this case the warp is set straight from the buoy to the net and back again. The spread of the net is all the width allowed to the set. This may seem rather little but in fact it is more than adequate if the fish have been properly surrounded.

To make sure that the net lands right on the fish, a few turns are taken around the cleat aft as the last few fathoms of rope run out. A crew member holds on to this while the skipper tows the warp in the direction of the fish shoal, keeping a careful eye on the echo sounder at the same time. As soon as the sounder marks the edge of the shoal, the rope is let go and the net runs out.

Sometimes, when speed is essential because of competition from other vessels in the vicinity, a free-floating dhan is thrown over at the spot where the shoal is located, and the net is set around it. However, in the excitement, other vessels have been known to set around a floating marker before the vessel that dropped it could get back to the starting position. See *Figs 44, 45*, pp 76, 77.

Charts A good chart is a great help to a seine net skipper, as to any other fisherman, especially when working in a new area. The British Admiralty charts are used greatly by these fishermen and many skippers add their own notes to the chart data in the area where they are fishing. Some companies produce charts especially for fishermen and these fishing charts contain much additional information about fishing grounds, their nature, and the names

81

used by fishermen for each area. A good example of these are the blue-back charts produced by Imray, Laurie, Norie and Wilson of St. Ives, Cambs, England, but other fishing charts are made in France, Germany and Norway.

In Britain, the White Fish Authority produce a number of fishing charts based on information gathered from fishing skippers on the different grounds. The series of charts produced are known as 'Kingfisher Charts'. Most of them are trawler charts but there are a few produced especially for seine net fishermen. They give the location in Decca readings of snags or fasteners in the area, in addition to general information about the sea bed. These charts were compiled under the direction of Skipper F S Johnson.

Seine net vessel landings
Most Scottish seine net boats make several landings each week. Vessels which operate within a few hours of their home port and return each evening are known as 'day boats'. Vessels fishing further afield and staying out for several days are known as 'trippers'. Most day boats tend to fish from their home ports all year round, but trippers may operate from a number of different ports in a year's time. They move to different areas as the fish stocks undergo seasonal changes in their location and density. There are very few seine net fishing grounds around Scotland that are not within a few hours distance of a fresh fish market. The East Coast is best served with these markets, especially the Moray Firth area. Apart from the Firth of Clyde, there are relatively few markets on the West coast.

When working among a fleet of vessels, the skippers keep in touch with each other over the radio-telephone, and they report their catches after each drag. Fishermen often joke about the element of truth in these reports and it is true that information is sometimes withheld for a while, but generally speaking, most of the skippers are quite fair with each other in this regard. Sometimes a few skippers will agree to pass information to each other by code, as is done by skippers of distant water trawlers, but with seine net fishermen the system is much less organized and often quite temporary. Some vessels carry VHF radios equipped with voice scramblers.

Few vessels will work on their own in remote or distant areas. If operating in an isolated area, boats will work in pairs or in threes or fours. The main reason for this is safety, but there are other factors. It is much easier to locate fish if three or four vessels spread out over an area than if the searching is done by only one vessel.

In a virgin area there may be relatively greater quantities of flatfish to be caught, but these will decline in number as fishing intensifies. Shallower areas inshore may be overgrown with seaweed. Vessels have been known to drag such areas clear of weed

82

and return later to find them teeming with fish. But if there are any virgin areas left in the northeast Atlantic they must be very few, small and isolated.

Successful fishing has been deemed to be largely a matter of being in the right place at the right time. To achieve this a skipper must draw from his experience, past records, the reports of other vessels, weather observations and a sixth sense, often referred to as the 'Captain's nose'!

6 Seine net gear

Seine net gear has undergone a number of changes since its introduction to Scotland in the early 1920s, but it still retains its characteristics as a light and comparatively delicate kind of gear. The gear, especially the net, needs to be balanced properly and rigged correctly.

The cost of a complete set of seine net gear is high (£2,000 to £4,000). The biggest part of this investment is the rope or warps. Since a seiner may wear out more than two complete sets of warp in a year, the importance of good ropes cannot be over-stressed.

Traditionally, seine net ropes were made of the best long-fibre manila which was specially constructed to produce a hard rope with considerable resistance to abrasion. These were 3-strand ropes of $2^3/_8$ or $2\frac{1}{2}$in (60 or 64mm) circumference, which are supplied in 120 fathom (220m) coils.

In recent years this kind of manila rope has become extremely expensive because of the scarcity of the raw material. Consequently substitutes, made of synthetic materials, have been used.

Fishermen often judge the quality of a seine net rope by the amount of 'creak' in the completed coil.

The main reasons for the need for such hard ropes are:

(1) To reduce water absorption.
(2) To enable the rope to fall in regular turns from an automatic coiler.
(3) To minimize the effect of abrasion on the sea bed and to allow sand and grit as little lodging space as possible in the interstices of the rope.
(4) To counteract the wear from the pulleys and rollers over which the rope is constantly running.

Rope manufacturers claim that there is a limit to the degree to which the tightness of the lay is beneficial as too much tightness can cause cross-cutting of the fibres. To meet all the requirements, the

84

hard-laid rope is made from densely compact yarns of fine counts and good fibre quality. Waterproofing treatments are also used to improve the performance of the rope. Where manila is not available or is in short supply, substitutes such as sisal have been used. Such substitute ropes require stronger treatment with waterproofing and preservative agents to increase their life.

For a long time, synthetic ropes were considered to be much too expensive to use as seine net warps, but the rising cost of good manila made their introduction feasible. The synthetic fibres chosen for this purpose were polyethylene and polypropylene. Both these materials have better resistance to internal abrasion than manila, and of course, they do not absorb water. When under constant use, any fibres that are broken on the outside of the rope 'weld' themselves around the other fibres, and afford protection to the rope. Since both polypropylene and polyethylene ropes are buoyant, a lead core must be inserted in each of the three strands to allow the rope to sink to the bottom.

Synthetic seine ropes are much more expensive than manila, but it is claimed that they will last three times as long as manila rope and this appears to be the case. Normally a fleet of manila ropes would have to be replaced about three time in one year, but the synthetic warps should last more than 12 months. A disadvantage to the use of the synthetic ropes is that they cause tremendous wear on the towing rollers and winch barrels. Conventional towing rollers made of the hardest steel lasted only a few weeks when synthetic warps were used.

Combination wire and manila rope has been tried by seine netters but has been found to be rather heavy, and too inflexible for the coiling operation.

The ends of the coils of seine net rope are either spliced into a 'G' link or directly into the end of the next coil. When setting a brand new coil for the first time, care must be taken to ensure that the end to go out first comes from inside the coil and comes out anti-clockwise.

The marker dhan is made of bamboo or aluminium pole about 15ft (4·5m) long, with a cork or plastic float. An iron or lead weight is attached to the foot and a few pieces of bunting are tied to the top of the pole. The buoys were formerly made of canvas but are now constructed of strong plastic or reinforced rubber. A short strop is attached to the dhan and the buoys to allow them to be fastened to the gear.

Nets The early seine nets were composed simply of a long bag and two long narrow wings to which were attached the floats and weights. As the gear developed, modifications were introduced to suit different grounds and different species of fish. There were two

85

basic designs of seine nets used until before World War II—the 'plaice' seine and the 'haddock' seine. The one had long narrow wings with little taper, and was designed to catch mainly flatfish, and the other had shorter, deeper wings resulting in a larger mouth opening which made it possible to catch more of the higher-swimming round fish (*Figs 49 and 50*).

There were considerable advances in gear design following the war. Today there are a myriad of designs for seine nets, but they fall broadly into five divisions: plaice seines; haddock seines; deep seines; wing trawls; and box trawls.

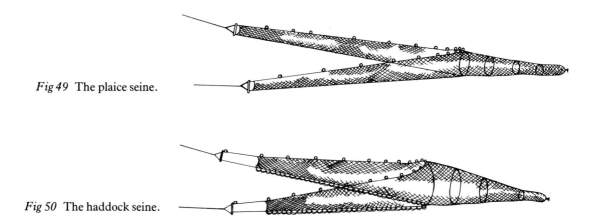

Fig 49 The plaice seine.

Fig 50 The haddock seine.

Plaice seines Plaice nets, or fluke nets are not in general use today as most vessels rely on round fish rather than flat fish to pay for their operation. However, one may still see a few of these nets being used by small inshore boats in Scotland. The original seine nets, or snurrevods were plaice seines, and the plaice nets used today are very similar to the gear first used by the Danes. The most striking features of the fluke net is the length and the shallowness of its wings. Flatfish are rarely found more than 2ft (0·6m) above the sea bed and the height of the net is therefore unimportant. What matters is the length of the wings which herd the fish into the mouth of the net. Thus a plaice seine may have a headline 220ft (67m) long. Such a net may be worked by a vessel with only a 50 or 100hp engine. The length of the wings adds little to the resistance of the net in the water. The size of the mouth of the net is the usual measure of the resistance, and a plaice seine may have a circumference of 120 meshes around the mouth compared to 420 or 520 in a wing trawl.

Plaice nets are heavily weighted with leads, but they do not normally carry a groundrope. The dan leno or spreader pole is attached directly to the wing end and the headline is more sparsely

86

floated than roundfish seines. Most plaice nets are worked on very smooth sandy bottoms and are towed at a slower speed than haddock seines.

Haddock seines Haddock seines or cod seines are much deeper nets than plaice seines and their larger mouth opening enables them to catch more of the higher-swimming species of fish. This does not mean that they will not catch flatfish; in fact the typical haddock seine net is probably the best all-round seine net used today. Its wings are relatively shorter than those of a fluke net, and they have a greater degree of taper. Where the wings meet the bag of the net, shoulders are inserted, and these are made of a slightly smaller mesh than is used in the wings. A coir groundrope is carried and sweeps or cables may be inserted between the wing ends and the spreader pole, at the discretion of the skipper.

Deep seines Increasing concentration on haddock, whiting and cod, led seine net fishermen to seek more headline height in their nets. At first the nets were simply made deeper at the shoulder and wings, and larger around the mouth, but results soon showed that the extra webbing billowed out and added to the drag on the gear without allowing the headline to rise any more.

It became apparent that there was a definite limit to the headline height on a seine net because of the tension it had to carry. A solution was found by adding a rope or lastridge of meshes down the centre of each wing and bag. A 'V'type wing end was inserted to allow the lastridge to bear some of the towing strain. This reduced the tension on the headline and allowed it to rise higher.

This modification was borrowed from the wing trawl and the modified type of seine was called the deep seine. One of the first of these was designed in 1959. Tests by the White Fish Authority the following year indicated that the deep seine caught more round fish than a conventional haddock seine at a ratio of 3·2 to 1·0 (*Fig 51*). *Fig 52* shows in diagram form, plaice, haddock, deep seine and wing trawl nets.

Apart from the 'V'-type wing end and lastridge arrangement, a deep seine is rigged in much the same way as a haddock seine except that it is almost always fitted with sweeps between the wing ends and the dan lenos. These sweeps may be ten fathoms (18m) long, or more.

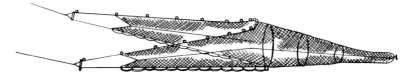

Fig 51 The deep seine.

87

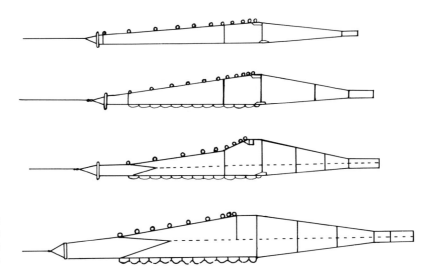

Fig 52 Schematic diagram of seine net types (plaice seine, haddock seine, deep seine and wing trawl).

Hanging Seine nets are hung directly to head and footropes made of half inch (12mm) diameter combination wire, or of Terylene rope. The wings are hung with a 5% loss in stretched length, *ie* every two meshes are hung on a staple the length of one and seven eighths stretched meshes. The shoulders are hung slacker on the headline than on the footrope. This results in the headline overhanging the footrope by anything from two to six feet (·6 to 1·8m). The crown piece at the head and bosom is hung-in about 50%.

Accurate rigging of a seine net is essential if the net is to fish properly. Often fishermen will check their nets by re-measuring the headline and footrope, or by 'pulling the tail'. To do this the bag or codend is made fast to a bollard and the crew pull on each wing, holding it at the shoulders on the head and foot. The headline should lift up as they pull, and the footrope should assume some tension, but remain on the ground. If it lifts up at the bosom, the net is considered out of trim and is rehung accordingly.

Wing trawl The wing trawl (or vinge trawl) was introduced to the Scottish seine net fishery in 1957. It had been developed in Sweden and in Denmark for both haddock and herring fishing, and was designed for use by small otter trawlers. Its use with seine net gear was a surprising development since seine nets were considered to be far better for their type of operation than any kind of otter trawl. One of the first skippers to use a wing trawl with his seine net gear was William Campbell of the MV *Argosy*, then fishing out of Oban on the southwest coast of Scotland.

The wing trawl is a large light net with a 'V'type wing end and wing lastridge rope. Its most characteristic feature is the tight hanging arrangement which places the towing strain on the

88

webbing of the net rather than the headline and the footrope as such. The strain on the webbing appears to elongate the meshes when the gear is being towed, and thus facilitate the capture of small fish. The tension on the netting appears to have no limiting effects on the mouth opening and the wing trawls are credited with remarkably good headline height. *Fig 53* shows a commercially designed cod seine.

In a few short years, the wing trawl established itself as one of the best and most effective nets available for seine netting. Its success in this respect is surprising since, like other trawls, the vinge has shorter wings than a seine net and has a square piece inserted over and above the mouth. The square would appear to be an encumbrance since the angle between the wings changes gradually from 180° to 0° during the seining operation. In otter trawling the wings lie at a constant angle of 20° to 30°.

One disadvantage to the use of the wing trawl in seining is that it must be set directly into or with the tide, in order to fish properly. If the tide is at an angle to the direction of the tow, then the trawl will be fouled, or fail to achieve its proper fishing shape.

Vinge trawls are hung tighter in the wings than seine nets. Often they are hung as tight as the meshes will allow. Across the square and bosom they are hung much slacker, usually between a third and a half (33% to 50%), but most fishermen prefer to hang this piece as tight as possible. When re-hanging a wing trawl, the original headline and footrope lengths are ignored. The proper 10 or 12ft

Fig 53 A cod seine net. Floats, 25 plastic 5in (127mm) circ; leads, 252 × 4oz (113g) rings; headrope, 110ft (33·5m); footrope, 120ft (36·6m); lines of 1³/₈in (34mm) circ. Terylene or stainless steel wire. (*Harry Franklin Ltd, Grimsby*)

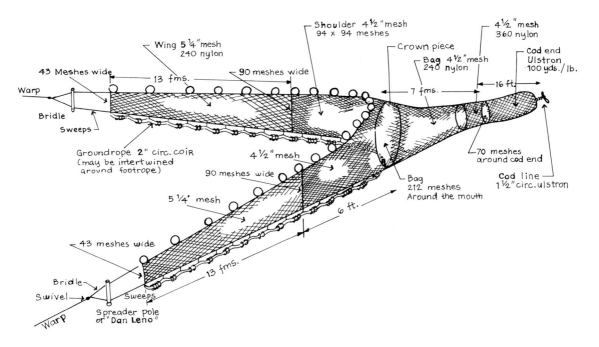

(3 or 3·6m) of cover is allowed for the square and then the shoulders and wings are hung as tight as they will allow. This method rectifies any stretch in the webbing.

A wing trawl usually carries more weight than a seine net of similar size, but they are still much more lightly rigged than conventional otter trawl nets. They also carry sweeps between the wing ends and the dan leno. When using a wing trawl, it is common practice to have a lazy line attached to the bosom to assist in hauling the net on board. See *Fig 63* p 109.

Box trawls   Box trawls or 4-seam trawls closely resemble the wing trawls having similarly proportioned wings and 'V'type wing ends. They differ in that they have side panels inserted to help increase the mouth opening and headline height. The side panels extend from the apex of the 'V' to a point halfway down the bag where it tapers to meet the codend.

That they do achieve a notable degree of headline height is not doubted. Whether the 4-seam design is a distinct improvement over the 2-seam wing trawl is still to be determined. Some skippers prefer a box trawl and others use only 2-seam nets. Where the box trawl is used it is generally thought to be more effective in deep water. Some of these nets have been used with remarkable success, and catches as high as 1,000 boxes (50 tons) have been reported.

Net performance   The performance of a seine net, or any net for that matter, is a subject of much debate. We know relatively little of what shape the net takes up under the water, and even less of the reaction of the fish to the net.

In 1953, the Department of Agriculture and Fisheries for Scotland produced a film of the seine net in operation. The film, 'Fish and the Seine Net', was shot in the shallow waters of Burghead Bay in the Moray Firth. It revealed for the first time the form of a seine net under water.

In the film, it was seen that the net billowed out in the water as it began to be towed, and all the meshes were wide open. Fish, mainly flounder (dabs and plaice) were herded along by the groundrope and eventually overtaken and led down the bag and into the codend. Small fish appeared to escape through the meshes without much trouble. While the fish seemed to sense the approach of the groundrope, they did not appear to notice the headrope and the crown of the net above them.

More detailed underwater observations of the reaction of fish to the seine net were made in 1964 by the Department of Agriculture and Fisheries for Scotland. This time they had an opportunity to observe the behaviour of haddock. The observations made in the daylight hours, at depths of 6 to 10 fathoms (11 to 18m) in the

90

Moray Firth, produced the following account.

(a) In most hauls, haddock were first seen at the bight of the net mouth in the later stages of closing. They were mostly swimming along the direction of the tow, and at the speed of the net.

(b) As the haul progressed the number of haddock in the mouth bight increased and tended to 'stack' upwards. This column of fish reached above the headline when the shoals were large.

(c) Fish were caught when they appeared to tire or 'give up', and stop swimming or swim slower so that they fell back into the mouth of the oncoming net.

(d) When the winch was put into fast gear, about 70% of the fish in the bight of the net mouth were caught, and the remainder spilled over the headline and escaped.

(e) At no time did the fish panic before the net.

(f) The reactions of the flatfish were similar to those observed in the film 'Fish and the Seine Net'.

(g) Only a small number of flatfish were observed near the warps in the vicinity of the net, but those that were seen were being herded along by the rope.

(h) The fish reacted in the same way, and were herded along at the mouth bight of a net which was set with netting in the wings and shoulder but no bag or codend. When a bight of rope with no net was used, the flatfish were herded along in front of it in much the same way.

Further observations in 1965 showed the fishing efficiency was high when the warp was on the bottom although many fish escaped where it was raised near the bridle pole.

It may be that the netting in the wings of a seine net could be reduced or perhaps a larger mesh could be used without much reduction in catch. The author recalls using a net with no yarn in the wings but the results did not indicate whether there was any loss of efficiency. The gear was used on hard bottom where stones and boulders were causing considerable damage to the net.

While headline height is an advantage when fishing for haddock and whiting, cod may often be caught in a seine net with a very low mouth opening. It appears to be the case that cod, when feeding or spawning, lie hard on the sea bed. There have been large catches of cod obtained on soft bottom when most of the lower half of the net

91

has been dragging in the mud. In such a case, and also when fishing for flatfish, a seine net holds a distinct advantage over a wing trawl.

Net materials The first major improvement to the gear was the introduction of synthetic fibres in the net twines. This was started in the early 1950s.

There are nine main kinds of synthetic fibres produced today, but only four have had widespread use in fishing nets in Europe. (Japan has utilized a greater variety of synthetic twines in fishing gear.)

The four that were prominent in Britain were, in order of their appearance, polyamide, polyester, polyethylene, and polypropylene, better known by their trade names of Nylon, Terylene, Courlene and Ulstron. Other trade names are:

Trade name	Country	Trade name	Country
Polyamide		**Polyester**	
Nylon	Britain	Terylene	Britain
Perlon	W Germany	Diolen	W Germany
Rilsan	France	Tergal	France
Enkalon	Holland	Terlenka	Holland
Amilan	Japan	Tetoran	Japan
Kapron	USSR	Alorsan	USSR
		Dacron	USA
Polyethylene		**Polypropylene**	
Courlene	Britain	Ulstron	Britain
Nymplex	Holland	Pylen	Japan
Hizex	Japan	Moplen	Italy
Reevon	USA		

These synthetic twines were superior to the traditional materials of cotton, manila, and hemp, in many ways. They were not affected by bacteria and consequently did not have to be treated or dried regularly. For the most part they were stronger and did not absorb water. They soon proved their worth and were readily adopted by the fishermen despite their increased cost.

The relative qualities of these new materials are still subject to debate and each skipper has his own preferences. *Table 1* gives some idea of their weight, strength and abrasion resistance.

Table 1 does not necessarily relate to conditions at sea and there are advantages to every type of twine used. Nylon is very strong and is still used extensively in seine nets. Terylene is also very strong but unfortunately because of its weight it is more expensive per yard which is what matters to the fisherman. However, it stretches

92

least of the four materials under consideration and as a result is used a lot for the headropes and footropes of the nets.

Courlene (polyethylene) and Ulstron (polyester) both float, and their use in light nets such as seines requires that they be rigged differently, *ie* with less floats and more weight.

Courlene twine proved to be extremely tough and durable in fishing nets and though its handling characteristics were not ideal, it was adopted on a wide scale in seine nets and wing trawls. Ulstron twine is also becoming very popular with seine net fishermen. It is much easier to handle and resembles nylon in appearance.

The use of these strong synthetic twines in their nets made it possible for seine netters to land huge catches of fish. Cotton nets have often been known to burst when the weight of fish caught was too great. The first seine nets with nylon and terylene bags amazed their owners by holding as much as 100 to 150 boxes of cod in a single drag. Later synthetic seine nets caught and held as much as 400 boxes of fish (20 tons).

Net manufacturers admit that the use of synthetic twines greatly prolonged the life of seine nets. This was particularly true in the case of Courlene.

Table 2 gives comparisons of filament yarn properties.

Table 1 Comparative properties of ropes of natural and synthetic fibres. Source: *Ropes made from man-made fibres*, British Ropes Ltd 1966.

Material	Specific gravity	Breaking loads for 3-in (76mm) circumference ropes	Abrasion resistance*
		tons	per cent
Nylon (Polyamide)	1·14	11·8	91·1
Terylene (Polyester)	1·38	9·0	94·2
Courlene (Polyethylene)	0·95	6·0	44·6
Ulstron (Polypropylene)	0·91	7·5	54·0
Manila	1·45	4·5	93·2
Sisal	1·45 app.	4·0	86·0

* Percentage of original strength after 2,000 rubs in dry sand.

Table 2 Comparative filament yarn properties. Source: Carter and West, ICI, *Modern Fishing Gear of the World 2* (1964).

Material	Extension at break	Elastic recovery from 5 per cent extension	Toughness $\times 10^3$ (Joules/G)
	per cent	per cent	
Nylon (Polyamide)	12–18	98	55–89
Terylene (Polyester)	6–14	90	28–50
Courlene (Polyethylene)	25–35	88	85–90
Ulstron (Polypropylene)	18–22	88	80–100
Manila	2–3	Breaks	4·0
Sisal	2–2·5	Breaks	3·0
Cotton	3–10	45	3·4–8·5

Groundropes Most seine nets carry a conventional groundrope made of 3in (76mm) circumference coir rope. The rope is hung from the foot of the net in bights and is attached by means of ossels made of braided nylon or manila trawl twine. The lead rings weighing four to eight ounces (100 to 200g) each, are strung on to the coir rope at intervals. A single net may carry one hundred four-ounce (100g) lead weights. They are strung close together at the bosom and the shoulders, and more widely spaced along the wings.

Plaice seines may carry no coir rope, but may have tubular lead weights strung directly on the footrope. If they do carry a coir rope it may be twisted around the footrope or lashed directly to it.

Short lengths of chain are often attached to the groundrope at the bosom and the wing ends to keep these parts right on the bottom while the net is fishing. A 'tickler' chain may also be inserted between the bridle pole and the warp end, but only when fishing very close to the bottom as too much weight could very easily 'kill' the net and keep it from assuming its proper form in the water. Types of seine net groundropes are shown in *Fig 54*.

In the past ten years, seine net fishermen have worked their gear increasingly on rough grounds. Since it is basically a light gear a seine net can suffer a tremendous amount of damage on rocky or stony bottom. Nets have been torn in shreds, broken in half, and even come to the surface with nothing left but the bare head and footropes! For this reason many fishermen attempted to modify the gear to enable it to come over rough bottom without damage.

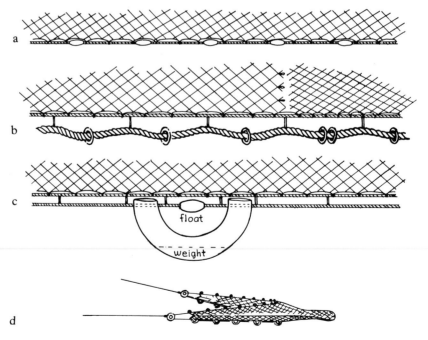

Fig 54 Seine net groundrope types: a: leads attached directly to footrope on small plaice seines; b: conventional coir groundrope with lead ring weights; c: rough bottom tyre type 'bouncer' groundrope; d: four half-tyres on each wing.

94

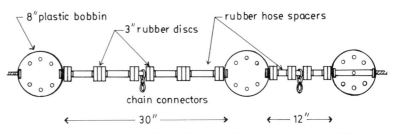

Fig 55 Arrangement of plastic bobbins for a seine net groundrope. *(Boris Net Co, Fleetwood)*

Trawl net bobbins could not be used for two reasons. First they were too heavy, and second, because of the change in the angle of the wings in a seine net during its operation, they would function only right at the bosom of the net. This would mean that only one bobbin could be used.

Some fishermen tried using weights or pieces of chain attached to the footrope by longer ossels, but these simply pulled the net down when they snagged on the sea bed.

Two types of groundrope rigs have been devised to overcome this problem. The first utilizes car tyres, cut in half and weighted at the bottom. Five or six of these half-tyres are attached to a groundrope of combination wire, and a light bobbin is encased in the tyre at the bosom. The dan lenos are each encased in a whole tyre and a small float is fixed to the 'top' of the half tyre at the groundrope, to keep them erect. When rigged properly, this 'bouncer' type groundrope can be used over rough ground without endangering the net.

The other type of rough bottom groundrope uses bobbins made of plastic or light aluminium alloy. Small rubber discs and lengths of rubber hose are used as spacers *(Fig 55)*. These rough bottom rigs are not in general use as on clean bottom they would have no advantage at all over the conventional coir groundropes.

Dan lenos Dan lenos or bridle poles may be made of wood or iron. The traditional wooden bridle pole is about 2½ft (0·75m) long and carries an iron weight on the foot. The bridle is made of a piece of polyethylene or manila rope about 3 or 4 fathoms (5 or 7m) long. The rope is lashed around an eye at the centre and the two ends are passed through holes in the bridle pole. It is common practice to knot the tails of the rope on the net side of the pole, to prevent them from slipping through the holes again. Eyes are spliced into each end of the bridle rope and the splices may be continued back around the pole into the fore part of the bridle. This also serves to secure the bridle pole. The wing ends or sweeps are tied into the eyes of the bridle and a swivel and 'G' link is connected to the front eye where the end of the warp will be attached *(Fig 56)*.

All-iron dan lenos are sometimes used, and these have no need of a rope bridle. If the gear is to be used on very rough bottom the iron frame may be encased in an old car tyre. Wooden hoop-type dan

95

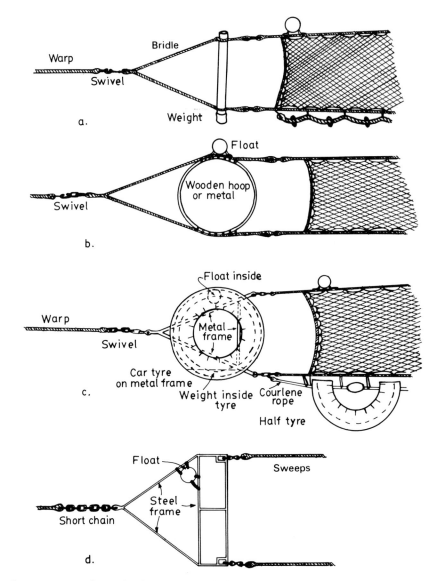

Fig 56 Seine net dan lenos: a: conventional bridle pole; b: Hoop-type for muddy bottom; c: rough bottom tyre type; d: welded steel frame.

lenos are preferred when the net is being worked on mud or soft sand type bottom.

Sweeps Sweeps or cables are wires or lines inserted between the wing end and the dan leno. They are used on most of the larger nets, particularly on the wing trawls. They resemble the Vigneron Dahl cables used on otter trawls, but serve a different purpose. Since they cannot keep the net open any more than the warps, their effect can only be to raise the headline slightly by increasing the distance from the bridle. Under normal conditions, a trawl net headline rises at an angle of no more than 1 in 10 (about 6°) when fishing. Therefore, a net with a headline of 120ft (37m) should achieve a 6ft (1·8m) vertical mouth opening (60ft × $^1/_{10}$ = 6ft). The same net with 10 fathom (18·3m) sweeps should achieve a much larger mouth opening providing there is sufficient depth of webbing in the wings (120ft × $^1/_{10}$ = 12ft). The maximum length of sweeps used is usually in the order of 15 fathoms (27m) (*Fig 57*). Detailed methods of hanging a seine net are shown in *Fig 58*.

Fig 57 Effect of sweeps: long sweeps allow headline to rise higher.

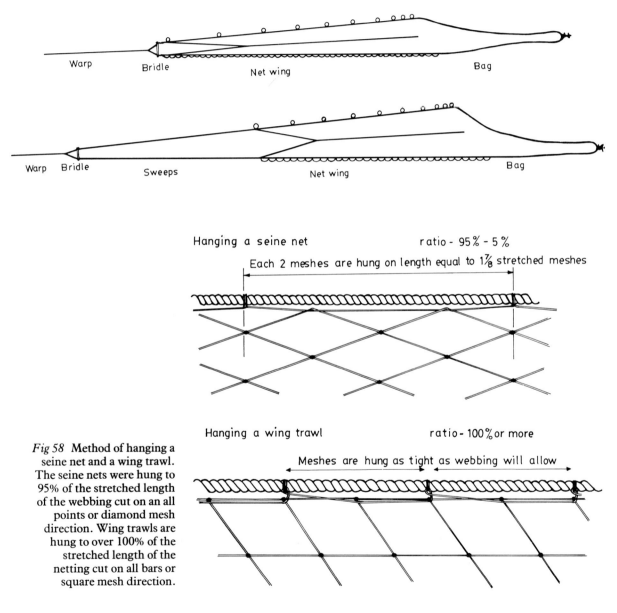

Hanging a seine net   ratio - 95% – 5%

Each 2 meshes are hung on length equal to 1⅞ stretched meshes

Hanging a wing trawl   ratio - 100% or more

Meshes are hung as tight as webbing will allow

Fig 58 Method of hanging a seine net and a wing trawl. The seine nets were hung to 95% of the stretched length of the webbing cut on an all points or diamond mesh direction. Wing trawls are hung to over 100% of the stretched length of the netting cut on all bars or square mesh direction.

97

Small otter boards   When fishing for prawns (Norway lobsters), it is common practice for seine netters to use small otter boards. The boards are attached directly to the wing ends and are used to disturb the sea bed and drive the prawns into the mouth of the net. They are too small to maintain a large mouth opening, but this is not their main purpose. The boards are used in areas where prawns are abundant and where otter boards are permitted by law. With development of a fleet of small trawlers working almost exclusively for prawns, the use of seine nets to catch these crustaceans has practically ceased. In 1965 Scottish seiners landed over 370 tons of Norway lobster. *Fig 59* illustrates a useful catch of *Nephrops* prawns taken in a seine net with small otter boards attached.

Fig 59 Catch of prawns. Note the small otter boards used with the gear in this case.

Net plans   A number of plans of seine nets are given in adjoining pages. *Fig 60* shows the basic parts. They are primarily now of only historical interest since most of the modern seine netters use wing trawls exclusively. The seine nets were made in two parts, each comprising one side of the net. Some strengthening was braided in around the crown and bosom and arranged in such a way that there was a very slight overhang. On most seine nets, the headline was only from two to six feet (·6 to 1·8m) shorter than the footrope. Most of this difference was achieved by hanging the head slightly tighter than the foot.

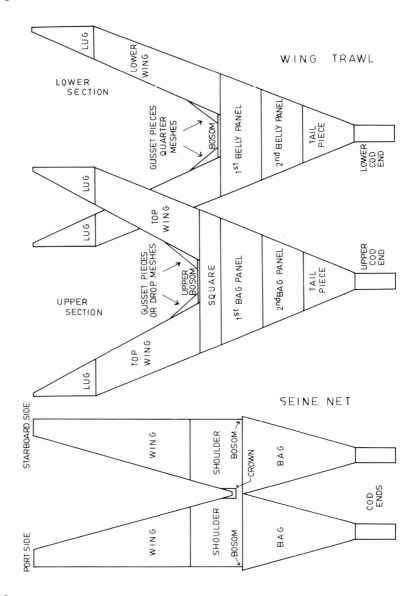

Fig 60 Diagram of net panels on seine net and wing trawl plans. The seine nets were made of two side pieces. Wing trawls are made of upper and lower parts.

The deep seine, described earlier in the chapter (*Fig 52* page 88) was constructed in an attempt to incorporate the advantages of a wing trawl into a seine net design. Although it was successful, it was soon discarded in favour of proper wing trawls. Just as in aviation, the biplane was superseded by the monoplane, so seine nets were followed by wing trawls or seine trawls as they are sometimes called to differentiate them from wing trawls used with otter board gear. The seine principle of operation remains the same.

The plan of a seine trawl differs as its two sections are upper and lower ones instead of port and starboard side sections in the older seines. The upper section has an overhang panel called a 'square'. (In the early beam trawls, this panel was literally square-shaped, but it is now shaped like a trapezium.) Apart from the square section, the upper and lower parts of a seine trawl are identical, except for a very slight difference in the length of the panels. The upper panels are usually shorter by anything from half a mesh (one row) to four or five meshes in the wings. There is also a difference in the taper or cutting rate in the upper and lower wings.

When illustrating trawl plans, it is customary to show only half of each section. The upper section is shown to the left and the lower section to the right. For a beginner, a net plan looks as confusing as a woman's knitting pattern does to a man, but once the terms and specifications are understood, they are quite simple to read. Professional net makers dispense with a lot of information that might be included in a complete plan. Much of the detail is 'understood' by the net maker as soon as he checks the basic specifications and he would know instinctively from experience what twine sizes and taper cuts would be appropriate.

It is difficult to draw net plans to scale because a sheet of netting is like a piece of elastic—it can be stretched in any direction and will then shrink automatically in the opposite dimension. The normal practice is to draw the plan at stretched mesh figures down the length (from wing end to cod end) and to draw the width at half mesh figures. The resulting shape is close to but of course, not identical to the shape the trawl will assume in the water.

The parts of a seine net are: the wings (two), shoulders (two), bag or belly sheets (two each), and cod end also in two parts. The parts of a wing trawl are: wing ends or lugs (two upper and two lower), top wings (two), lower wings (two), square (one), upper belly sheets and lower belly sheets (one each), upper and lower extension pieces (one each) and the cod end, upper and lower sections. The lower wings should extend the length of the top wings and square. In some nets, the lower wing section beneath the square is regarded as a separate panel, called the bunt or shoulder, but usually it is cut in one sheet with the whole lower wing. The size of the panels is usually given in number of meshes long and number of meshes

100

wide. Some manufacturers give the size in rows. The length of a sheet of netting can be calculated by multiplying the number of meshes by the mesh size. Net plans for seines and trawls of various shapes and sizes are shown in *Fig 61*.

Fig 61 Net plans

(1) Small plaice seine made of cotton. (*Franklin 1956*)

(2) Large plaice seine made of cotton. (*Gundry 1959*)

(3) Prawn seine made of cotton. (*Franklin 1960*)

(4) Haddock seine, nylon. (*Gundry 1959*)

(5) Cod seine, of nylon. (*Gundry 1959*)

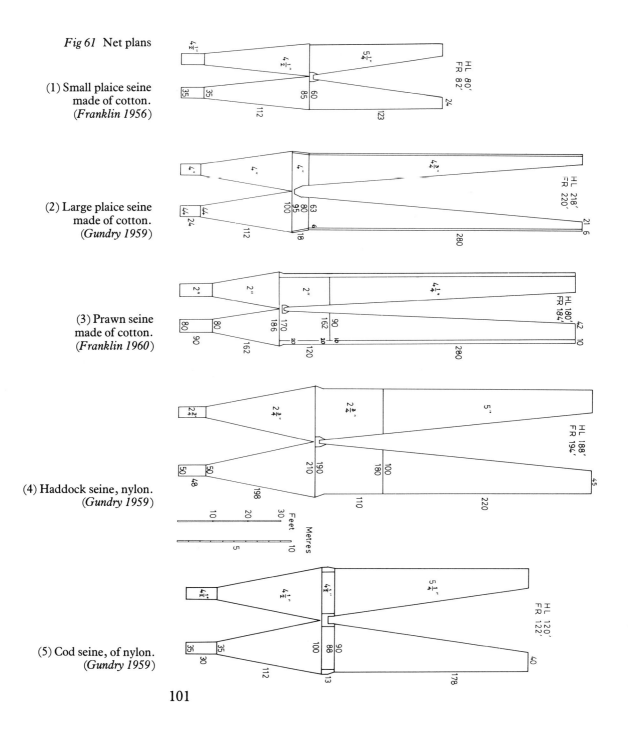

101

Fig 61 (cont.) Net plans

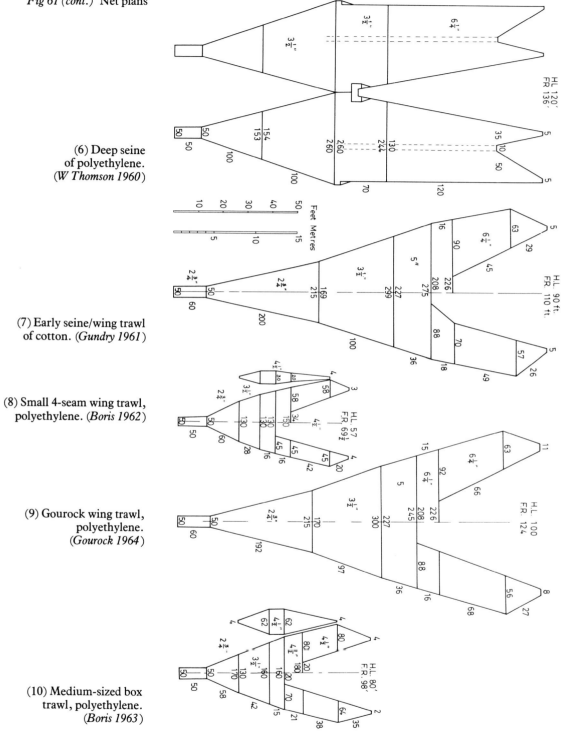

(6) Deep seine
of polyethylene.
(*W Thomson 1960*)

(7) Early seine/wing trawl
of cotton. (*Gundry 1961*)

(8) Small 4-seam wing trawl,
polyethylene. (*Boris 1962*)

(9) Gourock wing trawl,
polyethylene.
(*Gourock 1964*)

(10) Medium-sized box
trawl, polyethylene.
(*Boris 1963*)

102

Fig 61 (cont.) Net plans

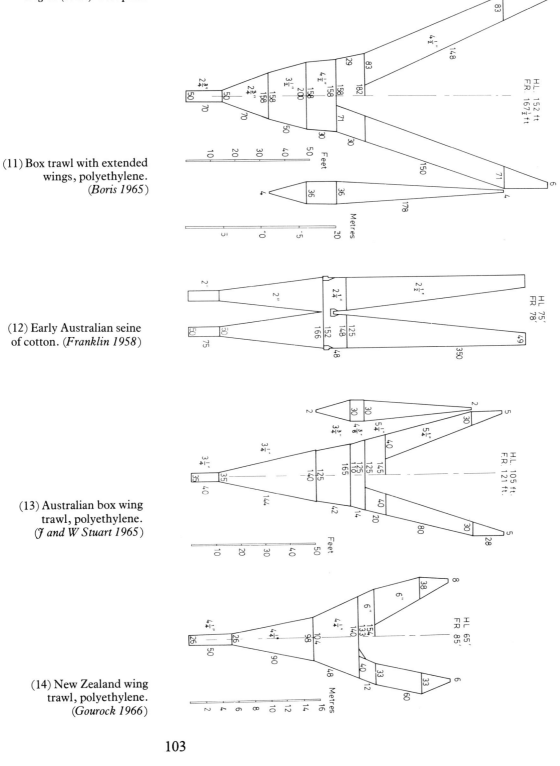

(11) Box trawl with extended wings, polyethylene. (*Boris 1965*)

(12) Early Australian seine of cotton. (*Franklin 1958*)

(13) Australian box wing trawl, polyethylene. (*J and W Stuart 1965*)

(14) New Zealand wing trawl, polyethylene. (*Gourock 1966*)

103

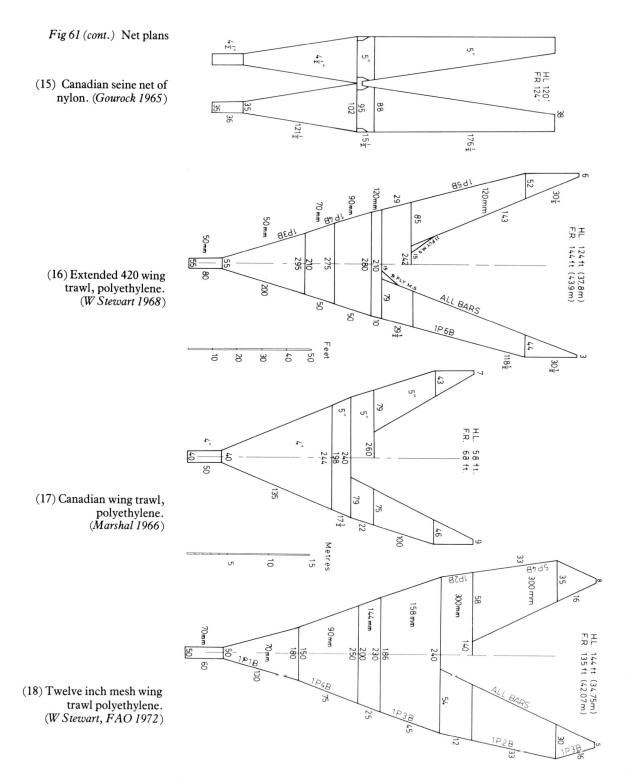

Fig 61 (cont.) Net plans

(15) Canadian seine net of nylon. (*Gourock 1965*)

(16) Extended 420 wing trawl, polyethylene. (*W Stewart 1968*)

(17) Canadian wing trawl, polyethylene. (*Marshal 1966*)

(18) Twelve inch mesh wing trawl polyethylene. (*W Stewart, FAO 1972*)

104

Headline and footrope length

The headline and footrope are measured from one wing tip to the other. Their length does not include that of the bridles or cables. On a complete net plan, the rope lengths will be given in sections starting from the centre of the square and bosom and working out to the wing ends. This is because the nets are mounted from those points and the hanging ratio changes at each section. The difference between the headrope and footrope length will give an indication of the size of the overhang or square.

Mesh sizes

Mesh sizes are always given in stretched mesh in Britain and in the American continent. This means the length of the mesh from one knot to the knot diagonally opposite when the mesh is pulled tight in that direction. The measure is made from the outside of one knot to the inside of the next. For legislation purposes, however, a 'V' shaped flat metal or plastic gauge is inserted inside the mesh and pushed down as far as it will go. Most net meshes will stretch with use so it is common practice when using meshes close to legal standard, to get 'tight measure' initially as it will expand with use.

Bar size is a common mesh measure used in Scandinavia and in some European countries. It is equal to half the stretched mesh. When studying a net plan, one should always check carefully whether bar size or stretched mesh size is used.

Many other old ways of gauging mesh size have (fortunately) long since been discarded. Some of them were incredibly complicated. Number of rows per yard was the system used by the British herring drift net fishermen. Such a system showed larger figures for smaller meshes. *Table 3* indicates some mesh sizes and their equivalents in different systems:

Table 3 Mesh sizes by different measuring systems. Stretched mesh size is the most commonly used notation. Bar size is much used in Europe and Scandinavia. Rows per yard is no longer in use. Herring drift net fishermen used this term.

Stretched mesh		Bar size		No. of rows per yard
inches	millimetres	inches	millimetres	
1	25	$\frac{1}{2}$	12·7	72
$1\frac{1}{2}$	38	$\frac{3}{4}$	19	48
2	51	1	25·5	36
$2\frac{1}{2}$	64	$1\frac{1}{4}$	32	29
$2\frac{3}{4}$	70	$1\frac{3}{8}$	35	26
3	76	$1\frac{1}{2}$	38	24
$3\frac{1}{2}$	89	$1\frac{3}{4}$	44	21
4	102	2	51	18
$4\frac{1}{2}$	115	$2\frac{1}{4}$	57	16
5	127	$2\frac{1}{2}$	63	$14\frac{1}{2}$
$5\frac{1}{2}$	140	$2\frac{3}{4}$	70	13
6	152	3	76	12
$6\frac{1}{2}$	165	$3\frac{1}{4}$	82	11
8	204	4	102	9
12	304	6	152	6

Net cutting   In the days of hand-made nets, the degree of taper in the shaped parts of the wing or bag was achieved by the insertion of batings or creasings. Batings decreased the number of meshes in a row by joining two into one. Creasings increased the number of meshes in a row by adding one between two. The wings of trawl nets were also shaped by having fly meshes (all bars) down one side. When repairing a tapered panel, the fishermen had always to note the formula 'one bating (or creasing) every x number of rows'.

Modern trawls are made almost entirely from machine made netting. The taper required is achieved by cutting to a formula of points and bars. A number of common taper cuts is given in the following table. Most net makers use a formula of their own to determine cuts as many tapers do not work out to simple cuts. If a complex cut is to be made, say 3 points 4 bars; it is divided into a series of simpler cuts, in this case:

$$3\,P\,4\,B = 1\,P\,1\,B + 1\,P\,1\,B + 1\,P\,2\,B$$

and the series is repeated all the way down the length of the panel. The steep cuts made around the shoulder or quarter of trawl nets consist of more bars than points. The long shallow cuts down the sides of the bag or belly consist of more points than bars.

The taper cut at the quarters, usually referred to as 'drop meshes' may be strengthened by hand-braiding over them with heavy twine or double twine. Sometimes a whole gusset section, several meshes deep, is hand woven at this point on the trawl.

Figure 62 illustrates examples of net cutting tapers.

Twine size   The designation of twine size is more complex than even the former confusing systems of indicating mesh size. Fortunately, for most fishermen and most net makers too, the most straightforward

Table 4 Net cutting tapers.

Symbol	Cut	Loss of meshes in number of rows
A P	All points	No loss – straight cut
A B	All Bars	One mesh every two rows
1 P 1 B	One point one bar	One mesh every six rows
2 P 1 B	Two points one bar	One mesh every ten rows
3 P 1 B	Three points one bar	One mesh every fourteen rows
4 P 1 B	Four points one bar	One mesh every eighteen rows
5 P 1 B	Five points one bar	One mesh every twenty-two rows
1 P 2 B	One point two bars	One mesh every four rows
1 P 3 B	One point three bars	One mesh every 3·3 rows
1 P 4 B	One point four bars	One mesh every three rows
1 P 5 B	One point five bars	One mesh every 2·8 rows

106

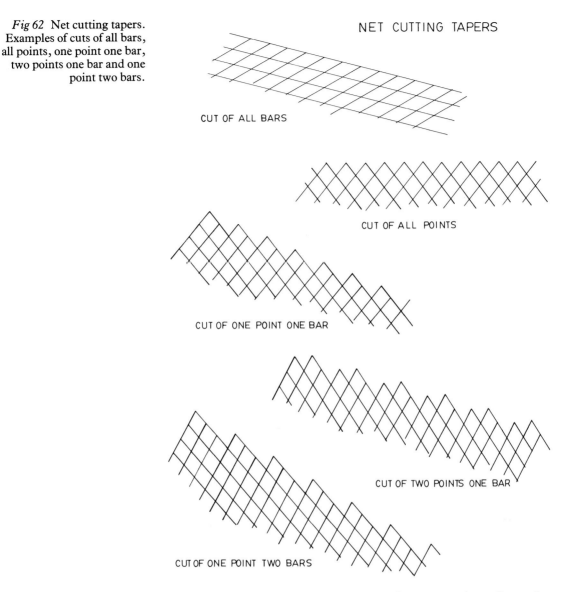

Fig 62 Net cutting tapers. Examples of cuts of all bars, all points, one point one bar, two points one bar and one point two bars.

CUT OF ALL BARS

CUT OF ALL POINTS

CUT OF ONE POINT ONE BAR

CUT OF TWO POINTS ONE BAR

CUT OF ONE POINT TWO BARS

solution is to select the required sizes from a number of samples, without going through the mathematical process of conversion from tex number to denier number or vice versa.

Denier number indicates the weight in grams of 9,000 metres length of the yarn thread. Most nylon twines are made up from 210 denier yarns. Depending on the number of yarns in a completed twine, the twine number will be 210/9 or 210/15 or 210/24 and so on.

The Tex system indicates, among other matters, the weight in grams of 1,000 metres of the yarn or twine. In the case of a finished

107

twine (which is all that really concerns the fisherman) the designation is R Tex.

Other methods of indicating twine size include runnage, *ie* number of yards per pound or number of metres per kilogram. Sometimes the breaking strain of a twine is indicated, but this is a very arbitrary figure and can vary immensely depending on the method of testing. In the days of cotton nets, the English cotton count system was used. It indicated the number of 840 yard (768m) lengths of the yarn required to weigh one pound (·45kg).

Some typical nylon and polyethylene twine sizes are given in the *Tables 5* and *6*.

Table 5 Nylon twines used in wing trawls.

Denier no.	R Tex	Diameter in mm	Runnage metres/kg.	Runnage yards/lb.	Breaking strain Kgf. dry
210/12	310	0·6	3230	1602	20
210/18	460	0·7	2175	1079	26
210/21	540	0·8	1850	918	32
210/24	620	0·85	1620	803	35
210/30	770	1·0	1300	645	44
210/45	1170	1·3	950	471	62
210/60	1550	1·4	650	322	80

Table 6 Polyethylene twines used in wing trawls.

Denier no.	R Tex	Diameter in mm	Runnage metres/kg.	Runnage yards/lb.	Breaking strain Kgf. dry
380/9	400	0·9	2500	1240	14
380/15	700	1·13	1430	709	26
380/24	1150	1·5	900	446	39
380/30	1410	1·6	710	352	48
380/36	1700	1·75	600	297	57
380/48	2250	2·05	445	221	75
380/60	2800	2·3	360	172	94
380/72	3400	2·55	294	146	115

Note: The size, runnage and strength figures must only be taken as approximations which may vary with different manufacturers.

Wing trawl development By the late 1960s seine nets had almost disappeared from use in favour of wing trawls designed for use with seine ropes. The trawls had a larger mouth opening and were more effective in catching haddock, whiting and cod. The first wing trawls had been similar in size and in netting to the seine nets. Larger wing trawls with bigger mouth openings were to follow. These nets carried more groundrope weight and their deeper mouth made them more difficult to haul by hand. The mechanization of net hauling by hydraulic power blocks was brought about at the time the heavier

108

nets were introduced. Much larger trawls were developed later for the large modern seiners which measured 80 ft (24·4m) in length or more. It would be extremely difficult for the crews to handle such nets without the aid of a powered sheave.

The overall dimensions of seine trawls increased dramatically following a surprise development in mesh size. Previously the largest meshes used in those nets were 6 or 6½in stretched length (152–165mm). Fishermen had long been aware of the fact however, that fish could be led into a net even if the meshes of the wing or leader were larger than the fish. Larger meshes are permitted a better flow of water through the net and fish were sensitive to the shock waves that a small-meshed net might build up in its path. Herring trawls were being fished successfully with enormous wing meshes, so a number of adventuresome skippers began to try large-meshed seine trawls. The results were quite dramatic.

The first trials were with nets of 8 inch wing mesh. These were so successful that nets with 12 inch wing meshes were introduced. Both the eight inch and the twelve inch nets worked so well they were soon adopted by most of the larger vessels in the fleet. Most of the big-mesh nets were made of polyethylene and they were mounted to ropes of the same length or even longer than the wing bar meshes. This tight hanging is an important factor in all wing trawls. From the net plan sketch in *Figs 61* to *64* one can see the enormous increase in overall size achieved by introducing the large-meshed nets. A modern wing trawl is illustrated in *Fig 63*.

Fig 63 Diagram of modern wing trawl. Note the relative positions of the different parts.

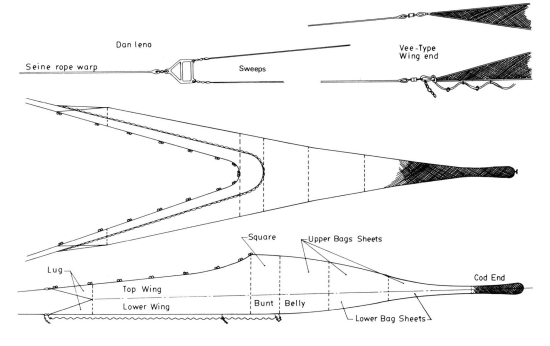

Among the first skippers to test the new trawls was Willie Hay of the *Illustrious* BF 438 who took 120 boxes of fish on the first tow with a Gourock 480/12 wing trawl. Skipper L Irvin of the Shetland seiner *Zephyr* had 17 hauls in excess of 100 boxes with a similar net in 1971. Twice he had hauls of over 200 boxes. Another skipper who pioneered with the twelve inch mesh seine trawl was Alex Sutherland of the *Internos* BCK 239 who used a Bridport Gundry net. Large meshed nets are difficult to haul and can be easily fouled as the floats tend to catch inside the meshes. Torpedo shaped floats may be used to avoid this problem but more commonly a pair of spherical floats are put inside a 'stocking' of small meshed webbing to protect them.

Ropes As the nets increased in size, so also did the ropes. Most seine net boats of the 1950s used ropes of only $2^3/_8$in (60mm) circumference. In the early 1960s only the biggest seiners used $2\frac{1}{2}$in (64mm) circumference rope. Synthetic ropes with lead core were fast displacing manila ropes and as the seiners increased in size and power, there was a corresponding demand for larger ropes. Warp sizes of $2\frac{3}{4}$ and 3in (70 and 76mm) were introduced and these were followed by larger ropes of $3\frac{1}{4}$ and even $3\frac{1}{2}$in (80 and 90mm) circumference. It should be borne in mind that a size increase of from $2^3/_8$ to $3^1/_2$in (60 to 90mm) circumference (19 to 28mm diameter) involves an increase of more than 100 per cent in volume and a corresponding increase in weight. It was very difficult to manhandle the large ropes on deck and some other means of stowing them had to be devised. At first some skippers fell back on the old system of using rope wells into which the warps were fed direct from the coiler. This system could work but it still resulted in numerous 'foul ropes' when setting the gear. Hydraulic rope reels developed first in Scandinavia proved to be much more efficient and despite their cost they soon replaced the rope bins. The warps were guided on to the reels by lead-in gear on an archimedes screw timed to suit the size of rope and width of drum. The neatly packed warps suffered minimal wear and there was no possibility of a foul-up when shooting. The rope reels are further discussed in the next chapter.

Whereas seiners formerly used only ten or twelve coils of $2^3/_8$in (60mm) rope, the large modern seiners began to fish regularly with fifteen, eighteen, or even more, coils of the larger warp. Eighteen coils equals 1·8 nautical miles or just under 4 kilometers. That length of warp on each side of the net encloses an area of about 660,000 square fathoms or over 500 acres. This kind of 'deep sea seining' is carried on mostly in the open parts of the North Sea.

Many smaller seiners still operate successfully inshore with lighter gear. The difference between 'deep sea' seiners and inshore seiners is almost as great as that between deep sea and inshore trawlers. The inshore boat may measure less than 25 tons and have an engine of 150hp. The larger seiner may measure 150 or 200 tons and have a main engine of over 500 or 600hp. The gear used by the bigger vessels weighs (and costs) twice that of the smaller inshore seiners. In both cases however, the aim and the result is the same—a productive and economical method of catching bottom fish.

Hanging, rigging and trimming a wing trawl

Wing trawls would normally be purchased already assembled by the net factory but to explain the hanging and rigging procedure we will assume that the netting panels only have been purchased and the buyer is to assemble the gear himself. The first step is to make absolutely sure that he has all the correct hanging dimensions from the manufacturer. Different manufacturer's nets will differ slightly from each other even if the overall dimensions are the same, and the mounting instructions must be followed correctly.

To commence assembly, the netting panels should be joined together. All of the upper panels are put together, and all of the lower panels before the two parts are laced together at the selvedge. Panels with equal numbers of meshes are woven together on a 1 to 1 basis. Where there is a difference in the number of meshes to be joined, a 'take-up' or bating rate is calculated accordingly. The bating rate applies to the sheet with the most meshes and is termed one bating every 2, 3, 4, 5 or more meshes as necessary. For instance 280 meshes being connected to 210 meshes would require a bating or take-up every third mesh. So every 3 meshes from the 210 sheet would be joined to 4 meshes on the 280 sheet.

The selvedges are laced together with several meshes bunched in on each side. At least 4 meshes are taken in to form the selvedge. Some fishermen prefer to take in more, but however many are used the number should be uniform in each panel. The selvedge or lastridge may be put together either before or after hanging to the head and footropes. When connecting the lastridge at the wing, shoulders and square it will be noticed that the lower panels are longer than the upper ones. They should be hitched correctly to each other at the seams and the slack in the lower sheet should be taken up gradually over the length of the panel. The amount of slack netting in the lower wings of modern trawls is much less than in older otter trawls but its incorporation is important to the fishing performance.

The head rope and foot rope are measured off and some extra length is allowed for eye splices. The mid-points and ends of each rope is carefully marked. Two more points must be marked. These are the points to which the bosom or square meshes are hung, and the points to which the drop-meshes or shoulder gussets are hung.

111

If one checks on a trawl plan one will see that between the bosom meshes and the straight bar wing meshes there is usually a tapered section of drop-meshes (points and bars) which requires a hanging ratio of its own. The bosom meshes are hung at 50% slack or less. The wing bars or fly meshes are hung as tight as the webbing will allow. The drop meshes are hung to a length determined by the manufacturer according to the taper and the mesh size. All these measurements must be obtained from the manufacturer. Only the most experienced fishermen or net repairmen will be able to calculate the distances themselves. Fishermen using wing trawls for the first time are well advised to get professional advice as incorrect hanging will seriously impair the net's efficiency.

The wing and bosom meshes are anchored at the seam points to the marks on the rope which is stretched out between two poles or bolts in the net loft or hanging bay. The mid-bosom meshes are anchored to the mid-point that was also marked. The bosom meshes and drop meshes are then hung to the appropriate lengths. Only the wing bar meshes will now remain to be hung and here there will appear to be an anomaly. At this point the rope is longer than the netting. Tension should be increased gradually until the netting stretches to equal the rope. Some pieces of light chain tied to the netting at the halfway point can help stretch it. The procedure is the same for the headrope and footrope, apart from the difference in lengths. A good strong staple nylon is best for hitching the meshes firmly on to the ropes. At the anchoring points and especially at the wing ends, particularly strong hitches should be used.

The 'vee' ropes may now be fitted, again following the manufacturer's instructions on their length. The end of the wing selvedge is firmly anchored to the point of the vee and the ends of the vee rope are spliced into the ends of the head and footropes.

Selvedge strain ropes may be fitted. These are usually made of light braided rope. They are attached to the selvedge at intervals so that the strain transmitted from the vee ropes is taken by the selvedge rope rather than the selvedge itself. Too much strain on the selvedge can burst the net at the seams. But the net will not achieve its proper headline height or mouth opening if there is not tension on the mid-seam. The strain ropes run only as far as the mouth section, but light belly lines may be attached to them there and they are run all the way to the codend. At the bag and codend the splitting ropes are run through nylon rings laced on to the netting. The codend rope is also run through such rings laced on to the end meshes.

All that now remains to be done is to attach the groundrope and floats. Sisal or some of the cheaper synthetics are now more commonly used for this than coir rope which is becoming difficult

112

to get. Some light chain (0.5 to 1.0kg per metre) is attached at the wing ends and around the bosom. The chain and the groundrope must be attached with sufficient slack so they do not crimp or shorten the footrope. The floats are attached as recommended or as preferred from experience. If the wing meshes are larger than the floats, a stocking of small-meshed netting may be placed over them to prevent their entanglement.

Trimming the net   During the fishing operation the skipper will keep a careful check on the net's performance, comparing his catches with those of boats alongside. He will watch the trawl as it surfaces since the way a net comes up is indicative of its fishing trim. He will check the chains for signs of 'polish' to make sure that they are touching the bottom.

When a net is suspected of being out of trim, the first thing to be checked is the bridle gear, or sweeps. These must be exactly equal in length. If one or more has stretched, then they must be evened up again. Should the bridles be all right and the chains well polished, it sometimes helps if the headline is slackened back slightly by inserting a shackle or a few links of chain between the headline and the bridle or between the bridle and the bridle pole. Floats may be added or removed. It may be that the upper netting has stretched in the square or bag. If so, the net will not fish well. The upper sheets are stretched lengthwise and measured against the lower sheets. If they have stretched, then one or more meshes may be cut out across the width of the sheet (bearing in mind that a half-mesh will be added when joining again). The selvedge is opened up and the shortened upper sheet is laced back to the lower sheet taking up the lower slack gradually along the lastridge. It is an established fact (though few people seem to understand why) that no trawl net, beam, otter, pair, midwater or seine, will fish well if the upper sheets are not tighter than the lower panels. If all else fails and the net still does not fish well, it may require complete re-hanging. If that does not remedy matters then there is probably something wrong in the way the sets are being made relative to the tide, or else the gear is not being closed properly before heaving up.

Fishing the wing trawl   The wing trawl is fished in much the same way as the seine net except that one must be more careful in setting the gear with respect to the direction of the tide. The skipper who takes most careful note of the strength and varying direction of the tide, and its effect on the gear, will generally catch more fish. The most common set is the one to tow before (or with) the tide. In this case the first warp is set more or less directly into the tide (*Fig 64*). The net is shot across the tide with the crew making sure that the bag and codend are well clear of the headline. After the two or three coils next the net are run out, the vessel makes for the dhan and

113

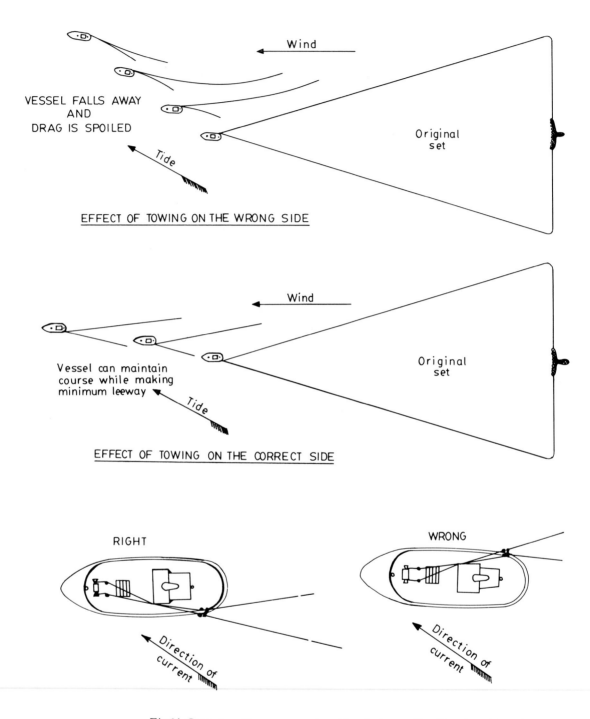

Wind

VESSEL FALLS AWAY
AND
DRAG IS SPOILED

Tide

Original
set

EFFECT OF TOWING ON THE WRONG SIDE

Wind

Vessel can maintain
course while making
minimum leeway

Tide

Original
set

EFFECT OF TOWING ON THE CORRECT SIDE

RIGHT

WRONG

Direction of
current

Direction of
current

Fig 64 Correct and incorrect towing side relative to tide. Showing effect of tide on vessels when towing on either side. The gear should always be towed on the tide- or weather-side.

buoys. The last of the second warp should run out about 200 or 300 yards (180 or 275m) from the buoys and the boat is slowed down and the rope towed gently up to the dhan. The skipper will check the tide flow on the buoys, possibly taking a transit bearing if possible. He will usually tow around 2 points (22½ degrees) past the direction of flow, with the gear on the 'tide' side of the vessel. There are occasions when wind and tide are both strong in different directions and the skipper might make a mistake when selecting the side to tow on. If he has erred, it will soon become apparent when the vessel falls by the tide and fails to keep her course. In such cases it is always best to fasten the warps aft and pass the ropes around the stern and back to the winch while still towing. Fly-dragging can then resume on the correct side and the drag can be saved. Otherwise very little fish would be taken. G-link shackles at the one coil and two coil marks make it easier to switch over to the other side at those points.

When shooting to tow into the tide the first warp is set about 3 or 3½ points by the tide (34–40 degrees) and the second warp is set directly into it. This way, there will still be some warp to run out as one approaches the buoys which will have been swept down tide a bit. The extra warp is usually dumped over the side before approaching the dhan. Alternatively the skipper could run it out and then come back up to the dhan on the first course. After the end of the first warp is secured to the winch the gear is towed into the tide a good distance to make up the ground lost by the buoys. Towing into the tide the gear will close more quickly than when towing before the tide. It may be difficult to maintain the towing course if the tide is very strong or if there is a stiff breeze in the same direction. In such cases the towing roller is shifted forward to the quarter and this usually enables the skipper to keep the boat's head up.

Figures 65 and *66* illustrate gear setting patterns and techniques.

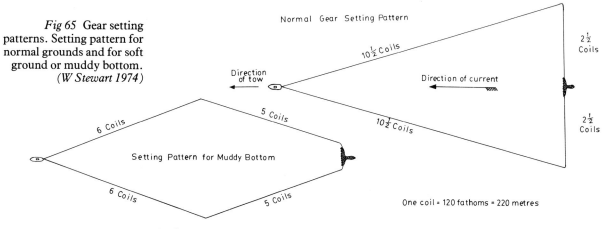

Fig 65 Gear setting patterns. Setting pattern for normal grounds and for soft ground or muddy bottom. (*W Stewart 1974*)

115

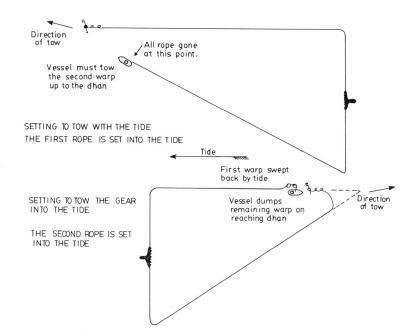

Fig 66 Gear setting techniques. Variation of setting pattern used when tides are strong. Note the different shape of the first and second warp sets. Once towing commences the gear will form a symmetrical shape if the tidal direction has been accurately determined. *(W Stewart 1974)*.

In the figure:

Direction of tow

All rope gone at this point.

Vessel must tow the second warp up to the dhan

SETTING TO TOW WITH THE TIDE
THE FIRST ROPE IS SET INTO THE TIDE

Tide

First warp swept back by tide

SETTING TO TOW THE GEAR INTO THE TIDE

THE SECOND ROPE IS SET INTO THE TIDE

Vessel dumps remaining warp on reaching dhan

Direction of tow

Towing speed: hauling speed ratio

The ratio of towing or propeller speed to the hauling or winch speed in fly-dragging is critical in determining how long the gear stays open. One normally aims to have the gear closed by the time half the warp is in. If one tows faster and hauls slower, the gear will close quickly. If one tows slower and hauls faster, the gear will stay open longer. This is good when fishing for flats. When working for cod and haddock it is better to close more quickly and the former approach is used. Skipper William Stewart gives a set of tables for engine-winch ratios in his very useful paper on Danish seining in Korea (*Table 7*).

Table 7 Fly-dragging speeds when fishing for flatfish or round fish.

Propeller shaft rpm	Winch barrels rpm	Ropes
Fishing for flat fish		
180–220	25	1–2 coils in
180–220	28–30	Until closed
180–220	50–60	1 coil more
180–	60–maximum	Remainder
Fishing for round fish		
210–250	18–20	1–2 coils in
210–250	20–23	Until nearly closed
210–250	23–28	Until fully closed
210–250	50–60	1 coil more
180–	60–maximum	Remainder

116

This table was developed for an 80 ton 250hp vessel with a mechanical winch. The propeller or engine rpm figures would have to be worked out from experience with each different vessel as the size and type of vessel, power and speed of engine, and the propeller type, are all influencing factors. Winch speeds are more easy to control in this day of hydraulic winches. In *Table 7*, a winch speed of 20 rpm would equal about 60ft (18m) per minute.

Successful skipper's experience

In a talk to fishermen attending an international exhibition in Canada, one of Scotland's best known seine net skippers, David Smith, summarised his experience with modern seine net gear. He said that the introduction of the hydraulic power block had enabled crews to handle big catches even in bad weather, when they would have been unmanageable by former hauling methods. When bigger seine net boats were built and heavy synthetic ropes were introduced, the handling problems were formidable. These problems were resolved with the introduction of hydraulic rope reels which accommodated all of the large heavy warps, spooling them in directly from the winch. The variable speed hydraulic winch gave enormous flexibility in relation to propeller speeds which was a great advantage in seining.

Describing the fishing operation on a modern seiner, skipper Smith said that the hunt for fish begins on reaching the fishing grounds. When fish traces are found, the gear is set around them in a huge triangle. The buoy with the first warp end is dropped into the sea about three-quarters of a mile up-tide or down-tide from the fish marks. When towing into the tide the vessel steams slowly ahead at about one knot (1.9km per hr) speed and commences heaving at around 70 feet (21m) per minute winch speed. The correct winch and propeller speeds can only be found out by experience. Speed increases slowly till the gear is closed by which time it will have been built up to around 140 feet (43m) per minute. A good rule of thumb is that the gear should be closed by the time half the ropes are in. The whole operation from dropping the dhan to taking the net and fish aboard takes about two hours. The success of the operation depends on accurately surrounding the fish with the ropes and net which sink to the bottom, and upon the herding of the fish by the ropes as they move inward over the grounds until they are driven into the mouth of the net just before the gear closes. Skipper Smith emphasized that engine power was not an all important factor in the fishing operation. Most seiners with large (500–600hp) engines, had them primarily for speed so they could cut down the travelling time to and from the fishing grounds.

117

7 Seine net vessels and equipment

Vessels Like all traditional Scottish fishing boats, seine net vessels are of heavy construction, built of oak and larch, to the most stringent specifications. Their design has developed over the years from that of the old fifie and zulu sailboats. The typical vessel is full and beamy, has a raked stem, cruiser stern and full round bilge. The wheelhouse is positioned just aft of amidships above the engine room. The crew's cabin is always right aft on Scottish seiners. Ring net vessels which used to go seining for part of the year had their cabins forward like those on the Danish seiners. Forward of the engine room is the large fishroom and then the fo'c'sle or forepeak store. A mainmast is fitted well forward and a mizzen just aft of the wheelhouse. On more modern vessels, the mizzen has been replaced with a short mast or goalpost supporting A-frame side derricks for taking the codend aboard. A landing derrick forward extends from the foremast to the wheelhouse, when in the lowered position. The galley occupies the after-part of the wheelhouse behind the raised bridge. On the bigger seiners, of 70ft (21m) and over, the mess table adjoins the galley. On smaller seiners the food is eaten below decks.

Seine boats are traditionally very 'stiff', having excellent stability, but as a result, are inclined to roll quickly. This motion may seem rather violent to a seaman used to slow rolling deep sea vessels. But it has its compensations and seine netters very rarely take 'green water' aboard, even in the worst of weathers. They are 'wet boats' only in the sense that they take a lot of spray which is no cause for concern. Their high stems and gentle sheer ensures a 'good head' or bow which can ride through the heaviest of seas. The cruiser stern is excellent for running before a heavy sea. A full vessel with a well-designed stern will not be 'broached' (be swamped from behind and turned broadside to the sea).

Figure 67 illustrates advances in size and design of Scottish seiners between 1927 and 1977.

Until 1965, all seine net boats were lightly powered and had the

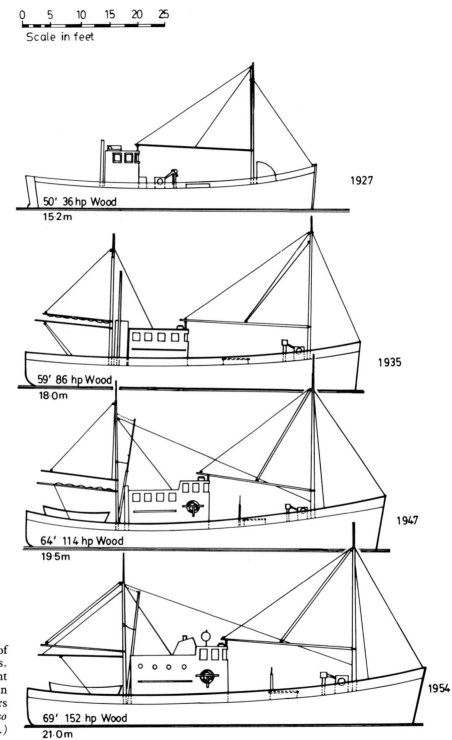

Scale in feet
0 5 10 15 20 25

1927
50' 36 hp Wood
15·2 m

1935
59' 86 hp Wood
18·0 m

1947
64' 114 hp Wood
19·5 m

1954
69' 152 hp Wood
21·0 m

Fig 67 Development of
Scottish seine net vessels.
Profile drawings of different
types showing advances in
size and design over 50 years
from 1927 to 1977. *(See also
following page.)*

119

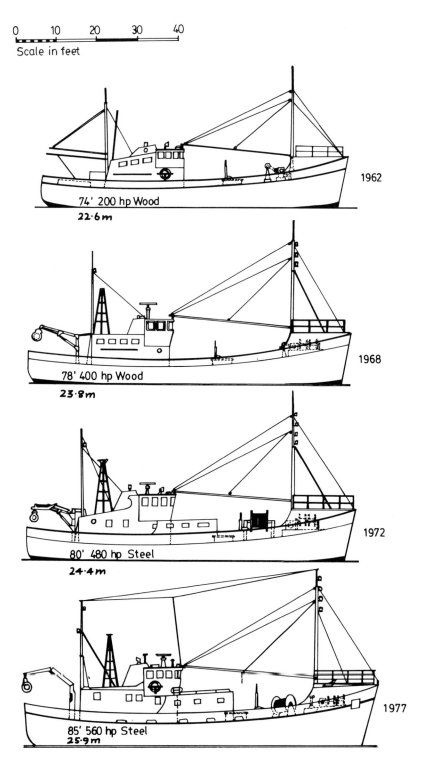

0 10 20 30 40
Scale in feet

74' 200 hp Wood
22·6 m
1962

78' 400 hp Wood
23·8 m
1968

80' 480 hp Steel
24·4 m
1972

85' 560 hp Steel
25·9 m
1977

minimum of deck machinery. The next decade saw a massive increase in power and mechanization on large new vessels built for seining. Main engine horsepower jumped from 152 to 230 then 400 then 500 and even over 600hp. Hydraulics were introduced, combination winches replaced single purpose seine winches; power blocks and hydraulic jibs were fitted and then huge rope reels were added. Whalebacks were constructed to shelter the foredeck and gutting shelters were added to the larger seiners operating year-round in the North Sea.

All this additional equipment brought about changes or modifications in vessel design. Stability could no longer be taken for granted, and had to be checked carefully in each new case. Steel began to be used widely for constructing large seine netters. A series of steel 'sputnik' seiner-trawlers built in the early 1960s had not proved popular. The steel seiners of the 70s were of better design (based primarily on the traditional wooden hull forms) and the steel was carefully sand-blasted or grit blasted and treated with anti-corrosive paints to increase its life.

Improved fish holds Fish holds had to be improved to facilitate longer sea voyages and this was done by improving insulation. Polyurethane or similar chemical mix foams were blown into the cavity between the ship's hull or deck and the fish room lining. Fishing trips for large seiners were increased from up to four days' to up to six days' duration without detracting from the quality of the catches. All the fish were gutted, washed, boxed and iced as before. The large Scottish seiners were able to land catches of 600, 700 or even 800 seven-stone boxes (44·5kgs) from a single trip. The fish would be mostly large haddock and cod. Vessels working for small haddock or whiting would usually make shorter trips.

Transom sterns Some modern seine netters were constructed with transom sterns. These gave much more room aft for the nets and for the crew accommodation below. Some seiner skippers felt that transom sterns would be dangerous in a following sea, that they would reduce speed, and that they would not permit the variation in towing positions that was possible on a cruiser-sterned vessel. Experience to date, however, seems to suggest that a properly designed transom stern may be just as workable on a seine netter as the traditional cruiser stern.

The *Fruitful Harvest* PD 247 *(Fig 68)* is an example of the best equipped modern Scottish seine netters in the lower-powered bracket. Measuring 65 × 22 ×8ft (19·8 × 6·7 × 2·5m) she was bigger and roomier than many former vessels of over 70ft (21.3m) in length. Built of wood by the Jas. Noble yard of Fraserburgh, she has a transom stern and a whaleback shelter forward. Her main

121

Fig 68 MV *Fruitful Harvest* PD 247 of Peterhead. One of the most modern and best equipped of seine netters in the 65ft (20m) range.

engine is an eight-cylinder Gardner marine diesel, possibly the most popular engine amongst Scottish seine fishermen over the past three decades. It is rated at 230bhp at 1150rpm and is fitted with a 4·5:1 reduction gear. Like practically all Scottish seiners, the vessel has a fixed blade propeller. The main engine is used for propulsion only and a second Gardner of 110bhp supplies power for the hydraulic machinery and alternator. On the foredeck, there is a Northern Tool and Gear Mastra hydraulic winch and three-drum system of rope reels supplied by the Lossie Hydraulic Company. Each reel holds 14 coils of 3in (76mm) circumference rope. The third reel enables one side of warp to be turned before setting so that the ropes will always be dragged in the same direction. This reduces the wear considerably. On the after deck is a Lossie 24in (61cm) sheave power block attached to a Lossie hydraulic jib arm. The *Fruitful Harvest*'s skipper, Robert Reid, has fingertip control of the winch and rope reels from his vantage point in the bridge which has all round vision of the working deck. Kelvin Hughes echo-sounder and fish detection equipment is supplemented with a Simrad sonar, and the vessel carries a Decca Navigator and track plotter, and a Decca radar. The vessel has 2,820ft³ (80m³) fish hold and can carry 2,000 gallons (9,090 litres) of fuel and 310 gallons (1,400 litres) of fresh water.

122

A larger vessel

Fig 69 Seine net vessel
MV *Sunbeam* INS 189 of
Lossiemouth. Built by
Richard Irvin & Sons Ltd
this vessel measures
86 × 23·8 × 11·5ft
(26·2 × 7·3 × 3·5m) and
has a 600hp Blackstone
engine.

A good example of the larger seine net vessel is the *Sunbeam* INS 189 completed in 1978 by Richard Irvin and Sons of Peterhead for Skipper William Smith of Lossiemouth (*Fig 69*). This stoutly built wooden vessel has all the features of the best traditional Scottish vessels. Built of oak and larch, she has a full cruiser stern and measures 86 × 23·8 × 11·5ft (26·2 × 7·25 × 3·5m). Deck beams, engine bearers and bulkheads are made of steel. She carries a whaleback forward and a gutting shelter around the fore part of the steel casing. The *Sunbeam*'s main power unit is a Mirrlees Blackstone four-stroke ELS6MGR diesel engine which delivers 600bhp at 750rpm. It drives a fixed four-blade Bruntons propeller via a 3:1 reduction gear. A Gardner diesel engine of 127hp drives the Dowty hydraulic winch pump, Vickers rope reels and block pump, and a Transmotor ACG 220 generator. A larger generator and back-up hydraulic pump unit are driven off the fore end of the main engine. Bilge pumps are GGG, Gilbert, Gilkes and Gordon, series M and there is a Wilson air compressor driven by the auxiliary.

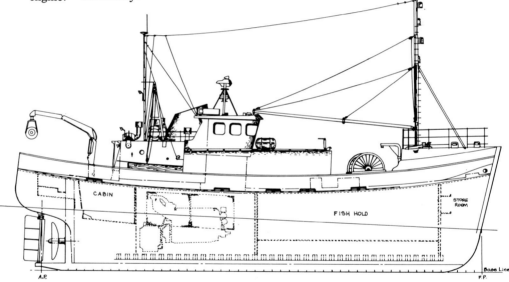

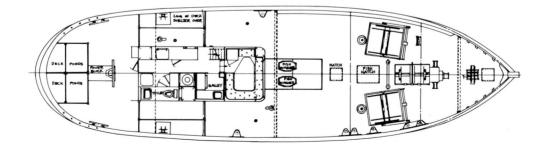

On deck, the *Sunbeam* is fitted with a Sutherland combination seine and trawl winch and two large rope reels from Lossie Hydraulic Ltd. each capable of holding 17 coils of 3½in (90mm) seine net rope. Aft of the wheelhouse is an Atlas hydraulic crane with a 24in (61cm) diameter Lossie power block. Cranes are used in preference to jibs by some large vessels to save on deck space, as they do not require to be supported by stays to the wheelhouse casing. To reduce the danger of fouling the propeller when shooting the warps, they are led through rollers on top of the gutting shelter instead of directly over the forward rail. They thus enter the water well aft where they have much less chance of ever touching the propeller.

Deck layout   There have been numerous attempts to vary the deck layout of modern seine net boats to gain some of the advantages of stern trawler or shelter deck trawler layouts. The Morse family of North Shields has pioneered such designs on their vessels, beginning with the 70ft (21·3m) *Conmoran* built by Jones Buckie shipyard in 1968, which had twin Gardner 150hp engines and twin controllable pitch screws, plus a third engine forward to drive the mechanical winch. The twin screw arrangement did not prove suitable for seine netting any more than otter trawling. But in 1977, the Morse family launched a much more advanced stern seiner named *Congener*, built in steel at Bideford, Devon. This boat is described further on in the chapter.

Other attempts at deck layout variation include the novel *Adelphi* of Fife which has net drum and power block aft and rope reels forward. The upper bridge is positioned aft so the skipper has an unimpeded view of the stern and net hauling area, at all times. A long gutting shelter extends on the foreside of the galley up to the rope reels. This vessel was built in steel by McTay's of Merseyside and outfitted by Miller's of St. Monance. Measuring 74 × 22 × 10ft (22·6 × 6·7 × 3·05m), she was powered by a 425hp Caterpillar engine. Her deck equipment was supplied by Fishing Hydraulics Ltd and the Arbroath Northern Tool and Gear Company.

The *Kestrel*, (*Fig 70*) owned by Skipper Ian Sutherland of Hopeman, provides another contrast in seiner deck layout. She has a full shelterdeck extending from the bow to the aft end of the casing. All her deck machinery for fishing is fitted aft of the wheelhouse. This includes Lossie hydraulic rope reels and power block, and a Norlau seine winch. A Lossie Hydraulics cargo winch and a Davey windlass are fitted forward. The *Kestrel* is one of the larger of the Campbeltown shipyard range of traditional style Scottish vessels built in steel. She measures 85 × 23·7 × 12ft (25·9 × 7·2 × 3·65 metres) and is powered by a 600hp Blackstone main engine and a 127hp Gardner auxiliary.

124

Fig 70 MV *Kestrel* INS 253 of Hopeman. Note the full shelter deck on this 85ft (25·9m) 600hp steel seine netter which operates out of Peterhead.

The Campbeltown range of traditional vessels are produced in three main sizes—75, 80 and 85 feet in length (22·8, 24·4 and 25·9m). The first of these boats with fine seaworthy lines and cruiser sterns was an eighty footer built for Skipper Willie Campbell of Lossiemouth. The yard's first 85 foot (25·9m) vessel was also built for Skipper Campbell, a well-known and highly successful fisherman with a good eye for a fishing vessel. His personal influence in the development of new boats and gear has been considerable.

Skipper and owner of the *Ajax*, William Campbell MBE went to sea first in 1942 when he was still only 13 years old and he was in command of his own vessel by 1954. All of the boats he has had built have incorporated some advance in equipment and layout. Beginning with his father's boat on which he served 30 years ago, we can trace some of the advances in seine net vessel technology in the subsequent vessels of the Campbell fleet.

125

Year	Vessel	Engine hp	Hull	$l \times b \times d$ in ft. and m	New equipment
1949	*ALLIANCE*	114 hp	wood	62 × 18 × 6 *18·9 × 5·5 × 1·8*	4-gear winch, echo-sounder, radio-telephone
1954	*ACORN*	152 hp	wood	69 × 19 × 7 *21·0 × 5·8 × 2·1*	Decca Navigator, fischelupe
1958	*ARGOSY*	152 hp	wood	70 × 20 × 8 *21·3 × 6·1 × 2·4*	6-gear winch, whale-back, radar
1962	*AJAX*	200 hp	wood	74 × 20·5 × 8·5 *22·6 × 6·3 × 2·6*	later developed hydraulic winch
1968	*AJAX II*	425 hp	wood	77 × 22 × 9 *23·5 × 6·7 × 2·7*	power block and hydraulic winch
1972	*AJAX III*	480 hp	steel	80 × 22 × 10 *24·4 × 6·7 × 3·1*	steel vessel, insu-lated fish hold
1976	*AJAX IV*	565 hp	steel	85 × 23 × 11 *25·9 × 7·0 × 3·4*	deck shelter, rope reels (later), Loran navigator
1980	*AJAX V*	575 hp	steel	85 × 24 × 12 *25·9 × 7·3 × 3·7*	colour video echo sounder, dual frequency sounder

Multi-purpose vessels Some seine net vessels spend part of each year engaged in bottom trawling, midwater trawling or pair trawling. These multi-purpose vessels are equipped to pursue two or more methods of fishing. The most common alternative is a switch to pelagic fishing for herring or sprats by single- or two-boat midwater trawling. But the actual methods pursued will depend on the area, the seasonal fish stocks, the local market, and the skipper's own preferences. Some seine skippers opt for herring fishing in the wintertime because it is generally carried on in more sheltered waters nearer shore, and not because it will necessarily be more lucrative. Two good examples of modern multi-purpose seiners are the *Christine Nielsen* and the *Congener*.

The *Christine Nielsen* GY298 (*Fig 71*) was built in Denmark, of steel construction. She measures 87 × 23 × 10 feet (26·5 × 7·0 × 3·05m) and is powered by a slow-running (400rpm) 500hp Alpha engine. The vessel is of traditional layout except that she has a transom stern. Aft of the wheelhouse she carried a 28in (71·1cm) Lossie Hydraulics power block and a net drum for trawling. The winch located forward is a Norlau combination seine and trawl unit and there are three seine rope reels of Grenaa manufacture. In the bridge the vessel carries a remarkable array of fish finding and navigation equipment, and the fish hold is insulated and cooled to preserve ice and fish. With a large fish capacity and fuel sufficient for extended voyages, the *Christine*

126

Fig 71 MV *Christine Nielsen*
GY 298 of North Shields.
Another multi-purpose
vessel, this Danish built
seine netter has a
three-drum rope reel system
and two fish holds.
(*T J M Wood, Grimsby*)

Nielsen can engage in several types of fishing on inshore or deep sea grounds. Her skipper Cliff Ellis of North Shields has held many fishing records in his career and has pioneered many new techniques such as the use of sonar for seine net operations, which take up the greater part of his time.

The *Congener* BCK 128 (*Fig 72*) which also operates from North Shields is of a stern trawler layout. Her skipper Alan Morse jr. belongs to a family that is renowned for pioneering new ideas in fishing. In the early 1960s on the vessel *Conmoran*, they had a separate engine to drive the winch, to give more flexibility in the fishing operation. The *Conduan*, a later vessel was powered by twin Gardner 150hp engines fitted with Slack and Parr controllable pitch propellers. She had a transom stern and a forward wheelhouse. Despite their many novel and daring features, all of the Morse family vessels were successful ventures. The new *Congener* is built of steel and measures 78 × 13 × 11 feet (23·9 × 7·2 × 3·4m). She is powered by a 640hp Hedomora diesel which drives an Ulstein controllable pitch propeller inside a steering Kort nozzle. A 60hp

127

Fig 72 MV *Congener* BCK 128 of North Shields. A fine example of a multi-purpose seine netter, this 78ft (23·9m) 630hp vessel was built for the Morse family by Bideford Shipyard, N Devon.

Gardner auxiliary drives a 30kw Stamford alternator and a back-up emergency hydraulic pump. On deck the *Congener* has a pair of Smallwood split trawl winches and an NTG hydraulic seine capstan which feeds the seine warps to a pair of Lossie hydraulic rope reels. A 24in (610mm) power block, cargo winch and gilson winch of Lossie manufacture, are also fitted. Like the *Christine Nielsen*, the *Congener* has a massive array of acoustical, navigational and communications equipment in the bridge. All the deck machinery apart from cargo winches, is placed aft of the fish hatch. The fish pounds are on the fore side of the hatch so the crew can handle the catch without any interference from the warps or nets. While she retains the stern trawler profile the *Congener* has her engine room positioned aft as preferred on most traditional vessels.

There are other multi-purpose boats that engage in seine netting sometimes, but which practice purse seining or midwater trawling for most of the year. Many of these are large vessels, 87ft (26·5m) in length, or bigger, and with main engines of 750hp or more. Because they require the deck space for other purposes, most of these boats use rope wells to accommodate the warps.

Engines A robust and dependable power unit is one of the most essential components of a seine net vessel. From their inception, Danish and Scottish seiners have been fitted with heavy slow running diesel engines. The earliest units were 'petrol-paraffin' engines but they were quickly replaced by two-stroke diesels which in turn were superseded by four-stroke diesel engines. Power was not a major requirement in these engines as seining did not demand the power needed in otter trawling. But dependability was paramount. The engines had to run non-stop five or six days a week, for around 48 weeks in the year. During the post-war years, the most popular

128

engines amongst seine fishermen were the Gardner and the Kelvin models in the 90 to 152hp range. Many of these units were still running well twenty or even thirty years later. They were normally fitted with a 2·5:1 or 3:1 reduction gear which would reduce maximum propeller rpm to around 300–400rpm. The winch drive-shaft was driven from the fore end of the engine by means of a dog-clutch and down-drive gear. The main engine also drove the generators or alternators and the sea-water pumps. Until the 1960s most seiners had only a small harbour generator rather than a proper auxiliary engine as such. Few seiners then had properly qualified engineers on board. Rather, one of the crew with some knowledge in that field was designated 'driver', and he had the duty of keeping the engine clean and attending to the lubrication, filters, dynamo belts, fuel supply, batteries and cooling system—all this in addition to normal deck duties. Since the engine was controlled completely from the wheelhouse, there was no need for a man to be stationed in the engine room.

The advent of multi-purpose fishing and the development of large deep-sea seiners brought about a remarkable increase in power and sophistication. Main engine power doubled and trebled. In order to conserve space, compact powerful diesels were installed and many of these had turbochargers to boost their power/weight ratio. The introduction of hydraulic winches, power blocks and rope reels put tremendous demands on the fore-end power take-off, and it became evident that a large auxiliary engine should be installed chiefly to power the deck machinery and electronic equipment. Some modern seine netters have auxiliary engines which are more powerful than the propulsion engines used by seine netters only twenty years ago. The engine rooms of those modern vessels are crammed full of sophisticated equipment which demands the attention of a qualified engineer and most such vessels prefer to employ a man who has completed an apprenticeship with a marine engine service and repair company. The modern equipment is necessary to drive the hydraulic and electrical gear, but the extra main engine power is primarily to give the vessel good speed and to enable it to engage in pair trawling when so required.

Multi-purpose vessels which engage in pair-trawling or purse seining most of the time and which may spend only two or three months in the year seine-netting, may have as much as 750hp or 800hp. But all the extra power is unnecessary when seine netting. Since the modern high speed turbo-charged diesels do not wear as well as the older naturally aspirated engines, many skippers prefer to purchase a larger engine than they require so that they can prolong its life by running it at less than maximum speed.

A large slow turning propeller is still preferred for seine netting and if high speed engines are installed, they must be fitted with

129

very big reduction gears. Strange to say, seine net fishermen do not like controllable pitch propellers which would give them more drive flexibility. The few seine netters with such propellers are ones which have them primarily for trawling purposes. Towing nozzles are not favoured by seine fishermen either, but this is due to the way seiners tow the gear on one side with the helm keeping the vessel's head away from leeward. For such situations a fixed towing nozzle is not effective.

There have been a few experiments with twin engine and twin screw installations in seiners, but they were not particularly successful. The single engine, single screw installation is universally accepted for seine netters as for most other fishing craft.

Seine net winches The seine winch is the most important piece of deck machinery on seine netters. It must be able to handle the miles of warp at hauling speeds varying from 50 to 500ft per min (15 to 150m per min) and at loads ranging from one to three tons or more for large vessels. Unlike trawl winches which operate only at the end of each tow, seine net winches must work for the full duration of each drag. This demands a robust and reliable machine. Fishermen who have attempted seine fishing with makeshift winches have invariably found that the efficiency achieved with a proper winch more than compensated for its extra cost.

The development of special winches for the fly-dragging operation in Scotland took many years. The Macduff Engineering Company was the first to produce a seine net winch in Scotland. The early seine net winches were of the open type, with two speeds and had gears made of cast iron. The firm of D F Sutherland, Lossiemouth, in answer to demands from fishermen, produced an enclosed four-gear winch in 1939. The winch had machine cut gears and was coupled to a lorry gear box. The first of these was installed in January of that year, and altogether, sixty-four of them were made. An improved model was introduced by the same firm during World War II. This model, with machine cut gears, was completely enclosed and had all parts running in oil. The lorry gear box was eliminated, and the resulting four-gear winch proved highly satisfactory. The first of these winches was made in May 1943, and by 1968 there were over 600 of them in service. Six-gear winches were produced first in 1955 and several hundred of them were made. For vessels which trawled for part of the year, combination seine and trawl winches were also produced.

A six-gear mechanical winch might have these gear ratios:

1	9·0 : 1		4	2·5 : 1
2	7·5 : 1		5	2·0 : 1
3	5·25 : 1		6	1·5 : 1

130

These winches were nearly all driven from the vessel's main engine. Since the winch was usually situated on the foredeck, a shaft had to be run under the fish hold to the forecastle. There, a belt and pulley transmission served to drive the winch on deck. The jockey pulley handle could be used as a clutch when changing gears. The power take-off from the fore-end of the engine to the after-end of the shaft, posed more of a problem. Since the shaft lay lower than the engine some kind of down-drive had to be fitted. At first this was done by chain and sprockets which were not enclosed. This drive suffered from excessive wear in the working parts owing to poor lubrication. The first enclosed chain drive was made in November 1947. One of the most important improvements to this drive has been the replacing of dog clutches with friction clutches which can be operated hydraulically from the wheelhouse. The

Fig 73 Combination seine–trawl winch. This hydraulic winch suitable for the larger seine netters is made by Andersen & Sorrig of Skagen, Denmark.

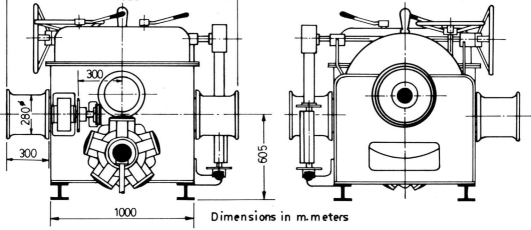

Dimensions in m.meters

131

advantage of this is obvious, especially with regard to the safety of the men at the winch which the skipper is then able to stop in an instant if necessary. The down drive also incorporated a reduction gear, usually in the order of 2:1. A seiner with 152hp engine with maximum of 1,000rpm (fishing rpm would be 10 to 30% less) might have such a reduction gear down-drive. Then at the belt drive forward it would be fitted with a 12in (300mm) diameter pulley at the end of the shaft, and an 18in (450mm) diameter pulley on deck. This gave a further 1·5:1 reduction. *Figure 73* illustrates a combination seine-trawl winch suitable for large seiners.

Coilers

The rope coiler is as essential to the operation as the seine winch and was used on all Danish and Scottish seiners until the advent of rope reels. Coilers were made by several Danish and British firms but the first and best known British coiler was the one manufactured by Elliott and Garrood of Beccles. It became known as the 'Beccles coiler' (*Fig 74*). The coilers were chain driven from the winch. The rope passed from the warping barrels to a vee wheel

Fig 74 Beccles coiler. Originally produced by Elliott and Garrood, this coiler has served the seine net industry for nearly fifty years. (*White Fish Authority*)

132

and tension wheel on the coiler and down through a revolving spout which laid the rope in bights of around three feet diameter.

The mechanically driven seine net winch and coiler served the industry well for over forty years. They were replaced by hydraulic machinery only after the introduction of other hydraulic items like power blocks. It made little sense to retain the mechanical drive for the winch when hydraulic systems were being installed for other purposes. Once satisfactory hydraulic winches had been developed, practically all new vessels were equipped entirely with hydraulic deck machinery. If seine netting was to be introduced to a developing country or to remote ports which did not have local hydraulic service engineers, mechanical driven equipment would offer the safest and cheapest way. It is never wise to apply sophisticated technology directly to a developing fishery where labour costs, fish prices and technical know-how do not match those in the industry where the technology is successfully used. Fishermen in Europe have qualified engineers to assist them in almost every port, and can purchase tools and spare parts 'off the shelf'. Fishermen in remote harbours in the southern hemisphere have neither the qualified personnel nor the specialist equipment on hand. So they must select equipment that they know they will be able to maintain and repair themselves.

Towing rollers and shooting rollers

The former towing rollers were adequate for 65ft (20m) 150hp boats using $2^3/_8$in (61·25mm) circumference manila ropes. But when seine net boats of 86ft (26m) and 600hp were built and began to use synthetic warps of up to $3\frac{1}{2}$in (82·5mm) circumference, heavier and more durable rollers had to be produced.

The new rollers are extremely hard wearing, being constructed of special steel or alloy. They have sealed bearings which use long-service marine greases. An extra horizontal roller above the two vertical rollers keeps the warps in place when fishing in heavy seas or deep swell, and reduces friction. The gate can only be opened by hand and the rail locking pin will take all loads without giving or bending.

Similar rollers are used for shooting ropes from rope reels and single vertical casing rollers of heavy duty design are available to replace the former open rope guides. One of the manufacturers of the new rollers, Shortway Rope Guides Ltd of Peterhead, won a TDC innovator award for their product (*Fig 75*).

On vessels with shelterdecks and rope reels, shooting rollers take a different form being either single horizontal rollers enclosed within guards, or fully enclosed units with both horizontal and vertical rollers. The ropes may be shot over the top, around the side, or underneath the shelterdeck. In the latter case the roller may be attached to the underside of the aft end of the shelterdeck.

133

Fig 75 Seine net rollers.

Hydraulic machinery Hydraulic seine net winches were developed in the mid 1960s. At first, they proved to be rather difficult machines to design and construct. The range of speeds required proved to be too much for most normal hydraulic pumps. Variable displacement pumps were needed in most cases for truly satisfactory operation. Many vessels which were also fitted with power blocks, hydraulic jibs and rope reels had an integrated hydraulic system installed. This was usually built around a 'power pack' unit like that produced by the Dowty company. The load of all these hydraulic circuits was rather much for the engine fore-end power takeoff and though a number were fitted there, the trend was for the hydraulics to be driven by a powerful auxiliary engine. An emergency retrieve system was installed on the larger vessels and it was powered by either the main or the auxiliary engine.

Once the hydraulic winches were satisfactorily developed, they very quickly replaced mechanical units on seiners in Scotland, Denmark, England and neighbouring countries. Many companies producing seine winches ceased manufacture of the mechanical units. This was unfortunate in one sense as there will probably be a continued need for a small number of mechanical winches. Most of the hydraulic winches produced were combination seine and trawl winches, with the seine winch set at right angles to the trawl drums. These compact units fitted on the foredeck under the whale-back shelter leaving plenty of clear deck space for ropes and fish.

134

The hydraulic winch is controlled directly from the bridge (although there is an emergency stop lever on the winch itself). The skipper has fingertip control and can adjust the hauling speed to any point between 0 and 100 barrel rpm. No gear changes are required on the hydraulic winches. The control lever is fitted to the starboard side of the wheelhouse, beside the main engine controls. From that point, the skipper should have a clear view aft and forward if the bridge has been properly designed. Far too many trawlers and seiners have been built with restricted vision aft. Their designers were apparently unaware of the fact that during the fishing operation it is vital that the skipper has a clear view aft as well as forward.

One of the first successful hydraulic seine net winches in Britain was that fitted to the *Ajax* INS 168 (the 1962 *Ajax*), and tested by White Fish Authority IDU engineers. In Canada, a hydraulic winch was successfully fitted to the *Cecilia II* in 1967.

There are three main types of hydraulic winch fitted to modern seine net boats. The most common is the combination winch which has seine barrels and winch drums incorporated in the same unit at right angles to each other. They are fitted on the foredeck with the seine winch athwart-ships and the winch drums lying fore and aft, usually on the forward side of the seine winch. The same basic winch and hydraulic power unit can thus be used for either trawling or seining. The second and less common winch is the single independent seine net winch. It is used by vessels which engage in seining year-round and by boats that prefer to have a separate trawl winch for better deck layout. Most of the stern fishing seiners are in this category.

The third and most recent winch is one that incorporates seine barrels and rope reels in a single unit. The first of these units, suitable for fly-dragging or anchor-dragging, was developed by Jimmy Allan of Lossie Hydraulic Company. It was installed successfully in 1978, in the Grimsby seiner, *Esme*, owned by an enterprising and progressive skipper, Jimmy Howard. The drums, made from mild steel tubing and weighing about 250 kilograms each are in a frame with the 2·5-ton full seine barrels located between them. The rope passes from the drum to the spooling gear on top of the reels and not across the deck as on units with a separate winch. Both seine barrels and both rope reels have independent hydraulic control from the wheelhouse so both speed and warp length adjustments can be made by the skipper at the touch of a lever. Compact winch-reel units like these are of particular interest to skippers of smaller seine net boats, a category that includes most Danish seiners and all of the under 60ft fly-draggers. Much more deck space is available for fish and gear handling than with separate winches and reels (*Fig 76*).

135

Fig 76 Lossie winch incorporating seine barrels and rope reels in a single unit.
(*T J M Wood, Grimsby*)

Power blocks

Hydraulic power blocks were developed in the United States and South American Pacific coast fisheries in the post war years. They were introduced to facilitate the hauling and handling of the huge purse seines being used to catch anchovy and tuna. Their application to the hauling of seine nets and light trawls came much later. Scandinavian fishermen were among the first to apply them to seine netting. The first Scottish seiner to have a power block fitted (in 1968) was the *Argonaut* KY 357 (the 1964 *Argonaut*) owned and skippered by David Smith. The main difference in the installation of power blocks to seine net boats as compared to purse seiners was the use of a hydraulic jib or crane on which the block was slung. On purse seiners, the block is fixed to the casing or hung from a strong high boom.

The use of a hydraulic jib makes it easy for the crew to slip the net into the block which can be lowered to rail level at the port or starboard aft quarter. The block is then raised to a suitable working height and hauling commences. The controls, fixed to the aft end of the casing, include a forward, reverse and stop valve lever and a speed control. The crew members still have to apply some weight when hauling, particularly with the bridles, and when fishing in heavy seas. But the danger of being pulled overboard is eliminated and the effort required in hauling is much less. It would be extremely difficult and time consuming to haul the large modern seine trawls by hand.

136

As when hauling by hand, two crewmen will place one wing ready for setting. The other wing will have to be inverted later. When the bag is reached and hauled in as far as the forward splitting strap or near it, the block will be stopped and swung towards the side the fish will be taken on board. While a crew man makes a turn of the bag round a cleat to hold it fast, the skipper will put the boat slow ahead with the wheel hard over. After a quick burst astern, the propeller is stopped and the codend should swing alongside. The fish tackle is hooked on to the becket or splitting strap and the codend is hoisted on board. If the catch is large, it is split into smaller lifts as described in *Chapter 4*. The power block can be useful in pulling the bag up to refill the codend after each lift when splitting is necessary.

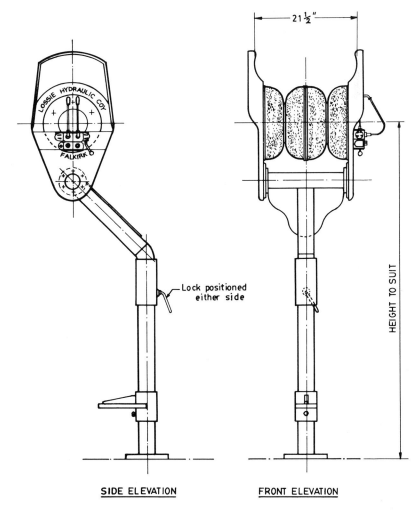

Fig 77 Pedestal type net hauler: double sheave type. (*Lossie Hydraulic Ltd*)

SIDE ELEVATION   FRONT ELEVATION

Smaller seine net boats and a number of Danish seiners use double or triple sheave power blocks fitted on pedestals instead of the single sheave hydraulic jib models. The pedestal block is fitted to one quarter aft or right at the stern. It can swivel to face the direction of the incoming net. Apart from its fixed location, the pedestal block is used in much the same way as the jib mounted block and it appears to be a more suitable unit for smaller boats, being simpler and more compact. *Figures 77, 78* and *79* illustrate net haulers and power blocks.

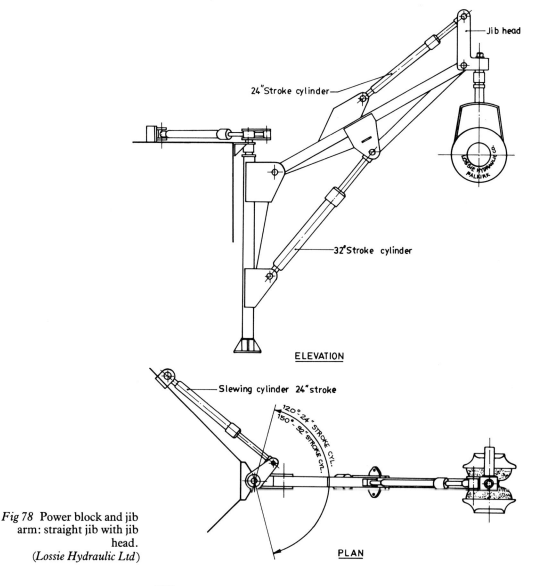

Fig 78 Power block and jib arm: straight jib with jib head.
(*Lossie Hydraulic Ltd*)

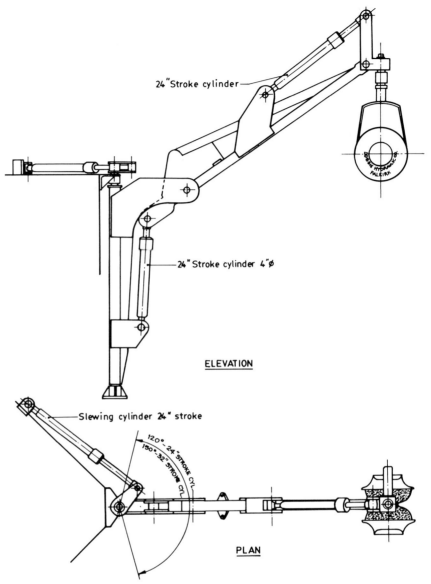

24" Stroke cylinder

24" Stroke cylinder 4"ø

ELEVATION

Slewing cylinder 24" stroke

120° - 24" STROKE CYL.
150° - 32" STROKE CYL.

PLAN

Fig 79 Power block and jib
arm: vertical cylinder
(*Lossie Hydraulic Ltd*)

Rope reels Seine rope reels along with the power block are probably the most
beneficial advance in deck machinery for seine netters since the
introduction of four-gear winches some forty years ago. The biggest
single obstacle to the mechanization of the operation had always
been the handling of the many coils of warp on deck. The coiler
provided a means of stacking the ropes neatly in bundles but these
still had to be manhandled by the crew. When a tow was in
progress, one crewman was needed to mind the winch and coiler
while the gear was still open, and two men were required to haul

139

away the ropes when heaving up. This meant less hands to attend to the time-consuming gutting of the catch. One crewman had to watch the ropes carefully when shooting the gear to make sure no fouled bights went out. The introduction of rope reels made it possible for most of this work to be controlled by the skipper from the bridge. He could even slack back on one side as necessary to even the warps, by means of a valve control. The reels also saved a great deal of wear on the ropes, so longer use could be obtained out of each coil.

Japanese fishermen had used rope reels on their large 'Danish' seiners and bull trawlers for many years. On smaller Asian seine netters in Japan, Korea and Taiwan, the warps were coiled by hand. But this was a laborious task and necessitated a large crew. On the bigger vessels, the warps were really too big to be manhandled efficiently and so reels were introduced on which the warps could be wound as they came from the winch. It was after the introduction of thicker, heavier synthetic ropes that Altantic seine net fishermen finally opted for reels to eliminate the need to manhandle the ropes. Rope wells were used for a short period on some vessels but this option was discarded owing to excessive wear on the ropes and the increased problem of foul ropes that they brought, not to mention the trouble with sand and mud accumulating in the bilges.

As usual, the Scandinavian fishermen led the way and the first commercially successful rope reels were made in Denmark. They were hydraulically powered and fitted to anchor-dragging Danish seiners. They proved to be almost immediately successful and with a minimum of modifications were soon in regular production. Grimsby-based Danish seiners followed suit and it was only a matter of time before most of the vessels in the fleet were equipped with the gear.

The first Scottish fisherman to fit a set of reels was the intrepid skipper of the *Argonaut III* KY 337 (the 1969 *Argonaut*), David Smith. Skipper Smith had been the first seine net skipper in his country to fit a power block and the first to have his vessel equipped with a deck shelter. In 1972 he led the way with the warp handling gear. A two-reel set was purchased from Norway and after some teething troubles was soon working efficiently in all weathers. When he built the larger and more powerful *Argonaut IV* KY 157 in 1976, he had no hesitation in having her equipped with the rope drums. But by that time, many other skippers had followed his example. Almost all who purchased rope reels were pleased with them, despite their cost, and by early 1977, more than 150 British seine net boats were equipped with the gear.

The rope reels are designed to accommodate all of the vessel's warp. This may amount to 15 or 18 coils each side, or more. The rope is fed to the reel from the winch by means of a guide-on gear which results in a beautifully neat pack which minimises wear on the warp (*Figs 80* and *81*). The sides of the reels are spoked for lightness and side flanges are sometimes fitted so that frayed and damaged sections can be led off to the side for easy access later. If two normal reels are used, then one side of rope must inevitably be 'turned around' each tow. When this happens, the warp suffers greater wear being rubbed both ways instead of always in the one direction. There are two installations that can be used to avoid this. One method is to fit three rope reels instead of two. Many Danish

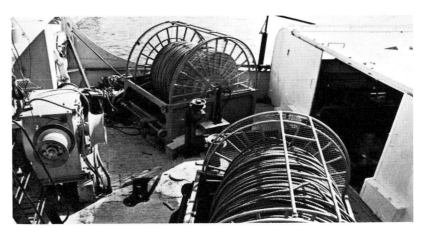

Fig 80 Seine rope drums on the *Loch Kildonan*—note bottom rope-laying guide.

Fig 81 MV *Loch Kildonan* of Peterhead. This is one of the largest seine netters in operation, measuring close on 100ft (30m).

141

seiners have a three-drum system. After each haul, the first side of warp (the side to be set first) is laid on to the third or empty drum which quickly reels in all the rope. The other method is to use only two drums but have one of the drums with double the capacity of the other. The warp from the dhan side is laid on to the larger reel, on top of the warp from the other side. Then both sides of warp are set from the one reel.

Shooting seine net warps from reels can be accomplished with or without hydraulic power. The better types of rope reels are fitted with hydraulic brakes to save the reel from over-running the warp. Reels may be fitted facing fore-and-aft, facing athwartships or at an angle between the two. There appears to be little difference in performance whichever way they are placed. Shooting bolts are still fitted to the rail to guide the warps over. When having to tow the warp off hard bottom or towards a school of fish, those vessels with good hydraulic braking systems can do so with the brake alone. A short length of rope with G-links is laid on to the winch and empty reels during the shooting operation and the ends of each side of warp are clipped on to these at the respective sides.

The use of rope reels has simplified warp handling and reduced deck work for the crew, leaving them free to attend to the fish catch. It has also reduced wear on the ropes. One of the few disadvantages of rope reels is the amount of deck space they take up. This is no problem to seine netters, but it creates difficulties for multi-purpose vessels. When switching over from seine netting to midwater pair-trawling for instance, the foredeck has to be cleared to accommodate the fish pounds needed to cope with large herring catches. Unless they are positioned well forward, rope reels would obviously interfere with the trawling requirements. They could be uncoupled and dismantled but that would involve time and specialist labour. For these reasons, only those vessels engaging in seine netting for all or most of the year normally fit rope reels. Boats which go seining for only a few months between herring seasons still use rope wells or deck stacking of the warps.

Deck shelters The North Sea and east Atlantic waters are well known for their stormy changeable weather. Seine net boats have fished these waters for over fifty years, summer and winter, storm and calm. When operating on inshore or nearwater grounds, the fleets could always make for port, or find shelter within a few hours, if the weather broke. But when the larger vessels began to fish more than 24 hours from the nearest haven, they could not run for shelter without losing valuable fishing time when the wind abated. So they chose to ride out the bad weather, keeping the vessel's head to wind until it was possible to resume fishing. The danger on a small boat in such heavy seas, for the crew on deck, is from 'lumps' of water

142

which can swamp the decks and wash a man overboard. When a man is handling fish on the side deck or fore deck, he cannot always be aware of the approach of a particularly high wave or sea. (Fishermen call them 'seas' or 'lumps of water' or 'green water' rather than 'waves'). Gutting shelters and whaleback or storm deck forward prevent water from coming aboard over the stern or bow. The writer can recall being lifted off his feet and swept right aft, ropes and all when shooting the warps in a lumpy sea on a vessel without a whaleback. Gutting shelters extend from the forward side of the wheelhouse (at the fish room hatch) to the aft end of the casing on each side. They are open aft and at the fish hatch forward. Inside the gutting shelter, the crew are safe from the danger of seas coming aboard amidships. They are made of aluminium or glass-fibre, strengthened as necessary, and may be fitted with windows or vents. (*Fig 81*).

Some seiners have been built with one side entirely enclosed by a shelter deck and there have been two vessels built with the whole deck area covered in, apart from the stern where the net and codend are taken aboard. These were the *Orion* KY 352 and the *Kestrel* INS 253 (see *Fig 70* p125), the former a 54 footer (16·5m) and the latter an 85 footer (25·9m). Many French stern trawlers are constructed with such shelter decks. Although they do add top weight to a vessel, shelter decks actually improve stability by increasing the 'free-board' a vessel has when rolling.

Fish holds   For a long time, there was little improvement in the design of the fish holds on seine net boats. What was needed was a hold that was big enough to accommodate the catch, the boxes and the ice, and one that was laid out to facilitate boxing and easy discharge of the boxes. Lined fish holds were not popular in the UK owing to the fear of dry rot which affected many vessels around 1960, possibly due to the use of timber from trees blown down in the 1953 gales. However, after that date, all timber for fishing craft was pressure impregnated with chemicals to prevent any recurrence of dry rot. So it became more feasible to insulate the fish holds. With steel vessels it was made easier still.

Fish hold insulation became popular when it was possible to blast-fill the cavities between the ship's side and the hold lining with polyurethane foam or similar material. This was formed by mixing chemicals just prior to injection. Insulated fish holds prevented the ice from melting in summertime and causing deterioration in the fish catch. It was hardly necessary on vessels making daily trips but for large seiners which were at sea for up to a week at a time, it became essential to maintain the high quality of seine net fish. Apart from the heat from the sun and the sea in late summer, there was considerable heat effect from the engine room,

143

particularly from the large turbocharged engines. The hold insulation protected the fish and ice.

A further development was refrigeration or cooling. The new wooden seiner *Rhodella* BCK 100 had a chilling plant installed. The steel seiner *Argonaut IV* was also equipped with a refrigeration system and in addition, she had two one-ton-per-day Promac flake ice machines installed.

Echo sounder   Correct interpretation of the echo sounder display is an essential part of seine net fishing.

Echo sounders operate on the principle of sound waves and their echoes. The sound transmissions are generated electrically and transmitted from a transducer attached to the under-hull of the fishing vessel. The transducer also receives the very faint echoes from the signals. The echoes are amplified and returned to the recorder machine where they may be displayed in different ways.

The main echo received is of course from the sea bed, but fish schools, water turbulence, or even plankton, will return echoes. Modern sensitive echo sounders can even detect single fish. The time lag between transmission and receipt of an echo can be measured electronically to indicate the distance or depth. The strength or intensity of the echo will provide some indication of the nature of the 'target'.

The first electrical sounding machines used by fishing boats in the 1930s were of the 'flashing' type which simply indicated the depth of the water and nothing more. Many small yachts use such sounders today.

Paper-recording echo sounders were produced after the Second World War, and they proved to be a tremendous boon to fishermen. They were so useful for bottom seining that in a short time all seine netters were equipped with one. They not only indicated the depth of the sea bed in a permanent manner, but also its contours and texture or consistency. Fish schools were also detected and represented on the recording.

As they were constantly on the lookout for 'snags' or 'fasteners', seine net fishermen were particularly impressed with the paper-recording sounder. Rocks, wrecks or patches of hard ground showed up clearly on the recording due both to the sharp change in bottom contour, and the heavier shading caused by an increase in echo strength. With the aid of the new echo sounders, boats could locate grounds quicker and could fish close to areas of rough or rocky ground with an accuracy and speed that was not possible when using a lead line and marker buoy.

Echo sounders may use dry or wet paper, or sometimes both. The wet paper has been treated with a chemical that will discolour when an electrical impulse passes through it. This happens as the

144

marker pen sends the signal through the paper to the metal plate behind. Dry or carbon paper burns slightly with the electrical impulse, revealing the carbon contained under the white paper surface.

Wet paper recordings are not really permanent, as the whole paper will eventually discolour and turn brown as it dries on exposure to air. But that process takes some days. Dry paper recordings are more permanent. One slight disadvantage to dry paper is that it releases black carbon dust which can interfere eventually with the machine's sensitivity if it is not cleaned regularly with a fine brush or air brush. However, neither of the disadvantages to wet or dry paper are serious. Most fishermen do not keep recordings longer than one trip, and usually they are discarded after one day.

For seine netting, one does not need a sounder with a range much beyond 100 fathoms (183m). Most echo sounders can record much greater depths but those deeper ranges are used only for navigational purposes. Seine nets are rarely ever set in depths over 120 fathoms (220m). Generally, the fishermen will use sounders with three depth ranges, usually about 0 to 40 fathoms (0 to 73m), 40 to 80 fathoms (73 to 146m) and 80 to 120 fathoms (146 to 220m). The precise ranges vary with units of different manufacture.

The frequency at which a sounder operates is important in seine netting. As the seine net skipper requires good ground discrimination in the bottom echoes, and as most of the fish he is after have air bladders, he needs a low frequency machine. That means one in the 20 to 50 kHz range. Echo sounders in the high frequency (200 kHz) are used chiefly by purse seiners or midwater trawlers fishing for species like mackerel which have no air bladder and are, therefore, more difficult to detect.

Fish echoes on a sounder recording are called 'spots' or 'marks'. The length and density of the echoes indicate the size and density of the school. Fishermen must be careful to have the gain and sensitivity controls at optimum setting. Too low a setting will reveal no fish, or only very large schools (which are a rare occurrence these days). Too high a setting will result in a multitude of marks from plankton or 'feeding', and real fish echoes will be obscured. The gain switch must be kept to a reasonable level much as an amateur radio 'ham' tries to keep static to a minimum yet still detect faint signals.

By the late 1950s, two additions to the echo sounder were becoming popular and by the 1960s, their use was widespread. The first of these was the CRT or cathode ray tube, scale expansion unit. This 'scope' or 'lupe' as it was called (from the German 'fischlupe') revealed that section of the echo signal from the 5 fathoms (9·1m) or so just above the sea bed. This is the important

145

part of the signal to a seine net or trawler skipper, for the fish they catch will be the ones lying on or close to the sea bed.

The CRT display showed a vertical bead of light, with a strong horizontal 'blip' formed by the sea bed echo. Any fish echoes showed as small horizontal blips on the central vertical echo line. The signals flashed regularly and it was one of the many modern bridge instruments that tended to strain a fishing skipper's eyes. Fish lying right on the sea bed were revealed in a shallow semi-circular shape of blip where the vertical bead touched the horizontal bottom echo. Many fishermen became expert at detecting fish schools with this instrument.

The next addition or modification to echo sounders came with the development of the white line or grey line. This was an effect produced by briefly blocking the heavy bottom echo. The fish echoes were then separated from the bottom echoes by a short gap which by its blank nature was termed the white line. It helped fishermen see whether there were fish lying on or very close to the sea bed, or whether the serrations in the bottom contour were due to undulations on the sea bed, or the movement of the vessel on the waves or swell.

Many seine net skippers do not shoot their gear until they have detected fish first. They may scour the grounds for days and nights before a school is seen. Thus, it becomes ever more necessary to have a fish finder that is both accurate and dependable.

By the 1970s, the CRT fish lupes were being replaced with scale expansion echo sounders. These were paper recording sounders which had the facility to display the 2·5, 5, or 10 fathoms (4, 5, 9 or 18m) immediately above the sea bed, at the turn of a switch. So at any moment a skipper wishing to take a closer view of the fish marks showing up to the main recording could have them magnified on the same paper recording. This relieved him of the tedious task of looking into a CRT unit to which he had to adjust his eyes and re-set the controls. As he would also have to be keeping an eye on the Decca Navigator, the sea and work-deck outside, not to mention the compass and radar, any added convenience in display was a big one.

The new scale expansion sounders also had a bottom lock facility. Regardless of the varying contours of the sea bed, the expanded scale echoes would be shown on a straight line. So one could watch the fish positions relative to the sea bed without having to adjust the depth control as on the former CRT units.

A modern echo sounder unit may cost as much or even more than a luxury saloon car. It is the single most expensive piece of electronic equipment on a seine netter's bridge. This indicates the value these fishermen place on the information the units provide about the sea bed and about the fish schools they seek.

146

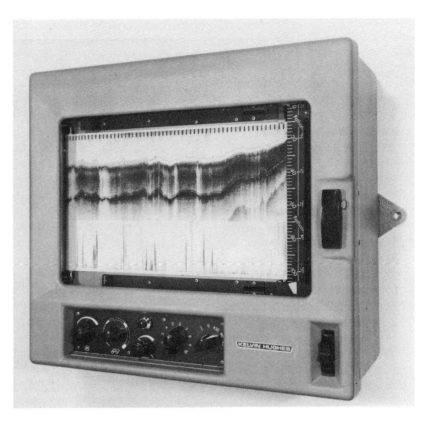

Fig 82 Kelvin Hughes MS
44 scale expansion echo
sounder.

A modern scale expansion echo sounder is shown in *Fig 82*.

The Decca Navigator   Accurate position-finding is an essential part of successful seining
since fly-draggers operate mainly close to rocks, wrecks, snags or
hard bottom where fish often congregate. Until the 1950s, the
positioning of one's vessel on the fishing grounds, and the accurate
setting of gear, was an art gained by long experience and by detailed
observations of depth, landmarks, type of bottom, wind, tide, and
course and distance run. All of this information would be recorded
carefully in a notebook which would become one of the skipper's
most prized possessions.

The electronic aid used in plotting the position of the vessel and
the fishing grounds before the 1950s, was the radio direction finder,
or RDF, but it was cumbersome to use and was not sufficiently
accurate. Loran was not used by seine netters since it is chiefly a
long-range system and seiners rarely operate more than 250 miles
from port.

Often a vessel would 'feel' its way around a particular fishing
ground and drop one or more marker buoys to help guide it in the
accurate setting of the gear. Many a time the result of all these

147

painstaking measures would be a net torn in shreds because of the element of human error involved.

The whole system of position finding was revolutionized in a way that previously, no one would have dreamed possible. The instrument responsible for this remarkable change was the Decca Navigator (*Fig 83*).

The Decca Navigator is an instrument that measures the phase difference in signals received continuously from three shore stations. These phase differences can be plotted on a chart in the form of a hyperbolic position lines.

The three stations transmitting the signals are positioned at the points of a triangle surrounding a central or 'Master' station. The slave stations are distinguished by the names of colours which are given to them, *ie* red, green, and purple. The position lines on a Decca chart are printed in the colour appropriate to the station from which they emanate.

A position fix is obtained by reading from two of the three position lines. In practice, fishermen use whichever two beams are running at right angles, or nearly right angles, to each other, in their particular area. Where the two lines cross is the vessel's position. It can be

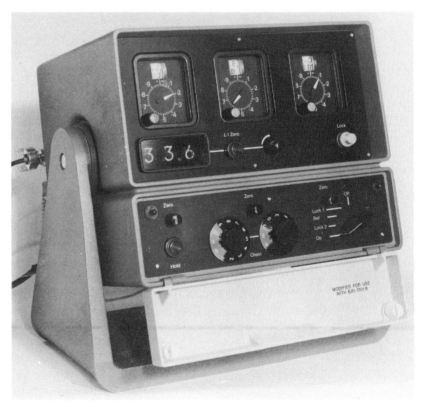

Fig 83 Decca Navigator Mark 21.

plotted on a chart, but when fishing, the readings themselves are used, without reference to a chart, unless one is unfamiliar with the area.

The current receiver unit, Decca Navigator Mark 21, is a solid state, microcircuit, multipulse receiver. Three decometer clocks provide continuous readings of red, green and purple lanes in decimal points. The lane numbers are shown in letters and digits above each clock. Lane identification is confirmed by a digital readout beneath the decometers, giving a reading for all three lanes every sixty seconds. On the earlier Mark 12 receivers, this was done by a master clock.

Once the instrument has been switched on and set up, usually on leaving port, it will run continuously for the duration of the voyage and the skipper needs only to refer to the decometers of whichever two lanes he is using. The lane identification or master readout is only for confirmation that each decometer is correctly set. If a vessel sails from the region of one Decca chain to another, the receiver can be switched over to receive signals from the other chain within a minute.

The track plotter (*Fig 84*) is an additional instrument which can

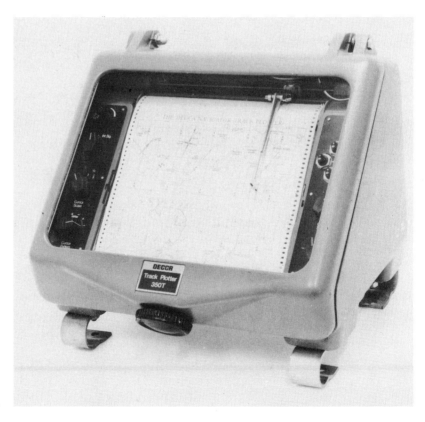

Fig 84 Decca track plotter.

149

be used in conjunction with the Navigator receiver. It records on a paper display the movements of the vessel relative to the two selected lanes. A vessel's track when fishing or steaming can thus be plotted or traced and the record retained indefinitely, along with any notes about the date, time and results of the tows in question.

Should the skipper be too busy to note the readings of a snag when hauling back the gear, he can refer later to the plotter chart for this information. When a set has been particularly successful, the gear can be set in exactly the same position by simply following the previous track on the plotter. When setting up the plotter upon reaching the fishing grounds, the skipper may mark the chart in advance with data on the location of the rough bottom, wrecks or snags. The visual display of the proximity of these hazards is very helpful in giving advance warning of the drift of the boat towards dangerous areas, particularly when strong tidal currents are at work.

The value of the Decca Navigator system to fishing cannot be overstressed. Practically all of the 2,000 seine net vessels in Europe and Scandinavia are fitted with the equipment which cannot be purchased but is rented from the company. It has simplifed what was once a time-consuming procedure while also greatly improving accuracy. All this has made the skipper's job a great deal easier. The result of its use in terms of savings in time and gear costs have made the Navigator one of the best investments a skipper can have. When it was introduced to the fishing fleets in the late 1950s, it produced savings of up to 30% in gear costs and increases of up to 25% in fish catches.

The system works well in daylight or darkness, in rain, fog or clear weather. It is not affected by strong winds, or by the rolling or pitching of the vessel in heavy seas. During winter nights, and especially when it is snowing, there may be some variation in the strength and precision of signals. Those who have not used the Decca Navigator find its accuracy hard to believe. Seine net fishermen have found it to be correct to within a boat's length; that is, to within 75 feet! To use a Scottish seiner skipper's expression, it makes it possible for him to 'drop his net on a sixpence' if so required.

Multi-chain fixing Approved range of Decca Navigator signals, by bodies such as the British Ministry of Transport, is in the order of 240 nautical miles from the master station. Accurate readings can be obtained at greater distances, but a new method of multi-chain fixing has become popular with fishermen working in the open parts of the North Sea.

To obtain a better cross fix, the fishermen take readings of lanes from two separate Decca chains. One of these chains might be the North Scottish one centred on the Orkney islands, and the other

150

might be the Northumbrian chain, or even the Vestlands chain centred near Bergen.

There are two ways of obtaining the readings. One is to switch the receiver over to the other chain. This would provide a cross fix within a minute. Many skippers, however, prefer to have continuous readouts from both chains, and they install two Navigator receivers instead of one. This way also, if they use the track plotter, they can have it plot the course relative to the chosen lanes from the two Decca chains via dual receiver interswitch. Most of the large seine net vessels operating in the North Sea now fit two receivers for inter-chain fixes (*Fig 85*).

A third system that vessels can use when working distant grounds is to get a fix from one Decca lane and one lane from the Loran C grid. For this, a Loran C receiver must be fitted but it also may be fed into a track plotter unit as with the inter-chain system. These long range systems are only used when vessels are fishing more than 200 miles from the nearest Decca Master station.

The skipper of the Fraserburgh seine netter *Constellation*, Joseph R Buchan has described the value of the Decca system as follows: 'I find the Decca Navigator absolutely essential for the job of seine netting. It has really contributed immensely to this form of

Fig 85 Skipper Bob Mainprize, MV *Pathfinder*, with dual Decca receivers.

151

fishing. Regularly, I work amongst wrecks and on rough bottom in a manner which would be quite impossible without the Decca Navigator. The Track Plotter is also of great value to me when I am going off track, and correct for tide and drift immediately. The Decca Navigator has really made this seine netting job.'

Jorgen Gjertsen, the skipper of the Danish seiner *Keimar* gave his opinion thus: 'Seine net fishing a few years ago was carried out mainly on fine grounds. Scarcity of fish however has meant moving to much more difficult fishing places where there are old wrecks. The Decca Navigator is essential to me for working in these places otherwise very expensive net damage can occur. Without Decca, I have to move away and in fact cannot really fish at all on a profitable basis.'

Decca Navigator chains cover the east Atlantic around the British Isles and Ireland, south as far as France, Spain and Morocco and north as far as the northern tip of Norway. There are also good chains established in the Canadian maritime provinces, in Japan, South Africa, West Africa, the Arabian Gulf, West India and Bangladesh. Loran C coverage is mainly around the United States, Japan, and across the north Atlantic and north Pacific oceans.

The coverage of the Decca Navigator system in the East Atlantic and throughout the world is shown in *Fig 86*.

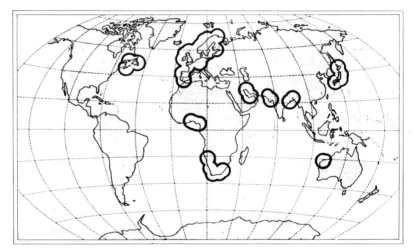

Fig 86 Decca Navigator system, world coverage 1979. (*Decca Navigator Company*)

152

8 Anchor seiner development

While in Scotland the trend towards larger, more powerful vessels continued through the 1970s, in Esbjerg and Grimsby, the chief anchor seining ports, fishermen preferred to stay with the smaller more lightly-powered craft which had proved to be so economical. The automation made possible with rope reels and power blocks was welcomed and there was widespread installation of these items on existing vessels.

New and more modern vessels were built, but they rarely exceeded 65ft (20m) in length and their engines were of modest size, the Gardner 230hp and the Kelvin 280hp models being most popular. Belt-driven winches were replaced with hydraulic models of Danish or Scottish manufacture.

There was little change to the common anchor seiner layout. The small wheelhouse was positioned aft and the crew's accommodation mostly remained forward. The installation of rope reels, whether two-drum or three-drum types, left much more clear working space on deck. Some of the more traditional aspects of Danish seiner design have remained despite all the modern gear. The main steadying sail and the cruiser stern are examples of these. The hull design is fuller but still follows the conventional Danish lines for anchor seiners. *Figures 87, 88* and *89* show typical modern anchor seining vessels.

Alternative methods of fishing

The pattern of fishing has also continued with perhaps only a slight shortening of the average trip length to around two weeks. Anchor-seining is not normally carried on during the worst of the winter months. The more modern boats may fish the year from February till November but most of the anchor seiners operate only from March to October. During the 1970s when pair trawling for cod became one of the most successful of fisheries, many anchor seiners were converted for two-boat fishing. However, only a few of the vessels made the change-over permanent. While the rewards for success at pair fishing were high, the skills involved were

153

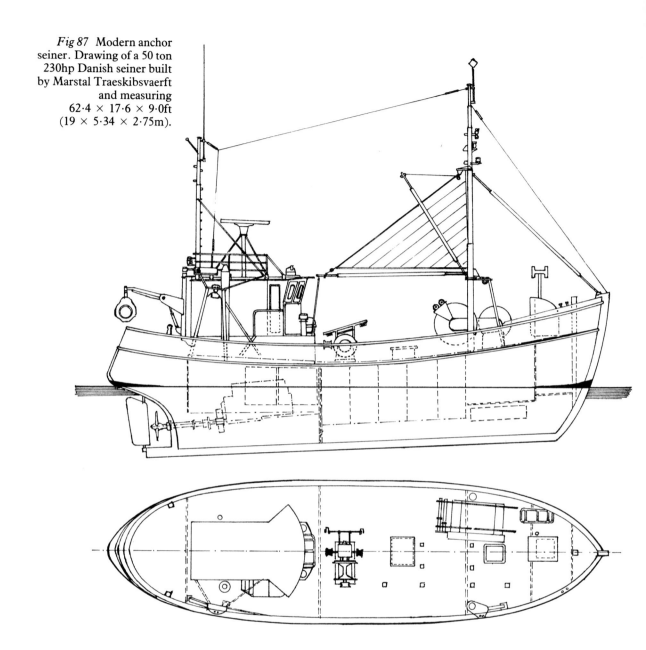

Fig 87 Modern anchor seiner. Drawing of a 50 ton 230hp Danish seiner built by Marstal Traeskibsvaerft and measuring 62·4 × 17·6 × 9·0ft (19 × 5·34 × 2·75m).

considerable and had to be developed with patience and perseverance. Anchor seining by contrast offered a more reliable if less spectacular income for those who were familiar with the gear. Another alternative for the smaller anchor-draggers was fishing for cod with gill nets set with great precision around wrecks on the sea bed. Some boats in the 40 to 50ft (12 to 16m) range adopted that gear to some profit.

154

Fig 88 Modern anchor seiner MV *Karen* GY 317.

Fig 89 Modern anchor seiner MV *Margaret* GY 334. Note the steadying sail, rope reels and pedestal power block.

155

A few anchor seiners are still registered at the ports of Fleetwood, Buckie, North Shields and Hull. But few if any of them fish from these ports. Grimsby remains the one chief port for anchor seiners in Britain as Esbjerg does for Denmark. Both Danish and British seiners land at Grimsby. Under the European Common Market rules, the landing of fish by member country vessels in other member country markets is much easier than before. During the difficult period following the extension of fishery limits to 200 miles by Iceland, Canada and other north Atlantic countries, the port of Grimsby had to rely on the small anchor seiners and pair trawlers to maintain a supply of fish. When the large distant water trawlers were forced to work closer to home it was soon apparent that they were much less efficient in the North Sea than the little economical anchor seiners and pair trawlers. Some trawling companies invested in smaller vessels. These were multi-purpose boats designed for light trawling, pair trawling and bottom seining on the Scottish fly-dragging pattern.

Low cost operation In retaining their small and low-cost character, the anchor seiners may have shown more foresight than their Scottish cousins who have gone in for much larger and more powerful vessels. Fuel oil prices are going to escalate throughout the 1980s and by the 1990s the very availability of diesel fuel at any price may be in question. It would be a most interesting and informative study for one of our fisheries research organisations to look into the capital and operational costs of fish production for each of the main methods used, in terms of fuel consumption. How much fuel oil is consumed to produce a certain type of vessel and its gear; how much fish will it produce; and what will be the weight of fish caught for each ton of fuel consumed during operation?

An analysis of the 101 best trips by anchor seiners landing at Grimsby in 1978 reveals surprisingly little change in catch rates from those of ten to twenty years before. Due to constant modernisation and a tendency towards overbuilding by all nations involved there, the North Sea must surely be the most competitive fishing area of the world. Yet the anchor seiners have continued to survive and to maintain their catch rates with only modest improvements to vessels and equipment. The daily fishing average for the hundred best landings in 1978 was over 21 kits or over 1·3 tons. In monetary terms that worked out at over £700 per day but as money values are depreciating rather rapidly, that may not mean much unless it is compared with the daily averages of other fishing craft for the same year. Large deep sea trawlers had to have average earnings of over £1,000 per day at sea just to break even in 1978. Many of them failed to do this and had subsequently to be scrapped.

156

Earnings During the year in question (1978), the largest single trip grossing by an anchor seiner was £16,684. This was by the seiner *Rasmine* skippered by Villy Thomsen and it was realised from a catch of 581 kits (36·83 tons). As the trip had been of only 13 days duration, the average daily earnings were well in excess of £1,000.

Danish seining by nature of its operation, does not often produce the kind of 'windfall' catches that can sometimes be obtained by Scottish seining or pair trawling. Nevertheless the top anchor seiners provide their crews and owners with very good incomes.

Annual grossing by Grimsby seiners in the seventies rose (as money values fell) till by 1978 and 1979 many of them were grossing over £100,000 a year. The *Rasmine* mentioned above made over £126,000 in 1978. Owing to their size the anchor seiners have a short operational year with few of them ever achieving 200 days sea time. Most Danish seiners will end the year with between 160 and 190 days sea time to their credit. So while a fisherman may receive several hundred pounds (or even a thousand pounds) as his share from a two week trip, his annual earnings may not be much above those of an industrial worker ashore.

Traditionally on Danish seiners the share-out is somewhat different to that on Scottish vessels where there is little difference in pay if any between skipper and deckhand. On an anchor seiner, the crew receives 50% of the net earnings. That is half of the trip grossing after the fuel, ice, food, insurance, sales, docking and hire charges have been paid. The other half goes to the 'boat' or to the vessel owners. But they will have to pay from it the annual cost of warps, nets, engine spares, docking and overhauling. The crew's share may be divided as follows, assuming a crew of four men: skipper 36%, mate 30%, deckhand 20% and cook 14%. If a 15 day trip grossed £8,500 then the net amount (less operational expenses) might be around £6,000, of which the crew's share would be £3,000. The actual share-outs might then be: skipper £1,080, mate £900, deckhand £600, and cook £420. Those figures multiplied by ten or twelve trips might give an indication of the gross annual salary of each.

The duties of engineer are carried out usually by the skipper himself, or by the mate, or the skipper and the mate together. All hands, including the skipper and the cook would help in sorting and gutting the fish, unless the catches were very small.

Fishing continues almost non-stop during the summer months. During this period an extra young crewman may be carried to provide each hand an extra few hours sleep, in rotation. In spring and autumn months the boat would lie at anchor during the hours of darkness unless there was a moon which would make night-time fishing feasible.

157

Continued success of seine net fishing It is now over 60 years since Danish seine net boats began to fish the North Sea and to land their catches in the port of Grimsby. During that period the fisheries have witnessed the decline of long-lining and the demise of drift netting. They have also seen the end of deep sea trawling as Britain knew it in the days when the distant-water grounds were open to all. In the same period the herring fishery has collapsed twice: first in the 1920s owing to marketing problems and then in the 1970s owing to drastic stock reduction through overfishing. But through all these ups and downs the Danish seine net has continued to flourish and to provide fish at modest cost without harming future stocks. If that is any indication we may assume that if and when the world enters the 21st century, there will still be some anchor-draggers fishing away around the Dogger Bank in the North Sea.

9 Seine net fishing in Scotland

One of the limitations of a technical book on fishing gear and methods is the impression it gives that a fisherman needs only to follow all the practical instructions given in order to fish successfully. This is not so. Fishing involves many factors some of which are only remotely concerned with the technicalities of fish capture. A successful skipper has to be a good businessman, a shrewd market analyst, a personnel manager, a meteorologist and an engineer, in addition to his recognised roles as navigator, fish finder and fish catching expert. Interwoven through all these activities is the background situation regarding his home port, his regular fishing grounds and the way in which the fleet operates in his area. The size and type of vessel used, the fishing grounds worked, the market supplied and the social and technical services situation in the home port will all have a bearing on the way a fishery is prosecuted.

Most fishing skippers will agree that their job consists of hundreds of small decisions. The success or failure of a fishing trip will relate directly to the correctness of those decisions. Few of the decisions a skipper must make are clear choices. Rather, they are value judgements on the marginal advantages or disadvantages of various courses of action such as: whether to steam ten hours in the hopes of finding more fish and risk worse weather conditions, or try one's luck on more sheltered grounds within five hours of the market; whether to shoot the net on rough bottom and risk serious damage to the gear, or set it on clean ground where the fish are less plentiful; whether to go ashore with a small catch and get a reasonable price or remain at sea till the catch is sizeable and risk poorer market prices. Most of the decisions will concern minor points of operation such as whether to adjust the net, or change the length of the warp, or tow into or with the wind, or move into deeper or shallower water, and so on. Very few businessmen ashore make as many decisions in one day as a fisherman does at sea.

To describe seine net fishing in Scotland with some accuracy, one has to look at the whole picture—the ports, the grounds, the fish, the markets, the vessels, and the personalities involved. This may be of limited interest to readers in the America or in Australasia, but perhaps even there, fishermen will appreciate common problems and derive some ideas on appropriate techniques for their particular situation. *Figure 90* shows seine net ports and fishing grounds in Scotland.

Moray Firth   The small ports of the Moray Firth are the 'home' of seine net fishing in Scotland. On the south shore of the Firth, there are five main ports, namely: Lossiemouth, Buckie, Whitehills, Macduff and Fraserburgh. Each of those harbours has a daily (Monday to Friday) auction market. In some ports, fish auctions are held twice daily. Near each of the market ports, there are smaller 'sister' ports which have some fishing vessels but no market. Some of the modern boats are too large for the small harbours and may dock permanently elsewhere, yet their skippers still faithfully paint the name of the real home port on the stern of the vessel.

There are two distinct fleets of vessels in each port; those which fish for most of the year at home and those which fish for the greater part of the year from some other port. The latter group of vessels are usually equipped with a boat's van which carries the crew to and from the port of operation. From Lossiemouth and its sister ports of Hopeman, Burghead and Nairn, fleets of vessels are based at Oban, Lochinver and Peterhead. From Macduff and Buckie, and their sister ports of Buckpool, Findochty, Portnockie, Portsoy, Whitehills, Banff and Gardenstown, many vessels are based at Kinlochbervie on the west coast and Peterhead on the east side. Some, working the Shetland grounds, spend alternate weekends in Lerwick and in their home ports.

Apart from the seine net, the most popular gear in the Moray Firth ports is the light trawl and the prawn trawl. Fraserburgh is primarily a herring port, and seining there is of less importance than midwater trawling and purse seining. A few Moray Firth vessels use bobbin trawls, and there are some small hand-line vessels. The local seine netters fish primarily for haddock, landing every day or two days to the fresh fish market. Cod, whiting, plaice and skate also figure prominently in the seine net catch.

The Moray Firth has been described as a mosaic of rocks, stones, sand and mud—an excellent natural habitat for many species of fish. The cleaner areas of sand and mud have long since been denuded of fish. But good catches of quality fish can still be taken at certain times in the 'rooms' close to the rocky and stony grounds. These inshore rooms are the hunting grounds of the smaller seiners. The bigger vessels may work the offshore rooms or the deep waters on the outer fringe of the Firth, bordering on the North Sea.

160

Noup
Deep

Rona

Sula Sgeir

Sule Skerry

ORKNEY

Stormy Bank

Butt of Lewis

SCRABSTER

Flannan
Is.

Bergen &
Viking Banks
180 miles from
Kinnairds Head

KINLOCHBERVIE

WICK

NORTH SEA

North
Minch

LOCHINVER

Smith's
Bank

Moray Firth

LOSSIEMOUTH

FRASERBURGH

BUCKIE MACDUFF

Buchan
Deep

PETERHEAD

South
Minch

CALEDONIAN CANAL

ABERDEEN

Forties

Fisher
Bank

Devil's
Hole

ARBROATH

Skerryvore

OBAN

• Bell Rock

Dubh
Artach

ANSTRUTHER
PITTENWEEM

• Bass Rock

St. Abb's Head

EYEMOUTH

Lindisfarne

Farne
Deep

AYR

Firth of Clyde

SEAHOUSES

Ailsa
Craig

AMBLE

NORTH
SHIELDS

Dogger Bank
100 miles + from
North Shields

Fig 90 Seine net ports and
fishing grounds in Scotland.

161

Total annual landings by seine netters at the southern Moray Firth ports is from 8,000 to 10,000 tons, worth in 1977 over £40 million.

Caithness, Orkney and Shetland

On the north side of the Moray Firth lies the port of Wick, once a thriving centre for the herring fisheries. Just through the dreaded Pentland Firth past John o'Groats is the other Caithness harbour of Scrabster. The two Caithness ports developed seine net fleets comprised chiefly of vessels in the 50 to 65ft size range (15 to 20 m) for working the inshore grounds of the north Moray Firth, Orkney Islands and the north Scottish coast from Dunnet Head west to Cape Wrath. Despite their distance from the British population centres, both Wick and Scrabster have maintained flourishing auction markets.

Orkney does not have any seine net vessels of its own although many Scottish vessels use Stromness and Kirkwall as temporary bases when fishing in the area.

Shetland by contrast has a large and prosperous fleet of seine netters, trawlers and purse seiners. Many Shetland seiners land catches at mainland Scottish ports and consequently the total production by Shetland's seine net fleet may be second only to that of the Peterhead and Aberdeen fleets.

An interesting development in the north Scottish fleets has been the adoption of long-lining as an alternative to seine netting during the off-season or to overcome species quotas and fishing controls. The normal alternative to seining is trawling with either light trawl, bobbin trawl, pair trawl or midwater trawl. Very little long-lining was practised after the war although a few boats continued to persevere with the gear. Now the introduction of automated long-line systems which drastically reduce the amount of labour involved, and the possibility of working grounds too rugged for trawlers, and catching fish not covered by quotas (such as ling, pollack, skate and eels), have combined to make long-lining an attractive alternative.

When in 1979, Norrie Bremnar of Wick replaced his highly successful 70 foot (21.3m) wooden seiner with an 85 foot (25.9m) steel vessel, he had her fitted out for automated long-lining as well as seine netting and trawling. The vessel was fitted with a full length shelter deck, the after part of which was removed when seining. Long lining involves rather longer trips in all weathers, on offshore grounds, and a full shelter deck is a great asset for that kind of operation.

The seine net boats of the Shetland and Caithness ports land over 8,000 tons of fish annually, worth (1978) over £2·5 million. They operate in very exposed waters and at a disadvantage distance-wise from the mainland markets.

162

West coast of Scotland Scotland's main west coast port is Mallaig in the southern Minch, but it is concerned almost exclusively with purse seiners and prawn trawlers. The west coast ports with seine net fleets are Kinlochbervie, Lochinver, Oban and Ayr. All of those ports have fleets of small trawlers. There seine net vessels provide the bulk of the demersal fish landings. The west coast produces around 8,000 tons of seine net caught fish realising (in 1978) over £2·0 million.

A unique feature of the west coast seine net fleet is that it is primarily owned and manned by east coast fishermen, chiefly from the Moray Firth ports. Since the 1950s these men have been basing their boats at west coast harbours. The skippers and crews travel home by car or van each weekend. Some well-known fishing families were involved in the development of these ports. Skipper William Campbell of the *Ajax* worked for many years out of Oban, while skipper John Thomson of the *St Kilda* fished most of the time from Lochinver. Both these skippers hail from Lossiemouth. *Figure 91* shows seiners and trawlers in the harbour of Lochinver. Others from the same town who have fished well on the west coast include: Benjie Scott, *Scotia*; Andrew Campbell, *Argosy*; Tommy Gault, *Colline*; Thomson Fiske, *Diadem*; John Stewart, *Ben Loyal*; and Eddie Fiske, *Amaranth*.

The port of Ayr in the Clyde used to see a huge influx of seine net boats from east coast ports during the early part of each year for the annual cod fishery. That, sadly, is a thing of the past and now there is only a modest seine net fishery in the Firth of Clyde, producing around 1,000 tons of fish a year.

From Oban, seine net boats have fished the south-west Scottish waters since the 1930s. The lack of a proper fish pier and market has always tended to discourage further development of Oban as a fishing port. The Oban grounds produce a mixed variety of species including whiting, hake, sole, skate, monkfish and haddock.

Fig 91 Seiners and trawlers in Lochinver.

163

Lochinver and Kinlochbervie serve the north Minch fleets, mostly vessels from the Lossiemouth, Buckie and Macduff ports although a significant number of west coast and Hebridean owned vessels are also based there. The main Minch fishing grounds lie between Sutherland on the mainland, and the island of Lewis, northernmost of the outer Hebrides. Outside of the Minch the larger vessels fish as far away as the Flannan Isles, St. Kilda and Rona.

The east coast South of Aberdeen, the main seine net ports of the east coast are Eyemouth, Arbroath, and the Fife ports of Pittenweem, Anstruther and St. Monance. Boats from these harbours fish the inshore North Sea waters though the larger ones may work as far afield as the Bergen bank to the north and the Fisher bank to the south and east. The larger seiners may be based for all or part of the year at ports like Aberdeen for the northern grounds, and North Shields in England for the southern or eastern grounds. Apart from seine netting, vessels from the east coast ports also engage in bobbin trawling, prawn trawling, and pair trawling. The east coast seine netters (south of Aberdeen) land over 8,000 tons of fish annually worth over £3·3 million (1978).

At Aberdeen, seine net boats land around 9,000 tons of fish annually, worth £4·5 million in 1978.

At one time Aberdeen was the base port for a larger number of seine net boats, but most of the fleet moved to Peterhead following a dispute over fish landing arrangements. Aberdeen is primarily a trawling port and deep sea trawler catches have traditionally been landed by teams of 'lumpers' or fish market workers. Union manning regulations allocated large numbers of men to each vessel. The seine net fishermen who had caught, gutted, iced and boxed their catches with crews of around seven men, objected to having to pay a day's wage to each of 15 or 25 men just to land the catch. In any case, most seine fishermen prefer to land their own catches. Discussions with union officials and harbour board representatives failed to resolve the arrangement to the satisfaction of most of the seine net men who moved permanently to Peterhead further north. The move of the seine fleet brought about a remarkable change in the relative fortunes of the north-east fishing ports. In a few years Peterhead became the premier fishing port in Scotland, vying with the great ports of Hull and Grimsby for the position of Britain's leading wet-fish (fresh fish) market.

Peterhead Scotland's chief fishing port is also the leading seine net port in Britain, and probably in the world. Some 50,000 tons of fish are landed by seine netters each year in Peterhead. The catch in 1978 was valued at over £22·7 million. A large fleet of well equipped local

164

vessels is supplemented by seine netters from Lossiemouth, Buckie, Hopeman, Wick, Lerwick and the Fife ports. Peterhead harbour has one of the finest fish markets in the world, and the support facilities are second to none. Ice plants, fish factories, slipways, dry-dock, engineering firms and companies making or servicing electronic gear, nets, deck machinery and superstructure, are all to be found near the harbour (*Fig 92*).

Peterhead may also be the port with the largest fleet of vessels which are privately owned or rather, which are owned chiefly by their skippers and crews. The fleets operating from the world's main trawler ports are owned chiefly by large companies and few if any of the skippers or crewmen have any shareholding in the vessels. With the exception of the dwindling deep sea trawler fleets of Aberdeen and Granton, Scottish fishing craft have been owned primarily by the men who man them. This probably accounts for their smart appearance and remarkable productivity.

Most of the Peterhead seiners operate well out into the North Sea, on grounds bordering on Norwegian waters. This may involve a steam of from 24 to 35 hours or more, just to get to the fishing grounds. That adds about three days to the length of each fishing trip. Actual fishing time may be from two to five days depending on the weather, the catch rate and the market fluctuations ashore. On

Fig 92 Some of the seine net fleet in Peterhead harbour.

'long trips' of five to eight days duration, catches are heavily iced and the insulated or chilled fish room proves to be a worthwhile investment.

In recent years fish buyers have been able to purchase round (or ungutted) haddock and whiting. Provided the fish are fresh, they can be machine filletted easily in the round condition. It is not possible to keep 'rounds' in good condition for long periods. Consequently on distant water seiners, all fish are gutted until the last day or day and a half when the small and medium fish may be left round. The gutting is not a major problem as much of the catch may be composed of cod or large haddock which would have to be gutted in any case. For smaller boats working day trips, the possibility of landing the smaller fish in the round condition has relieved the crews of a hitherto tedious and arduous task. Shipboard gutting machines have been available since the late 1960s but they found only limited acceptance on inshore fishing fleets. Perhaps it was a technology that was developed just as the need for it was about to decline. The seine net boats of the 1950–1965 era would have found the gutting machine most helpful.

English ports

Although they are located south of the border, it would be unfair not to mention the English ports where Scottish-style seining is practised. Chief among these is North Shields on the Tyne where a fleet of enterprising multi-purpose seiner-trawlers is based. This is the home of the Morse family who pioneered stern fishing and pair trawling from their seine-trawlers *Conmoran* and *Conduan*. Their latest vessel, the *Congener* is one of the finest multi-purpose seine netters in operation (see *Fig 72* p128). Another and larger seiner is the *Christine Nielsen* whose skipper Cliff Ellis formerly operated the wooden vessel *Lindisfarne*. Many of the Fife and Eyemouth seiners also operate from North Shields for much of the year. Further south at Scarborough there are a few seiner trawlers. Skipper Robert Mainprize did exceptionally well there, leading the way with this twin-engined seiner *Pathfinder* before she was accidentally sunk. There are also a few fly-dragging seiners operating from the southwest coast of England. Plymouth skipper Fred Ivey purchased the Lossiemouth seine netter *Atlantis* and with the help of her former skipper James Souter, was soon able to outfish local trawlers, particularly on the whiting grounds. Brixham skipper Tony Rae purchased the Peterhead seiner *Constant Friend* and began to fish her successfully on the south coast grounds. Both these vessels were fitted with Lossie hydraulic rope drums to improve their efficiency.

Comparison with other fishing methods

Relative to other types of fishing gear, the seine net still predominates in Scotland's fishing fleet. Throughout the 1970s it

166

maintained its position as the most productive type of gear. There are so many different methods of trawling now in use that it is necessary to sub-divide that category of gear into light trawls, bobbin trawls, prawn trawls, midwater trawls, pair trawls (demersal), and pair trawls (pelagic). Each is a distinct type of net used to catch particular species and requiring distinct operational techniques. The other chief methods of fishing are purse seining which has brought about the demise of ring netting, and long-lining which is in limited use. Many hundreds of small vessels also use hand lines and lobster traps or creels.

A disturbing trend throughout the seventies was the decline in the overall number of fishing boats and the increase in size and power of the average vessel. The development of purse seining was chiefly responsible for this trend but the building of large midwater trawlers and deep sea seine netters also contributed towards it. Hopefully the situation will stabilise before the inshore fleet is curtailed too drastically, which could cause serious unemployment of fishermen.

A seine net skipper's philosophy

Fishermen are naturally reticent persons, especially when pressmen or interviewers are around. While any fisherman may gladly share his views with friends at the fireside or in the cabin, he would be reluctant to put these views in print. So it is seldom that the public can get a detailed picture of a fisherman's philosophy or his approach to the job of hunting for fish. In 1971 the well known seine net skipper Willie Campbell MBE was interviewed at length by Gordon Eddie, then in charge of the White Fish Authority's Industrial Development Unit. The interview was first published in the Fisheries Industry Review. Much that skipper Campbell said could have come from any type of fisherman at any period of this century. Gordon Eddie opened the interview by commenting on his order for a new boat and asking his opinion of future fishing prospects.

Gordon Eddie: *Willie, I want to say how grateful we are to you for agreeing to make this recording—as an active fisherman you never get enough time at home. Perhaps we could begin by remarking on the fact that you have just ordered a new boat, which suggests you are pretty confident in the future.*

Willie Campbell: To my mind, prospects were never so good, as far as a young man is concerned. Everybody when you speak about new building quotes the excessive costs over the last number of years, but if you take a deckhand's wages on the better class of boat against the costs nowadays, and take a deckhand's wages against the costs when I started, I would say it is easier to get a boat nowadays than when I started.

Your own son, would you advise him to go into fishing?

167

This is the point. I was quite happy where I was in the present *Ajax*, but I am building this boat in the hope tht in five or six years years time he will be skipper and not me.

Each of your successive boats has been bigger and more powerful than the previous one. There is obviously a trend in this direction.

It is a bit of a dangerous trend as well, I think. Horsepower-wise I am beginning to get a bit worried because the thing reaches the stage where you lose sight of economics and it is power for power's sake. Fair enough, we need extra carrying capacity: the catches being landed by that class of seine net boat now would be considered very, very good in the normal middle water trawler. Per day at sea, they are fantastic as against the middle water trawler: they are landing 400, 500 and 600 cwts for an actual fishing time of 2 to $2\frac{1}{2}$ days. So hold capacity comes into it in a big way. With the development of herring trawling, powers have leapt ahead in the last few years. I like herring trawling, it is a change and you can get sheltered waters in the winter time and it makes a nice break, but I am not too happy about going to excessive powers just to be able to pair trawl. For the herring fisherman, pair trawling is a big thing and is going to be a bigger thing in this country. For the traditional white fish man like me, I want a seine net boat—with the capability of herring trawling when I want a break from the North Sea in the winter time.

Are you saying that there is a time in the winter when maybe the only way of keeping up the supplies of white fish, is to do it with a trawler rather than a seine net boat?

Oh, no, no. As far as North Sea fishing goes the weather's no problem, it is just the case that we are our own masters and can take the line of least resistance, and go to the Minch.

The so-called inshore boats are getting bigger and more powerful and there has been some anxiety expressed from time to time, from the direction of the Board of Trade, you might say, as to whether these boats are being pushed a bit too hard in the bad weather.

I would not say this, because I think that you will find that the average skipper-owned inshore vessel—'inshore' is a bit of a misnomer—the average inshore vessel is far beamier and fuller than the average trawler which belongs to a company. Fish room capacity, size for size, proves this. Sea-wise, or seakeeping-wise, ours are the finest boats that are built. Every improvement has been a general improvement through experience, sheer experience in all types of weather. They are not drawn out by a naval architect who does not have to spend time at sea in the boats he builds. If you look back to traditional models for a couple of hundred years, you will find that it has been a gradual evolution to the type of models we have got. Naval architects think we are a bit backward in not accepting their new ideas, but I think they have got an awful lot to

168

learn and it could do them the world of good if they could really see why our ideas have been arrived at. The stability criteria that we demand they say are nonsense because we have got too much stability. The boats are quick in the roll, they are uncomfortable and all that, but at least we know they will stand up straight. Quite a lot now in the inshore industry you are getting boats naval-architect designed, slow in the roll, but speak to any of the crews and they will tell you that they are up to their knees in water all the time, a thing that they never ever saw in a traditional boat in their lives.

Very often we have been fishing when the trawlers are complaining, but then they have got around this by going to stern trawling—to an extent.

Is there any advantage in having a trawler to fish the North Sea and the Western Approaches, then? Why should anybody build a trawler for three and four times the price of a seine netter with twice as many men on it?

This is a case of the company versus the skipper owner. The skipper owner is building a craft where he stands or falls by his own results and his boat is built to his own requirements. The company is building a ship for another man to work and pay. The vessel has to be designed to attract a crew and lots of things in the design do not affect the fishing capacity or anything else; it is just that the ship has got to be to that standard or they won't get men to go on it. Size for size the seine net boat is far more efficient, but it would not be so if the seine boat was share owned. You would arrive at the same stage as the trawler where you had to alter a whole lot of things to attract crews if you had the same payment system. I just think there will be trawlers fishing for flats in the North Sea and there will be seiners fishing in the North Sea for cod and haddocks.

I have never built a boat yet, but the day she was launched I always said 'I would like to be laying the keel today'. With the strides in fishing in the last ten years, your boat is out of date by the day she is launched. It has been the case for me that every time I have built a boat, usually by the day I stepped aboard and started fishing her, I was planning the next one, saying 'I will remember this the next time', and 'I will sort this the next time'. By the time you have built in all the improvements you find that they are out of date already. It is continual search for perfection, a thing that cannot be achieved, but it is fine to try.

As boats improve and competition gets hotter you find it a bit harder in the older boat; you have got to put in more work, it is more unpleasant, more uncomfortable and you reach the stage where you can achieve the same results with an awful lot less effort in a modern ship, because of mechanization, easier working conditions, more room, more power . . .

169

You feel there is still plenty of fish in the sea and that there will be a good demand for fish, which will justify your re-investment?

I think that the demand for fish is going to increase. It is only reaching the stage now where people are beginning to realise that fish is a food. I have got a brother-in-law who goes round the country with a van selling fish and he still gets the housewife going to him with 7½p expecting enough fish to feed a family of eight. And they tell him that the fisherman gets the fish for nothing, he just lifts them out of the sea. But this is changing through education of the public and mass advertising. People are beginning to realise that fish is a very, very, valuable food and worth the money that they pay for it, and other foodstuff costs have increased at such a rate that fish has got to increase in price. Frankly I see fish prices rising very, very fast in the next few years, especially quality fish.

In Norway and Denmark industrial fishing is a major part of the industry. The social conditions have forced them into it for the simple reason, I would say, that with full employment they can't find enough men for crews to carry on with human consumption fishing. They are working the same size of boat as us with half the crew.

If we can concentrate on fishing for the fresh fish market I am just not a bit worried about going in for new boats, I am quite confident that the rise in the cost of fish is going to more than meet the rise in the cost of the boats. If we can keep our crew situation as it is I think we are on to a very good thing. My fear in the future is not lack of fish, it is a lack of men to catch them.

You could obviously retire and dig your garden if you wanted to. What makes you keep going on?

I've aye been fascinated by the fishing industry, I think it is one of the few jobs left where, like me, you can get chased out of school at 13 and reach a stage where your earning capacity and the life attached to it are in many instances far better than a comparable job where a man has had schooling until he is 20-odd and has taken degrees and everything and had a late start to earning.

I like the job, it is a good job and if you are prepared to put something into it, you will get something out of it. We all have times when we say 'God, this is a terrible job, I wish I had bought a farm,' but there'd be a hue and cry if you stopped them tomorrow!

There is a very obvious difference between the success and attitude of this generation on the Moray Firth compared with the very sad times there were in the 1930s.

We in Lossie had a very, very prosperous fleet in the 1930s because my father and the others discarded the drifters quick and went right in for seine net boats. Lossie was in the happy position that it was a thriving port when other ports that were traditional herring ports hung on hoping for better times coming along. Take

170

the average age of the fleet in those days—the drifters, when you think back, were all built between 1906 and 1918: they were out of date during the 1930s and there was no money to replace them. In the herring fishing, the men owned the gear and to do away with the drift net was practically like doing away with a lifetime's work and saving. I think this influenced them to hang on to the drifter hoping things would take a change for the better; then they took the plunge and got rid of the lot and started from scratch.

The moral is to recognise when change is needed and still be able to make the change?

No matter how drastic it is.

What changes do you see coming in the next few years?

I am getting a bit worried that the young men do not seem to have the same incentive to own their own boats. I know when I left school—even when I could just walk to the harbour—my ambition was to own my own boat. No matter how distant or impossible it looked at the time, that was my ambition. Now you find that there is not this drive or interest even; it is lack of responsibility, they do not seem to have the same urge to be their own boss. There again I suppose it is the same sort of trouble as they are finding in the manufacturing industries—it is too easy not to work and still be able to live; there does not seem to be the same incentive.

Don't you think there is something extra, something special, about the successful fishing skipper? He has got to have a bit more dedication, a bit more ruthlessness than the average human being?

I wouldn't say it is ruthlessness it is just—though they would be the last men to admit it—it is a love of the job, I think. They would shoot you for saying it but it boils down to that. Any job you like to take—if you can come home at the weekend and say 'Well I did a good week's work this week' or if you did not, at least you know the reason why you did not, you can sit down satisfied.

To go to sea your own boss with your own boat and have a successful week, you have achieved something and you have carried out what you were thinking about during the weekend—as you'll hear by that 'phone before you go out of here, things happen at the weekend— it is a 24-hour a day job, seven days a week. You can never be too clever to learn—my father was a great lad for this. He said always remember that the poorest fisherman in the port, if you have a yarn with him, has a lot of ideas much better than your own but just does not seem able to pursue them or execute them.

How does one skipper always seem to be where the fish is and to find the fish and the next one does not?

I think this is just that one fellow approaches the job from the point of view that he likes the job and is interested in the job. The other skipper comes ashore and he could not care less though he never saw a boat again till the day he sails.

171

When I started skipper first of all I was fishing at Oban. At the time the average boat in Oban was 60 to 62ft with a 114 Gardner; I built the *Acorn* at 70ft with a 152 Gardner and the attitude was 'You will never make that pay, you will have to stay on the sea seven days a week,' and all that sort of business. (If I had a bit of the ruthlessness now that I had at that time, I would not be worried!) We just went into Oban and we said—'That's the top skipper in Oban, we are not concerned about anybody else, that's the fellow we have to beat'—and we did it with our youth and sheer hard graft. That man was an expert fisherman but he would not stand the punishment that we could stand because we were younger. But now I approach the job the way that he did: it is how *little* hard work I can put into it now!

I often wondered, that time when we were in Oban; you could stand on the pier on Sunday night and there would be about 50 boats and you could say 'Well, that one, and that one and that one, they're going to be the three top boats in Oban this week'. And often, going out of Oban going down Kerrera Sound, before the boats began to split up and steer their different ways, it was maybe just a bit of arrogance of youth on my part, but I used to say 'Well, that fellow hadn't much last week and he's not going to get much this week, the way that he's going—what's possessing him to go there? Because I know that if there's a box of fish there, there are ten boxes where I'm going, and he's more experienced, he's bound to know this'. Like any other job, I think you will get the fellow that plays safe for a living, he'll never take the gamble and win all or lose all. A pet saying of mine that I keep in the back of my mind is one Sir Andrew Cunningham used at the time of the war:

'He either fears his fate too much
Or his deserts are small
That puts it not unto the touch
To win or lose it all.' *

and I think there is a bit of this in the fisherman.

You never hear about it, but the top skipper makes some of the wildest boobs that ever were made. You never hear about them because he usually finishes up with a successful trip, but he does things that the conservative lad that is just scratching along with a good living and is not worried about anything else would think were just absolutely mad. It is just this drive that they have got—that you would sooner take a chance than just drudge along at the same old

*Footnote by the interviewer: the author of this was the great Marquess of Montrose and no friend to the Campbells.

172

rate every day, which gets a bit monotonous like everything else.

One of the biggest problems of fishing is deciding when it is profitable to shift ground. I can trudge in a day that I know we are not making a lot but we are keeping things ahead, and the time wasted steaming and the fishing otherwise does not justify a shift, but you have the other attitude of the fellow that does this all the time, irrespective. I could never give you the reason, but just the other week there we had had a good day on the Monday and we had shifted. We made a big shift, in fact, assuming a thing that happens fairly often, that if you get good fishing here today, you want to be somewhere else tomorrow. We had made this shift and we had two good hauls of good quality haddocks. For no reason whatsoever I took it into my head that we should be 40 miles further away. Now we were going to lose two hauls during that 40 miles steaming, and the type of fishing we were amongst it seemed a lot of fish, but as it turned out   why I arrived at the decision I don't know   but we made this shift and landed in twice as good fishing with better quality again.

Do you keep a black book, do you keep notebooks?

No. I did when I started first, and I found that you can be led astray oftener than you can be led right because it is very rare that you get the same day and the same conditions two years running; different broods of fish and things alter, this sort of thing. I have only fished the North Sea the last two years or so. But you can gather a lot of information by just weighing up the situation and how the boats behave. You usually find that 90 per cent of the boats behave in a certain way, but the other 10 per cent that are going to be the top boats, you will find that they just attack in a different method altogether. It is the element of competition, the ability to weigh up the economics, and to put more thought into your job: to one fellow it is an experience, to another fellow it is just a job.

It is still quite amazing that you can get a feeling for the movements and behaviour of animals that you never see.

This was a thing that my father aye drummed into us. When travelling, you can look out of the window of a car or train and see maybe 10 square miles of countryside; it is very thickly populated or highly intensified farming with cattle and things like that, and yet, in the area you see, the people and cattle seem to be concentrated in certain bits of it. There are reasons for this—there is shelter or better ground or better food supplies or transport, and the same thing happens with fish. You have deserts in the sea, you have areas where there has been good fishing and the fish seem to concentrate there. If they can get food and shelter and the conditions they like, that's where they will go. I always take notice of this because it is surprising how near the resemblance is with the behaviour of anything that is hunted. If you started hunting people

173

they will go where they can get protection. Fish are the same. If they can get feeding and protection in the same area they will naturally make for there. If I am in the car and passing a field—it is surprising how interesting it can be—you will see a farmer put 50 cattle into a great big park and they're up to their knees in grass, and yet they will all make for one corner of the park. They'll walk 100 yards through the same grass as where they are going, but there is something that draws them there and I often try to think the reason for it, and you usually find it is because it is sheltered or something—they aren't exactly dumb.

I aye tell our lads that fish are some like people. I mean, if you went out of here just now, on Saturday, and you wanted a lot of people, you would automatically go to High Street, you wouldn't go to Dava Moor. It is as simple as this.

How much of this skipper ability can be transmitted one man to another?

Oh, I think the total ability can be transferred. A complaint that you hear in the trawler industry—and it is a complaint you also hear in our industry—is that when the skipper comes ashore the boat's just as well to be tied up. But I would say that it is putting a black mark against yourself, if you cannot come ashore—it is a case of delegating authority and if you haven't the confidence in yourself to be able to teach your mate to be as good a fisherman as you, it's because you are scared he'll maybe come along and start beating you. I would be ashamed in fact if my mate could not make as good a job as me, because that's what he's for, and if I haven't got the confidence to take him into the wheelhouse and tell him why we are working a particular ground, and how we are working that particular ground . . . well! When I decide to shift, I usually try and put it in a way that he takes an active part in the decision (though my decision's already made) and agrees with it or disagrees with it. I would say it is sheer lack of training and very, very bad on the skipper's part, and I think very little of him, if he is scared to train his mate to be as good a hand as himself in case the mate goes and gets a boat and beats him.

Do you think there is a freer exchange of knowledge and information nowadays?

This is a problem that we in the northeast here have never been bothered with. I wouldn't say it is the same on other parts of the coast. But there has always been this lack of teaching the mate, and after all that's what he's there for. You get fellows reaching a stage where they alter Decca clocks and all this sort of thing before they go to their dinners so that the fellow that takes the watch when he is at his dinner doesn't know where he is. It is this fear of being replaced, and why it should be I don't know, because if you train a good mate to be a good skipper, it's the finest investment in the

174

world. But it is a lot commoner than is realised that the mate in a ship gets slated for making a poor job and the only reason is that the skipper just never gave him a chance.

People who go out fishing with you, like our own people from the IDU, notice that on your ship the fishing operations are carried out in almost complete silence.

I think this is a safety factor. I have been on boats where everybody was shouting and it was all Chiefs and no Indians and there are aye mistakes. I just tell everybody who comes aboard: 'If there is a shout there's something wrong. If you hear a voice here above normal speaking tone, drop everything, there's something wrong, see what it is.' If anybody shouts, the crew immediately look to see what has happened, and it is surprising the number of times you can avoid accidents. Also, when you get shouting you get confusion, because if a man is doing a job and he is concentrating on it there is nothing upsets him quicker than a shout, he just loses all concentration altogether. It is very rare, I think, that you will find where there's a lot of shouting that there's a lot of success. If a fellow signs, you know what he is at; just gradually through time, and being together so long, you know with a look what is wanted and what is happening, but with trying to watch the amount of instruments you have got to watch and navigate the vessel, and watch that things are OK outside, shouting would just confuse the issue until you did not realise what was going on.

I think you are also keen on quietness under water?

I think this is a great essential in fishing and to me it is the reason why the seine net is so good a method.

I suppose that I would be slated for saying this by the seiners, but I think that the seine net is a far more deadly method of fishing than the trawl.

Before our fellows changed over from line fishing and drift net fishing to seine net fishing, a trawler was regarded as just murdersome: it ploughed up the ground and all this. But a trawler ploughing up the ground is like a farmer ploughing up fields, he releases feeding and things like this. The seine net has stealth and quietness and efficiency; it is like brushing down a suit, it takes everything off without disturbing the bottom and you leave a barren bottom instead of a bottom that has been ploughed up. This applies to the land: if you skim the top and don't do something to the land you get barrenness.

A trawler can fish a ground for years until he thinks it is barren and along will come a seiner and he will take three times as much fish as the trawler got when he thought it was rich ground. It cannot be anything else but that it is just more deadly. Fishing alongside a trawler, if I had a good seiner I would say that per hour's effort, per hour the net is in the water, she more than outfishes a trawler; the

175

grounds worked by the seine net boats are grounds where the trawlers can't make a living.

It is the fishing potential per hour the net is in the water that interests me with the trawler versus the seiner. If you take our boats working east, you are a day steaming to the grounds, you are two days working, you are a day steaming home and you have three days at home; or you have three days working and you have two days at home. So over the fortnight you have actually either four or six days' fishing and you are never fishing day and night, because you are either fishing through the day or you are only fishing at night. A trawler has 12 days on the ground, 24 hours a day. The seine net fishermen that have changed over to trawling in the last number of years have been far more successful than the trawl skippers that changed over to seining, and it was just that they were brought up that the gear had to be quiet, there were no chains, bobbins, doors banging and things like this. They approach trawling in the same manner. You have got the Vinge trawls and the three bridle trawls, all with twine strengths and lightness and quietness the same as the seine net: everything should be as fine as it is possible to do the job economically.

The trawler up to now has always been able to go farther afield and get harder ground and bigger bobbins and things like this, but this is coming to a stop, because with the size of the fleets of freezers and factory ships from Russia and all those places, there is not a part of the sea now that if there's fish there's not a trawler. When they run out of pieces of hard ground that they were not capable of working on before and they have to start catching fish on bottoms they formerly gave up as unproductive, they will have to modify the gear to be able to catch this fish, because the type of gear they have got now, they scare them. This summer our fleet have proved they can fish with trawl gear as efficiently now as they can do with the seine net. But the type of nets when you look at them are just the same and the approach and ideas the same as they were using with seine nets: quietness and stealth. When you look at a great big freezer trawler with a 90ft headline it seems a bit ridiculous when you see a 45ft seine net boat working a Vinge trawl adapted for seine netting with a 120ft headline. Of course the big stern trawlers are going in for these very big pelagic trawls now, because economics are forcing them into using them. To me, maybe it was ignorance on my part, but I felt that a trawler seemed to be an awful waste of power and everything else, but it was profitable because there were plenty places with hard ground that were not being fished and the fish were that thick that it was a case of if you pulled a coal bag through them you would fill the bag. This is changing and this is what is forcing them to use the pelagic trawls on the big trawlers.

176

What about flatfish? Is it necessary to have tickler chains and all that sort of thing, making a noise no doubt? I think you fish sometimes alongside the chaps with the tickler chains on the Great Fisher Bank.

Flatfish, with us, is a very, very minor part of the catch. When we go flat fishing we usually just work the same gear as we have got now but with a bit more weight.

Still quiet?

Still quiet.

This is a thing that we can never understand. You could get a Lowestoft trawler with 1,200hp come along and a fleet of seine net boats there, getting 30, 40, 50 baskets a haul, cod and haddocks. Now their actual fishing time per haul is only something like 35 to 40 minutes. Working the Fisher Bank, 200cwts is a common day. It is not exceptional, it is fairly common. But those fellows are towing along for four to five kits of plaice, every four hours, 24 hours a day. We aren't getting the plaice. Along comes a Dutchman with a different method altogether with the same type of ship and he can take as big a drag of cod and haddocks as anybody can take, because he believes in high opening and lighter gear—his gear is in the style of ours. Surely if a seine net boat can catch £2,000 worth of cod and haddocks in two days, it is a better proposition than catching £4,000 worth of plaice in 12 days, 24 hours a day.*

Mind you, before the day of the power block and all that, seining was much harder physical work than trawling, wasn't it, because once the trawl was on the bottom and towing, then everybody could have a rest for a while?

This was just part of what we said at the start, that as regards the type of job and the ownership and pay system and everything, they are a different class of boats and a different class of men and the methods of working and everything are all different.

The mechanization has taken some of the physical work out of seining?

Mechanization has made a terrific difference because we are working bigger nets and everything now.

But I notice in your new ship you are sticking to the traditional layout with the wheelhouse and accommodation well aft and the cruiser stern and the fishroom forward. A growing number of skippers are going in for boats with transom sterns and one or two of them for net drums for hauling the trawl.

Fraserburgh I think you will find is the home of the transom stern. Fraserburgh was a herring port—it would not matter if the sea was full of cod, if somebody came on the wireless and said so-and-so had 20 cran of herring, they would think more of that 20 cran of herring—it is just natural because they are herring minded! The seine net with them is just a time-filler between seasons. They would be far happier if they could be pair trawling, herring fishing,

*These were 1971–72 figures.

177

all the year round and to save changing over and the maintenance of seine net gear for what might be an eight or ten week period, they are going in for bottom trawling. Pair trawling for, say eight months a year and bottom trawling for four months, they are more or less minded for designing their boats for trawling all the year round. I am the opposite. My boat I want for seining nine months of the year, three months pair trawling.

You think the cruiser stern still has advantages for seining?

I like the cruiser stern for seakeeping, especially if you are working in the North Sea in the winter time.

I would be far happier with a transom stern design if we were going in for trawling on the lines that you see happening a lot on the Continent. It is not so much that the transom stern gives you a blind area, but you haven't got a fixed towing point on a seine net boat. Your towing point can be from the point of the stern to the midships, depending on wind and tide and things like this, and you could be rubbing ropes there on the corner and things like that.

It's a matter of choice and I suppose the fellow with the transom stern would have as good arguments for as I have against.

With the wheelhouse aft, it doesn't matter what is happening on deck, you can see it. I just don't like the idea of being forward and everything going on behind my back, because with the amount of gear and things like this, an accident can happen, and it could be over before you turned round and saw it happening, because you have that many things on your mind in the wheelhouse that to me it is a far safer idea to have it aft. Looking at Deccas and things like this, you don't stand and stare at them, you automatically see them in your field of vision and it comes to the same on the deck—though you aren't actually looking at a man doing a thing, if he does something wrong you notice because something affects your eye because it was not done properly—the pattern is different. With the wheelhouse in the place it is, every man on deck is within your field of vision without having to take your eyes away from something else and it is a far, far safer way of working. Also working in bad weather you have always got a safe side to the boat, because the wheelhouse acts as a division to the gear. You have the gear on one side and you are working on the other.

Of course you haven't got a man at an after gallows or a towing block or anything like that in your case. I suppose a wheelhouse and accommodation forward in your size of ship would be physically very uncomfortable, too.

Well it's going back about 100 years, some of the boats that I see being built just now with transom sterns and wheelhouses where they are. We have put in some nights in the North Sea when I am damn glad that the *Ajax's* wheelhouse is not forward there, or it's a bundle of mince that they would have taken out in the morning. It's just not practical. Here again it is up to the man having the boat built, but if you want a long working deck, why not have the wheelhouse lifted above the decks, so that you can have your split winches away forward and heave the gear through under the wheelhouse or something, and still have the skipper aft where he can watch everything? I think there are a lot of ways to lay it out, but the wheelhouse forward I think is a bad one, I just have no time for it because you've got to turn your back on the working crew. It makes a grand layout if you are drawing it out in an office, but if you are at sea in it then it is not so hot. It's OK in the bigger trawler with the amount of men they have on deck; you have more comfort anyway, you have more room and when you are hauling everybody is facing aft, but on a seine net boat it is just impossible.

Seine netting seems to be a much more versatile thing than it used to be, which was shallow water and fine ground in the old days, wasn't it? What sort of depths of water do you reckon you can seine in?

This is true, I think, of any type of fishing. There's the big trawlers turning to pelagic nets now as against the Granton trawl; circumstances forced this change. I fished on the West Coast, at the back of St. Kilda, in 160, 180 fathoms, long ago, and the 60ft. boats were working 120, 140 fathoms in the Noup Deeps, for different classes of fish, in years when good fish were scarce, but you usually find that the 30- to 50-fathom water you could say around the British Isles is the best water for quality fish, for quality haddock and cod. If things scarcened in the North Sea and we had to go to the West Coast, we would think nothing of fishing in 140, 150, 160 fathoms.

For our class of boat certainly I would say that there is a lot of ground that we are not exploiting yet but as fish scarcens in traditional areas and you open up new areas, there'll aye be a lad that has the brains to get round the situation, to take advantage of it. This is one of the attractions of the job, I think—the continual challenge to adapt yourself to change.

Although you are building eighty-footers yourself, is there still a future for the fifty-five footers and thirty-five footers?

When you go down the coast a bit, they wouldn't build anything over 54ft. and it is as highly successful a fleet as there is in Britain. You don't read much about them in the papers or anything, but if you go down and have a close look around and have a yarn with them you will find it is one of the most thriving communities on the Scottish coast.

It gets to be a bit like driving a big car and then going back to driving a small car. You just feel that this is a hopeless sort of article and yet if you had been in a small car all the time you are as happy as Larry. It goes from A to B the very same. I think it is your mind and the way you are used to working. We had an instance the other day, when we were towing a boat in and we were making about a mile and a half less speed than we normally do, and my mind was going twice as fast as the boat and the boat didn't seem to be going. And yet when you sat down and thought about it, I realised this boat's going faster, towing a boat, than my previous boat did steaming free—and we thought we were really going when we were aboard her!

You started fishing when you left school just around the age of 13 or 14 and you spent National Service time in the Navy, but apart from that you have been fishing for the last 30 years nearly. Was your time in the Navy of any advantage to you, do you think?

I wouldn't say it did me any harm because it taught you to live with other people, and the discipline, did not do any harm, but in the two years that I spent in the Navy I could never understand the reason why I was there. I couldn't see that there was anything that I was doing that wouldn't have gone on though I hadn't been there. For the actual good that we were doing, it was totally wasted time as far as I was concerned. But the Navy for fishery protection and that—if they are going to be wasting fuel they might just as well waste it doing fishery protection as steaming up and down and this sort of carry-on. This was one of the things that bothered me in the Navy: you went aboard a ship, they said she had a lifetime of so many years but if she spent 24 hours at sea, she spent 24 months in the dock. At least they could have been doing a service of some sort.

You got married when you came out of the Navy, I think. How important is it to the successful fisherman to have the right kind of wife?

I think—you shouldn't tell them this—but it is the most important thing of the lot. This has been one of the changes that I have seen in our industry up here. Once upon a time a fisherman married a fisher lassie; he went to sea and that was that. She was quite used to it, she had been brought up in those circumstances. It's one of the reasons now I think that you are finding crews totally differ in their outlook, because on a Saturday night now a young lad hops into his car and he goes away to Aviemore to a dance or he goes to Inverness to a dance and you go down through the town and you see a chappie that you know and a lassie that you never saw in your life before and she has been brought up with a father who's home every night at tea time for his tea and her mother had a wage that she knew for the next 12 months—'that's what I've got on Friday, that's what I've got to live on'—she is far happier like that than she is with a big wage one week and nothing the next, and this is altering the thinking and approach of the younger men to the job. The wife influences the man's decisions all along his life and if she has been brought up that way it is natural for her to be that way. I can see a great future in this job but it's going to be lack of men to catch fish to supply the demand that's going to be the problem,

180

because changing social conditions are just changing the whole outlook of the industry. Wages are rising ashore and with shorter hours and longer holidays and all the benefits that can be got, these things usually affect the basic industries first as far as manpower is concerned and I think this is just a natural thing that will happen.

I believe that you very rarely have a holiday and when you do have a holiday you go to the seaside and you go and stand and look at fishing boats.

I'm not holiday minded a bit, and for me to go to a place where there's not a harbour—I'm quite content if I'm there for two hours or to be away home the next day. I'd rather be at the harbour at home than sitting in the sun somewhere. It's just that, maybe too much so, I like to see different modes of fishing and if I see a lad with a boat, how he's going about his problems. He's got the same basic problems as we have, and very often you find that he tackles them in a different way and in a way that it wouldn't do you any harm to learn. I reckon that though I live to be a thousand, there would aye be a lad working with a boat somewhere that I never saw and he would be doing something that I should know about. It is just a never-ending source of interest to me. I am not really a good fisherman from my own point of view because I am always too interested in what is going on somewhere else.

I think all the boats in your particular fleet have taken to landing at Peterhead in preference to Aberdeen when you are fishing in the North Sea. Can you see any other changes in the marketing side coming in the future?

We had some Canadians at sea with us this winter, who told me about contract buying. You hear a lot about the advantages, but if you go to any country where you have got contract buying you have got a very run down fishing fleet, because the producer doesn't get a decent return. Our system, certainly it's not a good system, but I think it is a case of better the devil you ken than the devil you dinna ken. At times of heavy supply and things like this you can alter your methods accordingly so that you don't go for bulk, you go for quality. But to be tied to a contract—if you squeeze out the local lad that's buying his few boxes here and there and you squeeze out the element of competition, before you look around you are at the mercy of maybe two processors. If they put their heads together, as it's natural for them to do, with costs and one thing and another, any extra costs that they get are going to be taken out of you and it is as simple as that.

Changes are the same in any job, people think it will never work, but they adapt very, very quickly. If contract buying is going to come—and I suppose it will, because they can make the incentive so good—I would say it's time that we were taking more thought along the lines that as well as being the producers, we will be the

181

contractors. With the big trawler owner with his seven, eight and nine ships, with a value of £7, £8 and £9 million, this had got to be, and it is easier done in the trawling industry. In our type of job I think there are too few fishermen travel abroad and take an interest in industries in other countries to see what has happened there through being forced into doing things through lack of marketing and lack of competition in marketing. On the other hand you have the Danish fisherman with his industrial fishing where he owns the fish meal plant. With the investment we have in boats and gear at the moment, I think if you put it alongside the investment that the shore side have, our investment is by far the bigger. The investment, as against the investment in the fleet we have got, would be very little per man or per boat to set up our own producing and marketing organisation, and I can see this coming. There are countless good buyers who know that their livelihood depends on healthy competition, which keeps the production side healthy, and I wouldn't like to see contract buying taking too big a hold; the essence of the thing is for the producer to have some processing facilities and marketing facilities under his own command to be able to keep the processor from ruling the roost altogether.

Are there species of fish in the sea that you think are being neglected because the British public doesn't know enough about them, aren't familiar enough with them to appreciate them?

I think it's just a matter of education. There are fish that we throw away that are perfectly edible and good to eat, tastewise and everything, but they have never seen them, they have never been used to them. If you filleted them and skinned them and said it was cod, 50 per cent of the fish buying public would eat them and think it was cod. When we were working on the West Coast we caught a lot of fish that weren't marketable here, not because they weren't good to eat but the public had just never heard about them, fish from the deeper water. When we went to the West Coast first in the late 1940s, early 1950s, prawns were a menace; it was 'Those damned things again!' destroying the fish, and we were shovelling hundreds of stones of them overboard. Then within two or three years they were the most sought after valuable fish you could catch.

It is surprising the change there has been in the eating habits of the public, but they don't change overnight, you find it is a gradual change over the years and I think the affluence in the country and the amount of people holidaying abroad have altered the British public's eating habits. This is also helping to stimulate the demand for fish. This is the thing I like about the industry now. It seems to be that the public seems to be consuming more fish and they're more interested in different kinds of fish, and where before you had

182

very few ways to turn, there's more and more ways to turn every year.

You are stressing once again the ability to adapt.

Yes. I'm very, very pleased to see the pelagic trawls and things like this coming in, because the trawler owner has been slated quite often for backwardness and not adapting; I haven't the same problems as he has: if I take aboard a different gear, we all muck in together, and sort it out, but the trawler owner is up against the problem of this skipper who can catch fish with a Granton trawl and isn't interested in changing to different gear until it is proved and proved beyond all reasonable doubt. However, there could be a revolution coming with the trawler skippers: new gears mean more problems, but it's more interesting. When you can catch fish with this new gear where you couldn't catch them before, it generates interest. You will find that even though they have never worked this type of gear and the Germans are recognised to be the experts and everything, in a few years the British will be the experts.

Is there room for more organised education and training for the average skipper?

This is a thing that cannot be emphasised enough. Ireland have done a very good job, considering the circumstances they have got, and I think that there's not enough of our skippers travelling to different countries to see the different set-ups and different ways of approaching problems, why they concentrate on this type of boat for this type of job, and this sort of thing, it's a subject you can never learn enough about. One of the things I would like to have is the time to see all that I want to see, because it's a lifetime's job and you would never even scratch the surface. Education of skippers is sadly, sadly lacking because the mate just learns his job by what he picks up and sees happening, it is very rarely that he is told what is happening.

It is terribly difficult to get a man—who must by nature be a very self-reliant man, with tremendous practical experience of the sea and so forth—to come ashore and learn things. And who will teach him?

This is a very hard problem. With the system of Government here and the system of promotion in the Civil Service, the Civil Servants would never agree that a man that had chucked schooling at 14 was worth a damn sight more than them. They would look on him as an ignorant sort of oaf, but that man can prove in hard black figures that he can go to sea and what his earning capacity and his worth is. They just would not wear it, but if we are going to get round this problem we have got to pay the man what he has proved he is worth.

This was Dick McNeely's point at our fishing gear meeting, wasn't it, how to pay the skippers of the research ships?

They found there was only one way that they could do it. We've

183

got as many useless research vessels manned by men who are completely out of touch with the fishing industry and scientists whose work . . . words fail me! These ships should be manned for the good of the industry instead of being an embarrassment to it, and should be answerable to a committee from all parts of the industry for their work programmes and even for the continued existence of most of them. The system has got to be taken from under the Civil Servants, with freedom for the man in charge to say 'Right, if we want the top man we have got to pay him accordingly.' It has to be separated from the normal method of doing things.

If a lad's a successful fisherman, he's a highly educated man in his own field, and placing his education alongside the normal standards is ignorant. But for a start he's assumed to ge ignorant because he's a fisherman.

On a slightly different but parallel point, the question of training people in the nuts and bolts of new methods and in the use of new instruments, like new echo sounders and Decca Navigators and so on. Do you think this is done in a reasonable way at the moment by the manufacturers?

No. You get a new echo sounder and you go away to sea and if you are interested, you learn about it, and if you aren't you switch it off and use it for holding up your mug of tea in the wheelhouse or something, and this happens more than anybody realises. I approach an instrument in the spirit that it can do a job; you usually find you finish up making it do jobs that the manufacturer never dreamed about. It is fascinating how it happens, because they make a machine and they make a specification and it does this and it does that, but they are no more qualified to train the man that's got to use it than he is to tell them. To teach the nuts and bolts of the thing needs somebody out of our own ranks that we have known, we know he's a good fisherman and we'll listen to him.

If you take Iceland and read about how they adapted sonar to herring fishing—they started off with a whale finder and this fellow just had the savvy, or the brilliance, you could say, to adapt it to what he wanted. Now it's recognised as one of the foremost means of fish finding in the world. You couldn't say that man was ignorant. I would say he was a very, very skilful lad in his own field. And this happens with a lot of electronics in boats, that the use they are designed for turns to be a minor one. The main use is one that the manufacturer neither designed nor credited the fisherman with being able to do or see.

You mentioned that man from Iceland. I've met that man and if you put him into a group of Moray Firth skippers you wouldn't be able to pick him out. He's a very typical fishing skipper.

This is the sort of thing that happens and it would be a shame if we allowed it to disappear. There should be a means for men of that

184

type to be able to channel their interests and energies to the benefit of the whole industry.

If you get a technical lad up from an electronics firm he can baffle you with technicalities, but he just can't tell you anything about how to use it or how to use it to advantage. To be able to get a man to liaise between him and the fisherman, is the big problem. As fish get scarcer and harder to catch and as gear gets more complicated, there's a bigger need coming on all the time for a means of bridging the gap between the manufacturer and the actual user. It's getting highly technical.

We have been very lucky with your people who will always come to sea to see our problems; you can speak to them and it's the only place that it happens.

How do you spot the fellow who is going to be a good skipper?

Well, funnily enough we had a youngster at sea this week; he's only 10 years old, but I would be quite happy to say that when that fellow's 22 he will be a skipper. He is just a young laddie, and when you saw him on the boat he was a natural. The next youngster you take to sea is interested the first couple of hours, fish splashing about the deck and things like this, and then 'I've seen it, let's finish with it.' To spot them when they start going to sea is even harder. You can see the potential when they are very young and then it disappears for a while because they start to run about with their chums and have different interests for a while and it seems to lie dormant, and it is dormant at the period when you need to make your decision. You have to wait then until you commit him to a ship where it's stand or fall before you find out your mistake. It's about the hardest decision to make. You usually find you have to commit yourself to the ship before you find out if he's got it or not, even in our section of the industry. But we're lucky in our industry in that the capital involved isn't so big as the trawler owner's and also with the different type of fishing you can put him in a small boat, a secondhand boat, where capital involvement is not very big. He can go to a place where he can scratch a living and you can afford to wait six months and see if he's going to come on a bit or not and there's no real loss, but when you go to a trawler—with the figures involved, every week's a big commitment.

Don't start getting like industry ashore and thinking that unless you have so many A-levels you are no use for anything. Don't start picking them out of University and the top of the class at school and all this, because funnily enough when I look at my own school days, the clever lads you will find are now the poor relations to the lads that were just harum scarum. It doesn't follow that because you are top of the class at school . . . I think this has got a bit out of hand.

I greatly regret the loss of education that I had. It doesn't bother me in my job or anything like that, but I feel sorry at times now that

185

I had not had more time schooling as things are getting more complicated, more complex in all different ways. It doesn't hold me back or anything like that, but I feel it would have been so much easier. Don't just get blinded with education altogether because fishing, after all, is just hunting. You have to be a bit of a 'Jock' along with being a bit educated.

One of the things that seems to be essential to your type of fishing is being backed up by a very good 'Office', because there are all sorts of things that you cannot possibly worry about if you are going to get on with your job of catching fish.

This is a thing that we have been very lucky with. Your hear a lot of talk about co-operatives. This is all very well, for if ten successful skippers form a co-operative, it cannot help but make money. But the time comes along when those ten men have ten sons needing new boats and if there are seven duds and three good hands, you will never convince the seven duds' fathers that their sons aren't entitled to a boat the same as the three good hands, and this is when the thing falls down, as against the type of 'Office' that we have. They can take a better look at it and give a more balanced judgment, no personalities enter into it.

I just wouldn't like to say how a co-operative would work out because fishermen being what they are and so highly independent, I just could not see ten of them sitting around a table and agreeing what's going to be done! It won't happen until circumstances force it, because they are too fiercely independent individuals. Of course they can be as fierce to make it work as they can be to keep out of it until such time as circumstances just start to dictate the co-operation.

You have been very successful with your move to Peterhead—the co-operation has been pretty good in that case.

The market in Aberdeen just reached a stage where you were paying fantastic dues and landing charges and being chucked into a spare corner that was 'good enough for the seine net boats' and yet they were supplying more than half of the revenue. It was a bit ridiculous that seven men could catch 500 boxes, gut them, ice them, pack them and then you had to take 28 men to land them and they got paid before you got paid. Peterhead has really gone out of their way to provide for the seine net fleet.

Just to sum it up, you are saying that you think that your section of the industry has a pretty bright future, depending only on getting a sufficient number of the right sort of men?

And this is going to be one of the main reasons for having an education scheme of some kind for training up the right kind of men and letting them see that there is a future in the industry.

Well, thank you very much, Willie for giving us all this time.

186

10 Costs and earnings of seine net vessels

For over sixty years seine netting has proved to be an economical and productive method of fishing. It has maintained this quality without any of the adverse side-effects that attend some other fishing methods such as beam trawling and purse seining. Part of the reason for its success is inherent in the nature of the gear and its operation. A great amount of credit must go first of all to the calibre of the men who have pioneered and developed the fishery. Their integrity, perseverance, ingenuity and enormous capacity for work are factors which one simply cannot evaluate in economic terms. Yet without men of such quality the seine net fishery would never have made the contribution it did, regardless of costs, productivity rates or technical superiority. No one should forget that commercial fishing of any kind involves men in arduous and demanding work, in extremely long hours, and in risks and discomforts which would be unacceptable to any type of industrial worker ashore. One can but touch upon this aspect of successful fishing, yet it should never be lost sight of. The data and figures given below in this chapter should be considered only in the light of the human element—the character and diligence of the fishermen themselves.

Seine netting is an appropriate technology in the sense used by the late E F Schumacher, author of 'Small is Beautiful'. It is relatively low-cost, it generates employment, and it is gentle on the environment. Perhaps the modern sophisticated deep sea seine netter does not fit that category in all respects, but certainly the small to medium sized fly-draggers and anchor-draggers do, relative to other fishing craft in the north Atlantic.

Increased costs of vessels and equipment

The tremendous inflation or deterioration of money values of the past decade adds considerable distortion to the overall picture of the economics of fishing vessels since the war. If we look back to the end of the First World War, to when the seine net was introduced to Britain, the distortion is even greater. In 1921 a seine net cost about £7.2s.6d. and a coil of rope £1.10s. By the 1960s nets were costing around £200 and ropes over £20 a coil. By the end of the 1970s a net could cost over £1,000 and a coil of rope from £100 to over £200. The first seine net winches cost £17.10s. Twenty-five years later they cost several hundred pounds, and today they cost several thousands. Inflation is not solely to blame of course as the size and complexity of the gear used has grown enormously over the years. The growth in cost, dimensions and sophistication is clearly apparent in the types of vessels built since the war, and in the prices of those boats over the years. In 1950 one could purchase a new 68 foot (20·7m) seiner (the biggest then available) for £12,000. By 1960 the same sized vessel cost over £20,000, and by 1970, over £50,000. Ten years later the same size of vessel, albeit much better equipped, was to cost around £350,000 or more. By that time the smallest of seine netters cost at least £200,000 and the largest ones about £750,000. There are seine net fishermen today operating vessels costing half-a-million pounds whose fathers or uncles bought their first seine net boats for around £500.

	Overall length			
Year	feet	metres	Horsepower	Range of prices
1952	50	15·2	76 hp	£ 6,000 – £ 8,000
	60	18·3	114 hp	9,000 – 11,000
	68	20·7	152 hp	12,000 – 14,000
1962	55	16·8	120 hp	12,000 – 15,000
	60	18·3	150 hp	17,000 – 20,000
	70	21·3	200 hp	23,000 – 26,000
1968	55	16·8	150 hp	38,000 – 44,000
	65	19·8	200 hp	46,000 – 52,000
	74	22·6	320 hp	54,000 – 60,000
	78	23·8	400 hp	65,000 – 75,000
1973	55	16·8	170 hp	65,000 – 75,000
	65	19·8	230 hp	90,000 – 105,000
	74	22·6	400 hp	110,000 – 130,000
	80	24·4	480 hp	140,000 – 160,000
1978	55	16·8	230 hp	180,000 – 220,000
	65	19·8	320 hp	260,000 – 320,000
	74	22·6	480 hp	380,000 – 420,000
	80	24·4	550 hp	460,000 – 500,000
	85	25·9	630 hp	550,000 – 640,000
1980	55	16·8	320 hp	250,000 – 320,000
	65	19·8	480 hp	330,000 – 430,000
	70	22·6	550 hp	450,000 – 550,000
	80	24·4	630 hp	550,000 – 650,000
	85	25·9	750 hp	650,000 – 750,000

Table 8 Approximate costs of new seine net vessels, complete, in £ sterling.

Fish prices Despite the tremendous increases in the costs of vessels and gear, the price paid for fish has not risen in anything like the same proportions. Like his colleagues in the other producer industries, the fisherman was for many years inadequately recompensed for his labour. In 1955 the average price paid for seine net fish in Scotland was still at its 1921 level of £2·50 per cwt or about 15 cents US per kilo. The price for fish paid to fishermen in Britain did not really begin to rise until the 1970s. From 1970 to 1980 the average price paid for seine net fish rose from £70 per ton to £500 per ton. In terms of price per 7 stone box (100lbs or 45 kilos) it represented a jump of from £3 to over £22 on average. When one considers that for 50 years the price per box had varied from below £2 to just over £3 one can get an idea of what the increases of the 70s meant to the fishermen. The reason prices never fell much below £2 per box was chiefly the minimum price regulations. Below a certain level, fish could not be sold for human consumption. If there was no bid above the minimum price, the fish had to be dumped or sent 'up the road' for fishmeal.

The seine net fleets went through a difficult period from the late 1950s to the end of the 60s due to costs increasing at a much more rapid rate than fish prices. Government subsidies alleviated the situation somewhat during that period. These subsidies were calculated at first on the weight or 'stonage' of gutted fish, and later on the length of each vessel and the number of days spent at sea. At the most it could add ten per cent to a vessel's annual earnings.

Table 9 Average prices paid for seine net fish, in pence per kilo (100 pence = £1) in selected years 1938–1978.

	1938	1953	1958	1963	1968	1971	1974	1976	1977	1979
Haddock	2·0	4·9	5·6	6·7	7·7	8·7	20·0	25·6	35·9	50·7
Whiting	1·7	3·8	4·2	4·9	6·5	7·3	14·5	18·5	29·1	33·5
Cod	1·8	4·7	6·2	7·9	7·4	12·7	24·7	36·0	51·5	62·6
Plaice	4·9	9·6	12·0	11·1	12·1	16·0	25·5	35·6	37·6	50·6
L Sole	7·0	13·6	16·8	18·9	19·8	28·3	37·8	53·5	62·2	80·0
Hake	3·4	11·7	15·4	15·3	15·8	26·7	33·5	55·0	76·8	83·5
Skate	1·8	4·4	4·9	6·6	8·4	10·7	14·9	21·4	25·4	34·2

Seiner trips and profits Using hypothetical figures, a 60 or 65 foot seiner (18 or 20m) with a 230hp engine might gross £1,900 for 80 or 90 boxes of fish. From that gross figure the week's expenses to be deducted might amount to £800. That would leave a net figure of £1,100. Half of this sum of £550 would go to the crew and a similar figure would be allocated to the boat or owner's account. If there are five crew men plus a cook or an apprentice, then the crew's portion might be divided into five and a half shares. That would give the cook £50

189

and the crew men £100 each. Note that the skipper is counted as an ordinary crew man in this respect and receives the same share-out as the deckhands. The Scottish fishing industry is probably unique in the world in this respect. It is always assumed that the skipper is the chief shareholder in the vessel and that he will consequently receive the major share of the profits from the boat's account, at the end of the year.

If the seiner in question was fortunate enough to average these weekly earnings throughout the year, and if it fished for 46 weeks out of the 52 (allowing for overhaul time, a trades holiday week, and time lost due to bad weather), then the gross annual deposits to the boat's account would be 46 × £550 or £25,300. From this figure the owners might have to pay £7,000 for nets, ropes and spare parts, plus some £3,300 for slipping, painting and overhauling the vessel. That would leave £15,000 before tax profits for the year. If the skipper owned 25% of the boat, he would receive just under £4,000 less tax which could be substantial. If the boat was relatively new, all of the sum would go towards repayment of the loan and interest charges.

The economics of large distant water seiners differs mainly in the volume of cash involved: the relative percentages remain much as on smaller boats. It is surprising that so many big vessels can operate on the same lay or share system as small vessels. Variations to the traditional system are referred to later in this section.

Few large seine netters (80 feet or 24 metres and over) can stick to a weekly trip schedule. Many of their trips extend to six or seven days or more. To that must be added the two or three days rest the crews are allowed with their families between trips. A few big boats do however manage to keep to the weekly schedule. Some of them do so out of respect to the traditional Scottish observance of Sunday as a day of rest. For the purposes of the following example we will consider a weekly-based operation which is easier to calculate.

An 86 footer (26m) vessel with a 600hp engine might gross £4,000 from around 190 boxes of fish in one week (8·5 tons). Expenses would amount to close on £2,000 for that size of boat, say £1,900. This would leave a net figure of £2,100 of which 50% or £1,050 would go to the crew. The crew would probably consist of seven men plus a cook or apprentice who would receive around £70 for his half-share. The crew's shares would come to £140 per man. The boat's share of £1,050 if averaged for a whole year would give the vessel £50,400 for 48 weeks. (Large expensive vessels do not stay in port for holidays or even for bad weather—only for necessary overhauls). The owners would have to pay around £12,000 for ropes, nets and spare parts, plus over £4,000 for an overhaul. That would leave them £34,000 pre-tax profits. This sum might just be sufficient to meet loan repayments if the boat was new.

190

Because of the excessive cost and the increased productivity of the large vessels, some of their owners have been departing from the traditional 50–50 split of net earnings between the vessel and the crew. This they do rather reluctantly as the traditional share out is a well established practice. There is no general rule followed in these cases, each skipper or group of owners doing what they believe to be fair with the consent of the other crew members. One approach is to give the boat two extra shares. A 'share' in this context is a crew man's percentage. If there are eight crew men including the skipper, then the net earnings are divided into 18 shares (8 + 8 +2). The boat receives 10 shares, and the crew, 8.

If, on the hypothetical 86 footer we considered, the net grossing was £2,160, then each share would amount to £130. This is what each crew man would receive. The boat would receive £1,300. On some vessels the extra share system is used partly to compensate particular crew men whose contribution to the operation may be particularly vital. Thus the mate and the engineer may, at the skipper's discretion, be given a half share bonus each. It is indicative of the integrity and the character of the men involved that such a system can work satisfactorily without any rancour, labour disputes or strikes. In the 60 years of seine net fishing in Scotland there has never been any such a thing as a strike or even a serious labour dispute. This is probably because the share system has been recognised as equitable by all parties. It resembles in effect, a common ownership system as pioneered and recommended by the humanitarian businessman Ernst Bader.

* Excepting strikes over national issues.

Running expenses Fuel costs have always been the biggest single item on the expenses bill. It was the cost of coal combined with poor market prices for herring that spelled the doom of the famous steam drifter and led Scots fishermen to replace their drifters with small motor boats in the period between the two world wars. But fuel costs doubled in proportion during the 1970s and they are likely to double again or even treble during the 1980s.

Vessel insurance costs have increased with the escalation in vessel prices. The increase in the cost of new boats is also a reflection of the escalation of fuel prices. Other expense items remained fairly constant (proportionally) during the two decades from 1960 to 1980 with the exception of Navigator hire costs which fell in proportion to others. Total expenses for one week's operation for a 70 foot (21m) seiner were £100 in 1960, £200 in 1970 and over £1,000 by 1980.

The following figures are approximations of the percentage of total expense bills of particular items for the periods 1967–70 and 1977–80.

191

	Late 1960s %	Late 1970s %
Diesel fuel	18	35
Vessel insurance	11	19
Food and galley stores	12	11
Salesman's commission and charges	12	10
Ice supplies	4	5
Decca rental and electronics	14	4
Twine and gear supplies	5	3
Miscellaneous labour	6	$2\frac{1}{2}$
National insurance	6	$2\frac{1}{2}$
Benevolent funds	2	2
Harbour dues	5	2
Miscellaneous items	5	4
Total	100	100

Although very few Scots fishermen are members of organized co-operatives almost all of them are members of fishermen's producer associations. These organisations deal with regional and national fisheries affairs. Smaller port associations are concerned with local services and it is through these groups that the fishermen can reduce costs by common ownership of marketing facilities or sharing of services such as transport and box washing.

Marine insurance costs are also kept to a reasonable level by co-operative action. Seine net fishermen mostly belong to mutual insurance associations. Fishermen act as directors and advisors on the boards of these insurances. When a member has a doubtful claim against the company, he faces a panel of his peers when he comes to defend the claim. Claims are kept to a reasonable level and fishermen feel honour-bound to prevent accidents as far as possible. Should a boat suffer a breakdown at sea, it will be towed to port by a vessel in the same insurance for an agreed modest fee. This avoids the danger of an expensive salvage claim. The profits made by the mutual insurances are ploughed back into the association in the form of reduced fees or no claims bonuses.

Productivity of seine net vessels

Although Scotland's fishery has long been regarded as one of the world's most well organised and technically advanced, there was always a feeling among foreign observers that the Scots would be wiser to change over entirely to otter trawling rather than seine netting. The Scots can hardly be regarded as lacking in versatility as they also engage in pair trawling, purse seining, midwater trawling, and prawn trawling. But the seine net has proved to be a most productive way of catching demersal fish. How productive was not really appreciated until the deep-sea trawling crisis of the mid 1970s forced the large distant-water vessels out of Icelandic and Canadian waters and back to the British grounds. They have found themselves competing with the very modern and efficient seine net fleet. Huge stern trawlers and side fishers 120 to 180 feet long (36 to 54m) with engines of 1,000 to 2,000hp were barely able to equal, far less surpass, the catch rates of the seine net boats. This was of course no discredit to the intrepid skippers and crews of the deep sea trawlers. It was just a simple case of an inappropriate technology. The era of the dominance of the deep sea trawler was over in the north Atlantic fisheries. They would continue to operate successfully in certain areas and for particular species, but on grounds within 200 miles of the national coastline, seine netting, pair trawling and light trawling were the most productive and most economical methods of bottom fishing. Some enterprising trawler companies began to invest money in seine netters and multi-purpose vessels. Several of these boats fished quite successfully but for some strange reason in general seine net boats have not performed as well under company ownership. The best fishing vessels are all run by skipper owners.

Grants and loans Fishing vessel investments in most north Atlantic countries are subsidised by government grants for new boats and for installations of new equipment on existing vessels. In Britain the White Fish Authority has, since 1951, provided grants of around 25% to 30% towards the cost of new fishing boat construction. Since 1973 some British fishermen have been able to get grants for new boats from the European Economic Community FEOGA fund. Fishermen purchasing a new boat have had to raise from 15% to 30% of the total cost in cash. The difference between the total cost and the grant plus deposit is made up from funds borrowed from the government (White Fish Authority) or the commerical banks. Fish selling companies may provide some assistance to fishermen buying boats provided that they get all the business from those boats when they are operative. That includes any commission on gear purchased as well as fish sold. It may also include oil or ice supplies or engineering service work in cases where the agencies also own or operate such facilities. The agency would normally have a small shareholding in any vessel whose skipper-owners they assisted. Government grants for new boats are smaller to shore based owners than they are to sea going shareholders. The agency or salesmen's offices also prepare the weekly and annual business settlements for their member vessels.

193

Vessel earnings A common rule of thumb when assessing fishing vessel performance is that if the boat grosses close to its capital cost in one year, then it is doing very well indeed. The best seine net boats have been able to do this over the years despite periods when market prices for fish were low. Comparisons are odious and a straight comparison of vessel earnings can be quite misleading. The capital and operating costs of the vessel must be considered in each case as well as the size of crew and number of days at sea. Many small seiners whose annual grossings are not spectacular are very profitable little units indeed, providing both crew and owners with a good livelihood. Another interesting aspect of the operation of these boats is that their crews mostly enjoy a five day working week—four days at sea and one on shore. But before any landlubbers jump to the conclusion that the inshore fisherman has an easy life, let us hasten to add that in those five days the fisherman puts in 80 or 90 hours of arduous work!

Quotas The earnings figures of the larger seine net vessels are spectacular from any point of view. The only other vessels of a similar size in Britain that can match their earnings are purse seiners and pair trawlers. But most purse seiners are now much larger than the biggest seine net boats. Drastic reductions in the stock of herring and other pelagic fish have considerably restricted the prospects for purse seiners and midwater trawlers in recent years. Seine net boats also face problems due to stock reductions which have resulted in quotas for some species including haddock which forms a large part of the seine net catch. The quotas are mainly issued on the basis of weight of fish per crewman per day at sea. To get around the quotas fishermen have gone after other species but there are not many available in any quantity that are not now under some kind of quota or fishing control

Grossings *Table 10* gives annual grossing figures for some of the best Scottish seiners during the 1970s. As the money values in themselves do not mean very much some grossing figures for top deep sea trawlers are given for comparative purposes. The capital and operating cost of each size of vessel is also provided. All of these figures are approximations since there are considerable variations in vessel prices and some variation in running costs. But a perusal of the figures will give any reader an indication of the relative profitability of the different vessels. The disappointing performance of the larger trawlers in the late 1970s was due to the loss of important fishing grounds off Iceland and other north Atlantic countries.

When studying the earnings of the most successful vessels one should remember that they represent only the best and most profitable sections of the fleet. The bulk of the seine net fleet

194

Table 10 Annual grossing by some of the best Scottish seiners, with figures of deep-sea trawler earnings for comparison. Figures are from press reports, and are given to the nearest £1,000. Some figures are estimated from total landings.

| Length | | | | | Annual grossings (£000s) | | | | | | |
ft	m	Type	Main engine hp	Main port of operations	1973	1974	1975	1976	1977	1978	1979
Scottish seiners											
78	23·8	wood	425	Aberdeen	153	191	200	231	304	343	365
70	21·3	wood	425	Peterhead	94	109	134	211	302	315	–
78	23·8	wood	425	Lochinver	120	130	145	215	258	–	–
75	22·9	wood	425	Peterhead	120	145	190	240	300	335	435**
80	24·4	steel	480	Peterhead	185	160	193	220	235	256	265
78	23·8	wood	425	Aberdeen	184	219	206	196	–	–	350
74	22·6	wood	425	N Shields	125	149	124	153	–	–	–
80	24·4	steel	480	Peterhead	–	–	180	261	323	305	310
87	26·5	steel	500	N Shields	–	–	174*	277	265	344	360
80	24·4	steel	565	Peterhead	–	–	–	190	240	294	320
86	26·2	steel	635	Peterhead	–	–	–	235	310	314	430
80	24·4	steel	565	Aberdeen	–	–	–	–	435	480	527
Deep-sea trawlers											
185	56·4	stern	1,950	Hull	327	438	528	692	739	653*	–
200	61·0	side	2,050	Grimsby	421	411	460	625	575	–	–
160	48·8	stern	1,900	Fleetwood	388	341	398	568	357	392*	–
145	44·2	stern	1,900	Aberdeen	220	281	262	410	447	–	–
130	39·6	side	750	Grimsby	205	190	252	353	402	423	423
140	42·7	stern	1,800	N Shields	–	137	240	316	–	–	–
130	39·6	side	1,350	Lowestoft	154	134	188	209	238	276	320
128	39·0	side	736	Grimsby	186	175	200	282	265	272	312
120	36·6	stern	1,095	Lowestoft	149	144	160	197	208	286	331
127	38·7	stern	–	Aberdeen	–	–	–	–	–	445	443

* Calculated for 12 months from figures reported for 6 or 9 months.
** This figure for a new 86ft (26·2m) 635hp vessel with the same skipper. See Table 11 for a comparison of capital costs and running costs.

Table 11 Comparative capital costs and weekly running expenses for deep-sea trawlers and Scottish seiners. All cost figures are approximate averages.

| Length | | | | Capital cost (£000s) | | Weekly running cost (£) | | |
ft	m	Type	hp.	1973	1976	1973–75	1976–78	1979–80
Scottish seiner								
74	22·6	wood	425	120	240	500	1,000	1,500
80	24·4	steel	565	150	300	750	1,500	2,500
86	26·2	steel	635	200	400	1,000	2,000	3,250
Deep-sea trawler								
100	30·5	stern	750	300	600	1,200	2,400	3,800
130	39·6	stern	1,200	450	900	1,600	3,200	5,000
160	48·4	stern	1,750	700	1,400	2,300	4,600	7,000
200	61·0	stern	2,000	900	1,800	3,000	6,000	9,000

195

provides a good though more modest livelihood for the fishermen. Many related factors cannot be measured in economic terms. They might include time at home with the family or less arduous or less dangerous work. For it should be made quite clear that the top earnings vessels, seiners and trawlers, work extremely hard in all kinds of weather. Scarcely a winter ever passes without one or more boats being lost with all hands in the worst of the severe North Sea weather.

Weekly grossings by successful seiners in the 1950s were in the range of £300 to £900. By the 1960s good weeks could amount to over £1,000 at times. When fish prices began to rise sharply in the 1970s, seiner grossings rose astronomically. Trips of £2,000 then £4,000 then £6,000 became commonplace. Soon the best vessels were able to break £10,000 some weeks. In 1976, Willie Campbell of the *Ajax* became the first to gross over £20,000 in a one week trip. This record was beaten several times in the next few years, the best grossing getting ever closer towards the £30,000 mark. These extremely large trip grossings were made possible not just by high prices, but by very large catches. Some of the 80 foot (24m) seiners were able to bring in over 700 boxes of fish (well over 30 tons). Their 140 cubic metre fishrooms would be very full with a catch of boxed and iced fish of that size.

Successful skippers The most successful seine net skipper of the past two decades without a doubt has been David Smith of Anstruther who has broken record after record in his vessels *Argonaut II*, *Argonaut III* and *Argonaut IV*. His annual grossings have rarely been bettered, even by boats twice the size or power of his seine netters.

Other big earning skippers of recent years include William Smith of the Lossiemouth seine netter *Sunbeam*, Ian Murray of the *Ocean Triumph II* of Pittenweem, George Hodge of the Aberdeen based *Forthright*, Ian Sutherland of the Hopeman vessel *Kestrel*, Alex Thomson of the *Emma Thomson* of Lossiemouth, David John Forman of the Peterhead seiner *Resplendent* and Norrie Bremnar of the *Boy Andrew* of Wick. Skipper Bremnar's performance in the previous *Boy Andrew*, a 70 foot (21m) wooden vessel was most remarkable, outgrossing most other seine netters many of which were 10 or 15 feet (3 or 4.5m) longer and more powerful.

In 1978 Skipper David Smith made his 80 foot (24m) 565hp seiner *Argonaut IV* (*Fig 93*) the second highest earning wet fish (demersal fish) vessel in Britain. Surpassed only by the 185 foot (56m) 1,950hp distant water stern trawler *C S Forester*, his grossing of £480,000 beat all other trawlers in the country including those at the deep sea ports of Grimsby, Fleetwood, Aberdeen and Lowestoft. In terms of return on her investement the only vessels that could bear comparison with the *Argonaut*'s performance were the top cod

Fig 93 MV *Argonaut* KY 157.

pair trawl team and the most successful of the country's fleet of purse seiners.

In 1979 the *Argonaut IV* grossed well over half a million pounds. She realised over £527,528 equal to over $1,213,438 at 1979 values.

Individual trip grossings by Scottish seiners exceeded £10,000 and even £20,000 during the 1970s. Those grossings were for trips of from five to eight days duration. In January 1980 the Lossiemouth seine netter *Sunbeam* set up a new record of £27,119. This was for a huge catch of 1,104 boxes (49 tonnes) of coalfish (pollock), cod, and haddock taken in during four days fishing time. More than half the catch had been taken in a single haul. In 1979 the *Sunbeam* was the leading seine net vessel landing fish at Peterhead, with a grossing in excess of £440,000. One year later the *Sunbeam's* record was surpassed by the *St. Kilda* INS 47 of Lossiemouth which grossed £27,554 in the first week of January 1981. This was from five separate landings at Lochinver between January 3 and January 8. The *St. Kilda* is an 80ft steel seiner built at the Herd and Mackenzie yard, Buckie, in 1978. Her skipper and owner, John Thomson, previously commanded the *Horizon* INS 21 and the *Caledonia* INS 311, both regular top vessels at Lochinver.

197

Success of the seine net fleet

The British seine net fleet lands over 10% of the country's total fish supply, and over 20% of the demersal fish catch. This 20% includes the bulk of the prime quality fresh fish produced by British vessels. The country's 400 or so seine netters are mostly owned by the fishermen who man them. They are relatively small vessels yet they provide full time employment for around 3,000 fishermen who in turn, it is estimated, create work for some 15,000 shore workers in related industries. The total British seine net catch has a landed value (1978) of well over £40 million. This flourishing national fishery has been established and maintained through skilful use of their gear and vessels by the country's enterprising, persevering and diligent seine net fishermen.

Bibliography

Arranged by date of publication

Books   Great Grimsby Coal Salt and Tanning Company, *Seine Fishing* (1935).

A C Strubberg, 'I. Fiskeredskaber' in *Fiskeriet 1 Danmark* (1946).

Dr Aage J C Jensen, 'Snurrevad' in *Havet Og Fiskeriene* (1947).

Peter F Anson, *Scots Fisherfolk* (1950).

Alan Glanville, *Danish Seining*, FAO (1953).

Atsushi Takagi, *Japanese Drag Net Boats*, FAO (1955).

John Tyrrell, *Irish Fishing Boats*, FAO (1955).

T N Stewart, *Danish Seining Explorations in Newfoundland and Cape Breton Areas* (1956).

Ichiro Saito, *Studies on One Boat Medium Trawl Fishery* (1957).

F M Davis, *An Account of the Fishing Gear of England and Wales* (revised) (1958).

William Dickson, *The Use of the Danish Seine Net*, FAO (1959).

Ichiro Saito, *Comparison of Starboard and Port Side Operation for Danish Seining* (1959).

Dr A Ritchie, *The Scottish Seine Net Fishery, 1921–57*, HMSO (1960).

White Fish Authority. Report on 'Comparative Trials with a Modified Seine Net and a Standard Haddock Net' (1960).

Ronnie Balls, MBE, *Fish Capture* (1961).

Gourock Ropework Company (John Garner), *Deep Sea Trawling and Wing Trawling* (1961).

Peter Buchan, *Mount Pleasant* (poems) (1961).

Ichiro Saito, *Illustration of Japanese Fishing Net* (1961).

John Garner, *How to Make and Set Nets* (1962).

Hiroshi Tominaga, *Mothership Fleets, Their Methods and Fishing Gear*, FAO (1964).

Japanese Government Agency, *Illustration of Japanese Fishing Boat and Gear* (1965).

Norio Fujinami, 'Japan—Modern Developments of the Fishing Industry', in *Fishing News International* (1965).

William Cowie, MBE, *Scottish Seine Net Fishing* (1965).

199

Gloria Wilson, *Scottish Fishing Craft* (1965).

N N Andreev, *Handbook of Fishing Gear and its Rigging* (1962). Translation (1966).

British Ropes Limited, *Ropes Made from Man-made Fibres* (1966).

Dr M Nomura, *Danish Seining in Japan* (1967).

John Proskie, *Costs and Earnings of Selected Fishing Enterprises, Atlantic Provinces*, 1964 (1967).

Port of Esbjerg, *Esbjerg Fiskeriet* (1967).

M Hatfield, *Measurements on Two Inshore Fishing Vessels*, FAO (1967).

Tatsuo Shimizu, *Development of Japanese Stern Trawlers*, FAO (1967).

B B Parrish, *A Review of Some Experimental Studies of Fish Reactions*, FAO (1967).

C C Hemmings, *Observations on the Behaviour of Fish during Capture by the Danish Seine Net*, FAO (1967).

Gerrit Van Dissel, *Recent Developments of Scottish Seining in the Canadian Maritimes and Potential for the US Fisheries* (1967).

G A Soppit, 'Developments in the Manufacture of Modern Seine Net Ropes', in *Fishing News* (1968).

Gloria Wilson, *More Scottish Fishing Craft and Their Work* (1968).

U Miers, 'The Hard and Soft of Scottish Seining', in *Fishing Gazette* (1968).

Dr Y Iitaka, *Fishing Gear* (1968).

Gerhard Klust, *Netting Materials for Fishing Gear*, FAO (1973).

M Libert, *Mending of Fishing Nets*, FAO (1974).

W Stewart, *Introduction of European Style of Danish Seining*, FAO (1974).

C Nédélec, *Catalogue of Small Scale Fishing Gear*, FAO (1975).

R Taber, *Scottish Seining Applied to Inshore Vessels in Southern New England*, University of Rhode Island, Marine Advisory Service, (1977).

FAO Fishery Industries Division, *Catalogue of Fishing Gear Designs* (1978).

FAO Fishery Industries Division, *Echo Sounding and Sonar for Fishing* (1980).

Reports, bulletins and periodicals, various years

Australian Fisheries

Canadian Fisherman. (Now ceased publication.)

Central Bureau of Statistics, Sweden, 'Fisheries'.

Commercial Fishing, Fleetwood, England.

Commercial Fishing, New Zealand.

Conseil Permanent International Pour L'Exploration De La Mer, Statistical Bulletins.

Department of Agriculture and Fisheries for Scotland
—Scottish Fishery Bulletins

—Fisheries Reports for Scotland
—Scottish Sea Fisheries Statistical Tables.
Fisheries of Canada.
Fishing Gazette.
Fishing News.
Fishing News International.
International Commission for the Northwest Atlantic Fisheries, Statistical Bulletins.
Irish Sea Fisheries Board Reports.
Irish Skipper.
Marine Department, New Zealand, Reports on Fisheries.
Ministry of Agriculture, Fisheries and Food (British), Sea Fisheries Statistical Tables.
Ministry of Fisheries, Denmark, 'Fiskeriberetning'.
National Fisherman.
Olsen's *Fisherman's Nautical Almanack.*
White Fish Authority, Annual Report and Accounts.
White Fish Authority, Fishery Industry Review.
World Fishing.

Index

**Other books published by Fishing News Books Limited
Farnham, Surrey, England**
Free catalogue available on request

Advances in aquaculture
Advances in fish science and technology
Aquaculture practices in Taiwan
Atlantic salmon: its future
Better angling with simple science
British freshwater fishes
Commercial fishing methods
Control of fish quality
Culture of bivalve molluscs
Echo sounding and sonar for fishing
The edible crab and its fishery in British waters
Eel capture, culture, processing and marketing
Eel culture
European inland water fish: a multilingual catalogue
FAO catalogue of fishing gear designs
FAO catalogue of small scale fishing gear
FAO investigates ferro-cement fishing craft
Farming the edge of the sea
Fish and shellfish farming in coastal waters
Fish catching methods of the world
Fish inspection and quality control
Fisheries of Australia
Fisheries oceanography
Fishermen's handbook
Fishery products
Fishing boats and their equipment
Fishing boats of the world 1
Fishing boats of the world 2
Fishing boats of the world 3
The fishing cadet's handbook
Fishing ports and markets
Fishing with electricity
Fishing with light

Freezing and irradiation of fish
Handbook of trout and salmon diseases
Handy medical guide for seafarers
How to make and set nets
Inshore fishing: its skills, risks, rewards
Introduction to fishery by-products
The lemon sole
A living from lobsters
Marine pollution and sea life
Marine fisheries ecosystem – its quantitive evaluation and
   management
The marketing of shellfish
Mending of fishing nets
Modern deep sea trawling gear
Modern fishing gear of the world 1
Modern fishing gear of the world 2
Modern fishing gear of the world 3
More Scottish fishing craft and their work
Multilingual dictionary of fish and fish products
Navigation primer for fishermen
Netting materials for fishing gear
Pair trawling and pair seining—the technology of two boat fishing
Pelagic and semi-pelagic trawling gear
Planning of aquaculture development—an introductory guide
Power transmission and automation for ships and submersibles
Refrigeration on fishing vessels
Salmon and trout farming in Norway
Salmon fisheries of Scotland
Scallops and the diver-fisherman
Seafood fishing for amateur and professional
Stability and trim of fishing vessels
The stern trawler
Textbook of fish culture: breeding and cultivation of fish
Training fishermen at sea
Trout farming manual
Tuna: distribution and migration
Tuna fishing with pole and line